Managing Internet and Intranet Technologies in Organizations: Challenges and Opportunities

Subhasish Dasgupta
George Washington University, USA

IDEA GROUP PUBLISHING
Hershey • London • Melbourne • Singapore

Acquisitions Editor: Mehdi Khosrowpour
Managing Editor: Jan Travers
Development Editor: Michele Rossi
Copy Editor: Maria Boyer
Typesetter: Tamara Gillis
Cover Design: Deb Andree
Printed at: Sheridan Books

Published in the United States of America by
        Idea Group Publishing
        1331 E. Chocolate Avenue
        Hershey PA 17033-1117
        Tel: 717-533-8845
        Fax: 717-533-8661
        E-mail: cust@idea-group.com
        Web site: http://www.idea-group.com

and in the United Kingdom by
        Idea Group Publishing
        3 Henrietta Street
        Covent Garden
        London WC2E 8LU
        Tel: 44 20 7240 0856
        Fax: 44 20 7379 3313
        Web site: http://www.eurospan.co.uk

Library of Congress Cataloging-in-Publication Data

Dasgupta, Subhasish, 1966-
  Managing internet and intranet technologies in organizations : challenges and opportunities/
Subhasish Dasgupta.
     p.cm.
   Includes bibliogaphical references and index.
   ISBN 1-878289-95-0 (pbk.)
     1. Internet. 2. Intranets (Computer networks) 3. Electronic commerce. I. Title.

HD30.37 .D37 2001
658.8'4--dc21   00-066081

British Cataloguing in Publication Data
A Cataloguing in Publication record for this book is available from the British Library.

Managing Internet and Intranet Technologies in Organizations: Challenges and Opportunities

Table of Contents

Preface

This book, *Managing Internet and Intranet Technologies in Organizations: Challenges and Opportunities*, brings together 12 essays that present real issues faced by organizations when they implement Internet and intranet technologies. We consider both intra-organizational as well as inter-organizational research. The book is separated into three distinct sections. The first section concentrates on intranet technology and its use within an organization. The second section addresses inter-organizational uses of Internet technology and includes research on business-to-business and business-to-consumer electronic commerce. Finally, the third section analyzes technical issues facing organizations. Following is a detailed look at each of the sections.

The first section on intra-organizational use of intranet technology consists of four papers. Rens Scheepers and Jeremy Rose, in "Organizational Intranets: Cultivating Information Technology for the People by the People," provide an introduction to intranet technology. Using a case study of a large telecommunications company in South Africa, the authors emphasize key challenges of implementing intranet technologies in an organization. In the second chapter, "Service Quality in the Virtual World: The Case Of Extranets," Beverley Hope looks at measurements of success in extranet systems. An extranet "is a private network that uses Internet protocol and the public telecommunication system to securely share part of a business information or operations with suppliers, vendors, partners, customers, or other businesses."[1] An extranet is a type of intranet that is extended to stakeholders outside the organization. The author extends our understanding of service quality, interface issues and Web usability to service quality in the virtual world. Dr. Hope uses the example of extranets to provide dimensions of service quality applied to the virtual world. The author also provides quality recommendations for implementing extranets in organizations. In a more specific application of intranet technology, Katia Passerini, Mary Granger and Kemal Cakici look at issues involved in the implementation of Web-based instruction in organizations. They present a review of the status of web-based education and their relationship in other types of distance education. The paper evaluates the perceived advantages and disadvantages for key stakeholders such as institutions, students and faculty. The authors also report on the results of an on-line survey conducted in a major East Coast university. The authors report that "expected disadvantages [of Web-based instruction] are in most cases lower than forecasted, except for the cases in which the Web is used as a substitute tool for instruction," and "faculty are interested and eager to use Web-based instruction in all its forms." The next paper also looks at the impact of Internet technology on education. Ashu Guru and Fui Hoon (Fiona) Nah, in "Effect of Hypertext and Animation on Learning," use concepts of "flow" and "media richness" to construct a model to explain the effect of hypertext and animation in the Web-based learning environment.

The second section looks at the use of Internet technology in an inter-organizational setting. Five papers are presented in this section. "Managing Value Creation in the Digital Economy: Information Types and E-Business Models," by John C. McIntosh and Keng Siau, investigates the role of information in the digital economy. They emphasize that the focus should not be on the management of information technology but on the manner in which different types of information can be used to create value. A classification scheme for information types and how to use these types for analyses in four e-business models is discussed. The efforts of nine cities in eight European countries to develop a 'service infrastructure' for organizations to efficiently deliver electronic services is previewed by Åke Grönlund in his chapter, "Building an Infrastructure to Manage Electronic Services." Dr. Grönlund found that the overall process was largely unstructured and improvised. He concludes that there is lack of strategic leadership in the field of electronic services in local European governments.

The next three chapters of this section evaluate more specific issues in the area of electronic commerce. I. Hakan Yetkiner and Csilla Horváth, in " Macroeconomic Implications of Virtual Shopping: A Theoretical Approach," present the economic implications of Internet shopping in a Ricardian equilibrium framework. They conclude that in the future, Internet shopping will have a significant role to play in the economy because more and more people will shop on-line. In a more applications-oriented approach to Internet technology, Raymond Panko in "M-Commerce: Mobile Electronic Commerce," looks at the next frontier of electronic commerce—mobile electronic commerce. Significant improvements in wireless technology led to small handheld access devices and personal digital assistants which constitute a major portion of mobile electronic commerce. This chapter looks at trends, potential applications and problems in the area of "m-commerce." The last chapter in this section is, "ERP + E-Business = A New Vision of Enterprise System," by Betty Wang and Fui Hoon (Fiona) Nah. Wang and Nah argue that the enterprise resource planning (ERP) model which connects organizational processes with one end-to-end application, may not be sufficient for today's fast-moving, interconnected enterprises. They extend the ERP model to electronic business (or e-business) and provide a new model that integrates the ERP model with tight business-to-business connections.

The third section consists of a collection of essays that focus on technical issues in Internet and intranets in organizations. Raymond R. Panko, in "Security: The Snake in the E-Commerce Garden," addresses one of the most important issues in Internet and Web-based systems. The paper provides an overview of different attacks that hackers may attempt against companies and methods used to combat each attack. The paper describes methods like the "denial-of-service" attacks and security mechanisms that include firewalls and authentication, to name a few. The paper evaluates the potential risks from lawsuits should a company experience a security breach. In the next paper, "Managing Web Site Performance and Reliability," Ross Lumley provides a number of different approaches to building reliable and high-performance Web sites. Dr. Lumley describes methods that include load distribution and load balancing and provides examples of how they can be effectively used to enhance Web site performance and reliability. In the final chapter of the technology section of the book, John Artz presents an overview of data warehousing, an emerging technology that extends capabilities of relational databases. A large number of companies analyze their Web server's Web log. This log provides information regarding visitors to a specific page or site. Web logs are time-oriented data that can provide valuable information about Web traffic. Dr. Artz uses this example to describe concepts in data warehousing, and shows how a simple data set from the Web log can be enhanced in a step-wise fashion, into a full-fledged market data warehouse.

Together, these 12 essays combine conceptual, survey and case study methodologies and provide a unique look at the challenges and opportunities faced by organizations in the area of Internet and intranet technologies.

Endnote

1 http://whatis.com/WhatIs_Definition_Page/0,4152,212089,00.html

Acknowledgments

With every publication there are many individuals and groups who are due thanks. This publication also benefits from the many contributions—not only from the guest authors but also editors, reviewers, and support of loved ones. I would like to take this opportunity to acknowledge those persons who have contributed so much to the development, shaping and subsequent publishing of *Managing Internet and Intranet Technologies in Organizations.*

It is always difficult to know where to begin, but begin I must. So I would express my warm appreciation to the reviewers of the many articles submitted. These individuals were responsible for the difficult task of evaluating, commenting, asking for further information and reading for clarity that is always a difficult task. Their valuable contribution of time and energy is appreciated. I especially want to add my sincere thanks to Nina McGarry, Beverley Hope, Mary Granger, Ross Lumley, Katia Passerini, Srinivas Prasad, and Rens Scheepers.

The authors who gratefully submitted articles for review also deserve recognition. It is always a difficult task to offer your work for comment and then find that someone, somewhere will comment. As authors you soldiered the effort well and I look forward to working with you again in the very near future.

Special thanks are due to my wife, Anju, and son, Rudra. Their continued support and encouragement were with me throughout and helped to sustain me. I also would like to thank my parents Purnendu and Gouri Dasgupta for their support throughout my education that has continued into my professional career.

The entire Idea Group Publishing team made compiling the effort fun and informative. Michele Rossi provided with me with a time schedule to work within and helped me focus on the project during the long summer months of 2000. Mehdi Khosrowpour, the editor-in-chief of Idea Group Publishing, is recognized for offering me the opportunity to undertake such a large production of editing essays on Internet and Intranets. Thank you all.

I would be remiss if I did not recognize the support provided in the form of time and materials by the Department of Management Science, School of Business and Public Management, The George Washington University. Erik Winslow, Sergio D'Onofrio and Emilie Artiga, all of whom knowingly or unknowingly helped me in compiling this collection of chapters. My graduate assistants Richa Kohli, Rupan Sood, and Li Xiao facilitated this effort.

Thanks to all and I look forward to working with you again.

CHAPTER ONE

Organizational Intranets: Cultivating Information Technology for the People by the People

Rens Scheepers
Swinburne University of Technology, Victoria, Australia

Jeremy Rose
Manchester Metropolitan University, England

INTRODUCTION

Fueled by the overwhelming media attention to the Internet and the explosive growth in World Wide Web usage during the mid-1990s, many organizations began to establish their own Internet presence and harness the Web's electronic commerce potential. The Web was a breakthrough in terms of global connectivity, because it allowed organizations to locate and disseminate information in a standard, user-friendly manner across a variety of incompatible technical platforms and across geographical boundaries (Castells, 1996). In the course of their Internet efforts, organizations realized the potential to apply the very same technology, but this time with an intra-organizational focus to overcome similar problems associated with intra-organizational connectivity. Intranet technology has subsequently opened up a wealth of possibilities in terms of its organizational application (Goles & Hirschheim, 1997). By utilizing their intranet, organizations have the ability to share information, collaborate and transact across various incompatible technical platforms and information systems, and across functional, structural and geographical boundaries within the organization, in a standard and user-friendly manner (Bernard, 1996; Isakowitz et al., 1998; Cecez-Kecmanovic et al., 1999; McNaughton et al., 1999; Damsgaard & Scheepers, 2000). Intranets are now also envisioned as platforms for organizational knowledge management (Davenport & Pruzak, 1998).

We believe that the organizational rollout of such an emergent and ubiquitous information conduit poses several new and unique challenges for IT management. Much has become known about various aspects of the organizational application of computer-based information systems and technologies since the early days of computerization. This knowledge is rooted in studies that were typically based on a centralized computing paradigm at the time (for example Nolan, 1973; Tornatzky & Klein, 1982; Markus, 1983; Srinivasan & Davis, 1987; Kwon & Zmud, 1987). The more decentralized computing paradigm associated with information technologies such as office automation, e-mail, groupware and so forth, required an extension of this knowledge (as reflected in studies such as Hirschheim, 1986; Orlikowski & Gash, 1994; Grudin & Palen, 1995; Orlikowski et al., 1995; Dennis, 1996; Ciborra, 1996). The advent of the organizational application of Internet-based technologies now marks the ubiquitous computing paradigm (Lyytinen et al., 1998) that weaves together a complex array of existing communication and information technologies into one rich medium (Dahlbom, 1996) that may involve numerous organizational units and role players (Scheepers, 1999a). As an example of this class of technologies, intranet technology calls into question some of our traditional IT implementation wisdom and presents new challenges for organizations seeking to implement the technology (Balasubramanian & Bashian, 1998; Scheepers, 1999b). Indeed, approaching intranet implementation with a traditional managerial mindset may be the reason why some intranets do not become organizationally embedded. A survey conducted in 1997 showed that half of the respondents indicated that although their intranets were deployed, they were by no means organizationally pervasive (Gartner Group, 1997), while more recently Romm and Wong (1998) reported on the stagnation of an intranet effort in an Australian University setting due to an insufficient level of information content. In addition, and importantly from an intranet practitioners perspective, Rein et al. (1997) note that "this internal Web, as an environment for supporting organizational work, is falling short of our expectations and hopes in significant ways."

Thus despite the promise that intranet technology holds, there are already some disappointing intranet outcomes. This chapter will not attempt to provide IT managers with an intranet rollout panacea. In fact we will argue that such simplistic conceptions of the intranet implementation process that are proffered by some consultants and intranet service vendors are not only misleading, but may lull managers into a false sense of security. Rather, by means of a case study, this chapter highlights some key implementation challenges associated with the introduction of intranet technology. Based on the case we will argue for a different managerial mindset, given the nature of intranet technology itself and context-specific issues. In light of this mindset, we offer intranet managers a way forward and compare our advice against some recent intranet research findings. Finally we will examine some current trends and also discuss avenues that we believe warrant further research attention.

BACKGROUND

Defined technically, intranets are the application of Internet technology (and specifically the World Wide Web service) for a prescribed community of users. Well-understood and widely available Internet technology and standards (Web servers, browsers, protocols) are employed, but access is restricted exclusively to specified organizational members, typically by means of passwords, firewalls (Oppliger, 1997; Laudon & Laudon, 2000) or even by physically separating the intranet from external networks (firebreaks).

Damsgaard and Scheepers (1999) describe intranet technology as multipurpose, richly networked and malleable in terms of its application. They isolate a number of intranet technology 'use modes.' These range from simple uses such as the publishing of home pages, newsletters, technical documents, product catalogues or employee directories, to more advanced uses. Advanced uses include interaction between individuals and groups (via discussion groups and collaborative applications), transacting with other organizational computer-based information systems, organization-wide information searches, and recording of best practices and business processes on the intranet in support of knowledge management.

Intranets may be implemented centrally in the organization as a corporate intranet, but units (such as divisions, departments or functional groups) and even individual actors often play an active role in establishing "child Webs" (Bhattacherjee, 1998). Setting up a simple intranet Web site (e.g., only to publish information) does not involve a major learning or financial commitment, provided the supporting networking and computing infrastructure exists (Ciborra & Hanseth, 1998). Unlike many other information technologies which may involve proprietary software, standards, technologies, licensing, etc., the software (such as server software, authoring tools and so forth) to start a basic intranet site is free or relatively inexpensive and can be quite powerful and easy to use and install. As such, it is quite common to find so-called bottom-up or grassroots intranet efforts (Jarvenpaa & Ives, 1996; Hills, 1997). Thus in terms of scope, various levels of intranets can coexist, the technology may even emerge without a grand plan in the organization (Ciborra & Hanseth, 1998) and the technology can involve a wide range of organizational actors. In these respects, implementation of intranet technology differs from the more traditional systems and technologies that often make up the organizational computing landscape (such as MIS, payroll systems, e-mail, etc.). The ubiquitous and emergent nature of intranet technology (as described by Lyytinen, et al., 1998) means that a wide variety of organizational units (and even individual actors) can independently establish their own intranet sites without being dependent on the organization's central information technology (IT) function. Indeed, where the organization's central IT function typically spearheads the organization-wide introduction of many other types of IT, this is often not the case with intranet technology (Jarvenpaa & Ives, 1996; Bhattacherjee, 1998; Ciborra & Hanseth, 1998). Jarvenpaa and Ives (1996) found that the technology was neither initiated by the organization's central IT function nor by senior management. Rather, it was initiated by decentralized "technology champions" in a variety of organizational functions *outside* the IT function.

From a managerial perspective intranet technology's cost, flexibility, open standards base and wide spectrum of uses does indeed render it an attractive information technology in the organizational environment. However, the technology also introduces a number of unique dilemmas when it comes to managing its organizational rollout process. For example, how should managers approach such an emergent and ubiquitous type of technology where numerous other organizational parties can vigorously be pursuing their own child intranet implementations? We will take a closer look at some of these issues by means of a case study.

INTRANET IMPLEMENTATION AT PHONECO

Like many large organizations worldwide, the South African company PhoneCo developed its own intranet during the 1990s. PhoneCo (a pseudonym) is a large telecommunications service provider with branches across Southern Africa. PhoneCo has around 50,000 employees in total. The organization consists of a corporate office and has a typical hierarchical structure with a number of large, specialized service groups. The service groups are geographically located in a large number of regional offices in all the main centers of southern Africa. Prior to the development of the intranet, the organization already had an advanced internal communications infrastructure consisting of fast local area and wide area networks. There are about 35,000 interconnected desktop computers in operation throughout the organization. We now examine the development and implementation of PhoneCo's corporate intranet "Content Book" in more detail.

Data collection, analysis and interpretation

The data collection for this case was done between December 1997 and January 1998, with a second round of follow-up interviews with the same interviewees in November 1998. A flexible but rigorous data-gathering strategy was used, which sought to discover a representative set of data (Benbasat, Goldstein, & Mead, 1987). Formal semi-structured interviews of about one and a half hours each were complemented with informal discussions. All interviews were tape-recorded and notes were taken during the interview. Other data collected (Yin, 1989) included notes from discussions, e-mails, policies, reports, demonstrations, intranet usage statistics, our own inspection of the intranet and, in some cases, promotional material (used during the intranet implementation). The interview transcripts were shared with the interviewees to check for possible errors and omissions and to evaluate the validity of our transcription. We interviewed a range of actors who were involved with the intranet. We followed a referral strategy, covering both IT managers responsible for the development of the intranet, as well as other parties

Table 1: Details of interviewees, their roles and data collected

Position of actor	Location in PhoneCo	Intranet involvement	Data source
Information Executive (senior managerial position)	Corporate Office	Intranet sponsor; has official overall responsibility for PhoneCo intranet	Discussions, documentation, demonstration
IT Specialist (junior manager)	Corporate Office, IT Services Group	Intranet coordinator; reports to Information Executive, official project manager for corporate intranet	Recorded interviews, documentation, demonstration, usage statistics
Network specialist (technical position)		Responsible for intranet security, reports to IT Specialist	Discussions, documentation, intranet inspection
Graphics designer (junior appointment)		Intranet content developer	Discussions, documentation, intranet inspection
Project Manager Y2K (junior appointment)	Corporate Office, Y2K Project Office	Intranet user and developer of child Y2K intranet site	Recorded interviews, documentation
Account Executive (senior manager)	Manager responsible for one of the PhoneCo Service Groups	Intranet User; also owner of his group's intranet site	Recorded interviews, documentation
Technical official (junior appointment)	One of the PhoneCo Regional Offices	Intranet user; "unofficial" intranet developer	Recorded interviews, intranet inspection

who were involved with the intranet. The details of the interviewees and the data we collected appear in Table 1.

The processes of data collection, analysis and interpretation overlapped in the study. As Patton (1990) argues, this provided opportunities to improve the quality of data collection and analysis from initial findings. The collected empirical evidence was first organized by event sequences to analyze the unfolding intranet implementation process over time (Sabherwal & Robey, 1993; Robey & Newman, 1996). Subsequent finer levels of analysis were done according to themes (Miles & Huberman, 1984) for example, to identify specific implementation challenges. These different analyses enabled the writing of the implementation accounts that follow below.

We present two seemingly contrasting accounts of the PhoneCo intranet development. Account A is based largely on the perspective of IT managers, while Account B is based on data collected from a variety of other involved parties in the company. We offer an interpretation of each account by drawing upon a different theoretical lens. The two contrasting perspectives and interpretations will serve to illustrate some of the complexities associated with managing organizational intranet developments.

Account A: Intranet take-up at PhoneCo

Like many large hierarchically structured organizations, PhoneCo faces problems with sharing information across functional and unit boundaries. Such information sharing is vital for initiatives such as business process re-engineering (BPR), total quality management (TQM) and cross-functional project collaboration.

Realizing the potential of intranet technology to address these problems, PhoneCo's Information Executive established a small team (four staff members within the IT Services Group) with the responsibility of establishing a corporate intranet for the organization. The team consisted of an intranet coordinator, a graphics designer, a Web developer and a network security expert. The team designed the basic corporate intranet structure in the form of a homepage and a series of structured indexes that cascaded to unit level intranet home pages. Hence the name of the intranet: 'Content Book.' Implementation started in February 1997.

The Information Executive then developed an intranet policy for the organization that enforced professional standards. Procedures were introduced to ensure proper business-related intranet use, quality assurance of content and a standard look and feel. The Executive also recommended hypertext standards and the obligatory tracking of site usage (hit counters), issued firewall guidelines and set up company-wide intranet training courses. PhoneCo's communications department appointed a specialist to advise units on intranet information quality.

The intranet team launched an internal marketing campaign with posters advertising the corporate intranet (*"Get a life, get a website"*) and encouraging people to adopt and apply the technology. In addition, an intranet forum was established, a monthly 'best intranet site' was chosen, and information about Content Book was distributed to all employees via their pay slips. Despite this, some top managers remained skeptical about the technology and were concerned that "surfing the intranet means playing around all day." The coordinator addressed their concerns and aimed to convince these managers that the intranet is "of business value to them." For example, she was planning to set up an intranet café within the head-office restaurant in order to acquaint these managers with the new technology and demonstrate its potential. The coordinator summarized the devolution of page authoring:

"Content creation is widespread. One cannot single out specific users, but staff with IT knowledge in PhoneCo create a lot of Web sites since they know the technology."

The intranet coordinator reflected on the implementation:

"It's successful, even though it's early days. It's not where I would like it to be, but I think it is successful and it's going to be more successful in the future."

Interpretation of Account A

In analyzing Account A and especially in the way this account was presented to us during data collection, one is tempted to view the account as the classical organizational diffusion of an information technology innovation.

Classical diffusion of innovation theory (e.g., Rogers, 1995) is useful in understanding the process through which a new innovation (often initiated by a single individual or small group of actors) spreads to a much larger group of actors who adopt it and ultimately put it into use. Diffusion theory has been widely applied in the study of information technology in an organizational context (Tornatzky & Klein, 1982; Kwon & Zmud, 1987; Cooper & Zmud, 1990; Attewell, 1992). In this respect, information technology implementation is seen as part of an organizational diffusion process, with the focal technology as the innovation. For example, the much-cited Cooper and Zmud model (1990), drawing on Zmud's earlier work (Kwon & Zmud, 1987), proposes six stages of information technology implementation:

1. Initiation
2. Adoption
3. Adaptation
4. Acceptance
5. Routinization
6. Infusion

Initiation concerns the active or passive scanning of organizational problems and opportunities, together with IT solutions. The initiation stage is triggered by change pressures emanating from either an organizational need (pull) or technology innovation (push) or both. Initiation is followed by the adoption stage that features rational and political negotiations to gain organizational backing for the implementation. This stage is marked by a decision to invest organizational resources to sustain the implementation. Following adoption, the process proceeds through an adaptation stage that involves the installation and maintenance of the information technology. During the adaptation stage organizational procedures may be altered and developed due to the information technology, and organizational actors are trained both in terms of the technology and new procedures. An acceptance stage follows where the technology is employed in organizational work and actors are encouraged to commit to using the technology. After the acceptance stage, the routinization stage follows where the information technology becomes a normal part of the organizational activity. The final stage in the Cooper and Zmud implementation model describes an infusion stage where increased organizational effectiveness results from use of the information technology. At this stage, realization of the technology's fullest potential occurs and it supports higher-level aspects of organizational work.

Using such a diffusion approach to conceptualize the intranet introduction at PhoneCo would yield the following plausible analysis of Account A:

1. **Initiation**. The Internet craze during the mid-1990s provided the technology

push. The organizational need (pull) was the need to change to flatter structures with much more information openness, together with the need to work across traditional intra-organizational boundaries. The Information Executive, realizing the fit between technological opportunity and organizational problem, commissioned the intranet project.

2. **Adoption**. The costs of the development were low, and the Executive was able to commit organizational resources (the development team). The establishment of the team marks the start of the project and formal adoption of the intranet technology.

3. **Adaptation**. 'Content Book' was developed to reflect the organizational structure and was launched. Training programs were initiated and sets of procedures devised to help the organization adapt and to align with the new ways of working offered by the development.

4. **Acceptance**. With the infrastructure and procedures in place, the attention shifted to inducing the wider organizational community to accept and apply the technology in their work processes. The marketing campaign was aimed both at staff in general and some laggard managers who were still skeptical.

5. **Routinization**. The PhoneCo diffusion process at the time of our research can be categorized as moving from the acceptance stage to the routinization stage. Although many staff members had bought into the new technology, it was only beginning to become widely incorporated into the day-to-day routines of organizational life at PhoneCo.

6. **Infusion**. The realization of the full potential of the technology was anticipated, but not yet achieved (as is evident from the final comment of the intranet coordinator).

Account B: Intranet take-up at PhoneCo

In contrast to the clear, orderly diffusion account presented above, we however also uncovered a second "version of the truth" during our empirical research at PhoneCo. This second account represents a much less unified story, more a number of seemingly unconnected and out-of-sequence mini-stories.

"Island" intranets

Well before the development of 'Content Book' in 1996, several individuals in dispersed service groups and regional offices within PhoneCo started to "play" with intranet technology. A number of island intranet sites emerged. These intranet initiatives often took place quite informally, and outside the auspices of PhoneCo's central IT Services Group. The developers of these sites usually had a personal interest in the Internet and were using IT in their day-to-day activities.

The technical official

One such island intranet initiative involved a technical official at a regional office. The official was not formally trained as an IT practitioner, nor did he hold an IT position. His normal duties included extracting telephone line statistics from monitoring equipment for reports for regional managers. Since he was an avid Internet surfer in his private time, the technician started to play with intranet technology and, teaching himself as he went along and borrowing server space from his friends in PhoneCo's formal IT environments, he developed his own intranet site. This served to disseminate the information that his unit had previously distributed on paper. Although the unit's clients, the regional managers, preferred their information delivered in this way, the technical official commented:

> "I'm not officially supposed to be involved with the intranet. I just started using it to make my job easier. They [my own unit's management] can say to me tomorrow to leave it and focus on what I'm supposed to do."

"The Wall"

During PhoneCo's merger with two equity partners, an intranet discussion forum was created. It became known as "the Wall" because the interface cleverly took the form of a brick wall with graffiti (the discussion messages). Users could post graffiti to the Wall about their concerns during the merger talks. The discussions were threaded, so one could follow trails, but all messages were anonymous. Following the merger, the Wall became a place where people discussed general PhoneCo issues. One intranet user (a relatively junior appointment) said the Wall was great—it gave employees a way of airing their concerns and venting their frustration. He read the Wall on a daily basis to see what was being discussed, and he liked to post messages to it. By contrast, a more senior manager had a different perspective. He called it the "Wailing Wall." He considered it to be of no value, very negative and he thought it should be shut down.

The project manager

Around December 1996, the project manager tasked to coordinate PhoneCo's Year 2000 compliance project started to use intranet technology for coordinating the effort. He created an intranet site with links to the various Y2K sub-projects that were being coordinated through his office. He commented:

> "The intranet is not our main focus—the Y2K project is. The intranet is just a tool for us for the project."

The Y2K sub-projects were responsible for their own intranet sites. The project manager was also a keen contributor to the Wall. He always referred to the Y2K intranet as *the* intranet and had no interest in Content Book. The centralized procedures required him, for example, to incorporate a hit counter, but he had no idea how to do that.

The information executive

The emergence of many of these initiatives throughout the organization coincided with the decision of a head office Information Executive to commission the development of a corporate intranet. This marked the formal start of PhoneCo's Content Book project in February 1997.

The senior manager

Various PhoneCo service units started actively to establish their own intranet presence. A senior manager of one such department contacted an outside supplier to develop their department intranet site, because "it was taking too long for my people to do as a sideline." An IT specialist remarked of these intranet efforts:

> "…some departments are creating Web sites purely because they want to learn the technology. Everybody else is creating Web sites, so they got to keep up with it."

Interpretation of Account B

How can we interpret these rather messy, unrelated, confusing mini-stories presented above? One way could be to examine this account using a different theoretical lens, one that is more oriented towards understanding the social practices in which the innovation is embedded. In structuration theory, Giddens provides us with one such lens. Structuration theory seeks to explain how the knowledgeable actions of human agents recursively invoke the sets of rules and understandings that make up structure. At the same time the theory describes how the social practice of individuals (doing things together within the context of structure) reproducing across time and space makes up the constitution of society. Thus, 'social practices, biting into time and space, are considered to be at the root of both subject and social objects' (Giddens, 1984). Human agency, in Giddens' formulation, is the 'capacity to make a difference' (Giddens, 1984). He defines structure as:

> 'rules and resources recursively implicated in social reproduction; institutionalized features of social systems have structural properties in the sense that relationships are stabilized across time and space. Structure…exists only as memory traces, the organic basis of human knowledgeability, and is instantiated in action' (Giddens, 1984).

Giddens thus recasts the two independent sets of phenomena (dualism) of structure and agency as a 'duality'—two concepts which are dependent upon each other and recursively related. 'The structural properties of social systems are both medium and outcome of the practices they recursively organize' (Giddens, 1984). Structuration is therefore the process whereby the duality of interaction and structure evolves and is reproduced over time and space. Agents in their actions constantly reproduce and develop the social structures that both constrain and enable them. In structuration theory, information technology is a resource that actors employ in social practice (Jones, 1997; Rose, 1999). As that practice spreads over time and space, the technology may become embedded in the practice

Drawing upon structuration theory to interpret the richer account of the intranet implementation at PhoneCo yields the following: PhoneCo, like any other organization, is made up of individuals trying to do things that they perceive to be useful, in the situation they perceive themselves to be in. They use all kinds of tools and technologies to help themselves. In structuration theory these are theorized as actions (doing things), structure (the situation) and resources (tools). The Y2K project manager has a need to coordinate a number of different projects (action); his situation involves an awareness of the technical possibilities (structure); the resource is intranet technology. When he implements the Web site and his colleagues start to use it, a new social practice emerges, but one that has strong roots in previous practices. There have always been projects that need coordinating and ways of communicating about them (memo, phone, e-mail, discussion group). When his colleagues use the site, the possibilities of the technology also become part of their awareness. If in the future they had a similar need, they would then have to consider the same technological resource, however fleetingly. Other examples in the company can be analyzed in the same way; for instance the practice of distributing telephone statistics evolves into a new practice incorporating intranet technology. Whereas these examples focus on action (things that need to be done), we can also find examples that are driven by the emerging structure. The senior manager who contracts out his department's intranet development is not reflecting the task needs of his department so much as the pressure resulting from other department's developments. Since everyone else is doing it, he has to follow suit, otherwise he may lose face. He will have a very attractive site (at some monetary cost), but without distracting his staff from their more important tasks. The technology has taken on significance beyond its ability to contribute to task efficiency and become a legitimizing device. The manager must comply with the trend or risk his power base eroding. Now we must also observe that these actors are not merely members of PhoneCo, but of many overlapping social collectivities: families, societies, clubs—ultimately of society itself. Though the idea of organizational intranets may be relatively new, the Internet technology, together with the social practices that surround it, has been established for some time. Through the mechanisms of time space distanciation, system and social integration, the technology and social practice have become well embedded in the organizational domain and form a routine part of many people's lives. Though we did not think to collect this data, it seems reasonable to assume that all these actors may already have had considerable experience with the protocols, standards and software outside their work lives. They may have children with Internet access in their schools, PCs at home, be familiar with e-mail, e-commerce, seen their colleagues' business processes re-engineered and so on. In fact the technology itself is a powerful driver of system integration—social integration over distance. Since the PhoneCo actors are familiar both with the technology and the idea that they can improve their work lives with it, it does not seem particularly remarkable that islands of intranet practice should emerge spontaneously within the company. One of the islands of practice, the Wailing Wall, no longer serves the purposes of the dominant management group. This is not part of the official PhoneCo corporate intranet; nevertheless it has become so well embedded that, for the moment, it cannot be closed down.

DISCUSSION AND
MANAGERIAL IMPLICATIONS

What should we make of these two seemingly contradictory accounts of the intranet take-up at PhoneCo? More importantly, what managerial implications can we draw from the accounts? Account A is rational, orderly, top-down and maps well onto traditional IT implementation models. For some managers it may be a comforting tale, but we believe it is also a "convenient fiction" (Kling, 1991) if one is oblivious to the social reality as illustrated in Account B. Account B is messy, disorderly and a bottom-up description of a number of social practices in which the innovation is embedded. Curiously, both accounts were reflected equally well in our empirical research base.

We believe the two accounts are not contradictory, but rather complementary of each other. Both make up parts of the complex technical and social reality of the intranet at PhoneCo. Of course, these two accounts are just examples of many such stories; we focus on them in particular, because for us they exemplify perspectives that may lead to questionable decisions if they are considered in isolation. For example, by fixating on Account A, IT Managers may be lured into developing a series of classical step-by-step, top-down, action steps to coordinate and control the intranet implementation process. Such an approach could deny the many local, child-level intranet initiatives, which may already be flourishing unofficially. In fact these informal efforts can actually predate the formal intranet and a heavy-handed top-down management approach may leave the pioneers of these efforts feeling alienated. Furthermore, an overemphasis on control mechanisms (e.g., intranet usage and content standards) may stifle users' creativity and even deter users from establishing new intranet sites. The end-result can be an intranet with insufficient information content to attract further users. On the other hand, considering Account B in isolation, IT managers may be lured into abdicating their responsibility and leaving the intranet to grow wild. This can rapidly result in a proliferating mess of unrelated intranet developments, useless content, information overload and even network congestion. Such a managerial approach also holds the danger that planned intranet initiatives become diluted in the process, since the seamless nature of the technology can have a ripple effect on the perception of the whole intranet user community. For example, organization-wide intranet searches that reveal outdated information or broken hyperlinks on some sites can quickly lead to a general distrust of the intranet and prompt users to revert to alternative information sources.

We offer some managerial guidelines based on both accounts, and we compare our suggestions to some recent intranet implementation research in the following section.

Balance control and individual ownership

We argue that the key challenge is to find a balance between the organized, controlled and directed approach of Account A (for another example see Bidgoli,

1999), while at the same time fostering the kind of individual initiative and interest which feeds the local developments (as Account B exemplifies). Too much control and the individual interest dies, too little control and intranet chaos results (Phillips, 1998). The end result is the same in both cases: intranet stagnation (as described by Damsgaard & Scheepers, 2000). Over time the nature of this managerial challenge shifts, as the intranet evolves in content and technological sophistication. Hence it is necessary to continually evaluate the appropriateness and timing of managerial interventions.

Cultivate the intranet as a medium, do not manage it as a system

Furthermore, as Account B illustrates, the time/space notions of different social practices means that both formal, child and informal intranet levels can coexist within the same organization; they can be at different stages of development, with varying degrees of sophistication, and can have different associated user bases and use practices. This observation is also supported by Cecez-Kecmanovic et al. (1999). Consequently we argue that it is vital to take context-specific issues (also at unit levels) into account when formulating intranet implementation plans. Intranet managers should be cautious of classical IT perspectives that often treat the IT innovation as constant and homogeneous (as also argued by Lyytinen & Damsgaard, 1998). We warn against regarding the intranet as if it is a homogenous system that can be controlled with blanket usage standards and policies. Instead we concur that it should be conceptualized and managed as a connection medium (Dahlbom, 1996) that consists of a mosaic of related components (with decentralized ownership), each evolving over time and space. The latter view would demand a more collaborative and facilitative managerial style that acknowledges diversity and individual contributions.

Aim towards a self-sustaining intranet

Intranet technology is essentially a pull technology and intranet use is largely voluntary (Lyytinen et al., 1998). Hence, tactics such as enhancing intranet awareness through intranet campaigns, ongoing education, presentations, intranet treasure hunts and the use of other promotional activities should be considered to foster individual initiative and draw users to the intranet (Hills, 1997; Damsgaard & Scheepers, 1999). Initially, potential intranet users need to be convinced of the benefits of the intranet (Laudon & Laudon, 2000) so that they do in fact adopt and start using the technology. The essence of the managerial challenge during the early stage of intranet introduction is the following: how to convince employees to adopt the technology when there is not yet a real benefit to the individual user (little or no useful intranet content may exist at this stage). One way of meeting this challenge is for managers to identify the intranet killer applications in their specific contexts that will induce and sustain usage and content creation (e.g., intranet-based phone/

employee directories, document management applications, externally sourced intranet content, support for staff home pages, Web-enablement of legacy systems, etc. [Rein et al., 1997; Balasubramanian & Bashian, 1998]). Factors such as top management sponsorship and funding (Bhattacherjee, 1998; Bidgoli, 1999), an established networking and computing infrastructure (Chellapa et al., 1997) and the necessary intranet technical expertise (Lau, 1999; Scheepers, 1999a) should also foster the rollout process.

Given the wide variety of organizational actors who can potentially be involved with the intranet, we concur that organizational coordination and control mechanisms (e.g., Web councils, intranet steering groups) are indeed necessary once the intranet has taken off in the organization (Hills, 1997; Bidgoli, 1999). However, given the nature of the technology, we argue that such coordination mechanisms should be facilitative and inclusive rather than exclusive. In organizations that are comprised of loosely coupled units with their own child intranets, it will probably make more sense for intranet coordination responsibility to be devolved to unit levels (see e.g., Bhattacherjee, 1998). Items such as an intranet policy, usage and content guidelines, the standardization of the look and feel of intranet pages should be on the intranet managerial agenda as the technology becomes organizationally more pervasive to prevent information chaos (Damsgaard & Scheepers, 2000). As indicated earlier, the timing of such controls need, however, to be considered carefully so as not to stifle creativity or content creation (Bansler et al., 2000; Laudon & Laudon, 2000).

FURTHER MANAGERIAL AND RESEARCH ISSUES

As more and more organizations begin to harness the fruits of the Internet revolution (Castells, 1996), new opportunities continue to arise, but these are often accompanied by new managerial and technical challenges, not to mention legal and ethical considerations. In this chapter we purposefully restricted the scope to organizational intranets and we explored some key managerial challenges that we believe are associated with this technology. However, we will highlight a few issues beyond the narrow scope of the presented case that we feel deserve further managerial and research attention.

Given the empirical base and timeframe of the case we examined here, we focused on the situation where an intranet is essentially homegrown and developed by the organization itself. However, a recent trend (as the intranet consulting and service sectors mature) is the increasing number of off-the-shelf (or so-called "intranet-in-a-box") solutions that are now available commercially. Such packages typically offer the organization a basic intranet framework and templates for departmental home pages, product directories and other organizational information sets that can be customized according to specific requirements. Intranet-in-a-box packages can also offer some basic functionality such as search, authoring and quality management tools. Such packages allow organizations to begin with at least some intranet base, albeit only skeletal. This raises the managerial consideration of whether to buy a packaged intranet solution and customize that further or whether to build an intranet from scratch. We will not debate this buy-versus-build decision here, but we do argue that even if the organization opts to buy an off-the-shelf intranet solution, our managerial advice does still hold. An off-the-shelf intranet solution may allow the organization to leapfrog the pioneering stages of its intranet development process. Furthermore, it may provide a more standardized intranet in terms of look and feel, especially if authoring features are included in the packaged solution. Despite this, we maintain that intranet stagnation can still occur due to a lack of customized content creation or due to a mass of useless or low quality content. We argue that the key managerial challenge remains the same, also in the packaged scenario: to find the right balance between top-down control while cultivating bottom-up intranet initiatives and content creation. We speculate that in the case of a packaged intranet solution, the need for managerial controls may arise sooner, if indeed it accelerates the intranet take-up process.

As illustrated by the case and also reported in some other intranet research (e.g. Jarvenpaa & Ives, 1996), organizational intranet introduction was initiated by actors (technology champions) outside the IT function. This may create the impression that the organization's central IT function has a passive or reactive role or even that it is bypassed in the case of intranet implementation. We believe this to be a misconception. Although some limelight may be stolen by all the decentralized child intranet efforts, we argue that the organization's central IT department has a fundamental role to play to cultivate a richer intranet content and usage base, but also in intranet control. The IT unit usually houses the skills that enable more advanced organizational application of the technology (beyond only the publication of static intranet pages). For this reason, the IT unit should lead technical intranet infrastructure developments to allow organization-wide searching (e.g., implementing organizational search engines) and transacting (building links to legacy systems and integrating existing organizational databases with the intranet). We also argue that the central IT unit has a key role to play in establishing intranet training programs, policy formulation, risk management and information quality monitoring.

From a research perspective, we do not think that linear diffusion models adequately capture, or wholly analytically inform, the take-up of intranet technology in organizations. This technology is much more accessible and pervasive, with greater interpretive flexibility (Orlikowski, 1992; Lyytinen & Damsgaard, 1998) than more traditional technologies (for which such diffusion models may have been appropriate). There is a critical need for complementary, richer, more organic theories and analytical approaches in this particular research domain. In particular, we caution intranet consultants and researchers who conduct studies in this domain to be alert and suspicious (Klein & Myers, 1999) and careful not to be lured into skewed interpretations of the phenomena they encounter. During our fieldwork, interviewees had divergent notions of the intranet, often seeing their own child Web intranet as *the* intranet. The intranet concept thus incorporates different meanings for different actors, and we urge researchers to accommodate for this in their empirical research designs. Lastly, we believe there is an urgent need for empirical studies of packaged intranet implementations that could, for example, examine issues such as the timing of managerial controls.

CONCLUSION

This chapter has investigated the implementation of an organizational intranet in a large South African company. We found that the IT managers told a conventional management story that was easy to interpret with classical diffusion theory. In this story, the managers are the principal actors and they are diffusing the new technology from the center to the rest of the organization in a rational, planned, stepwise fashion. Conversely, this story masked many other events in the company that could not be interpreted in this way, or by using this theory. In order to make sense of the actions of other independent actors also introducing intranet technology, we had to employ ideas from the realm of social theory—in this case structuration theory. This helped to explain the emergent disjointed picture of individuals and groups working with the new technology for their own purposes in more random and haphazard ways.

We conclude that intranet management approaches based solely on traditional implementation thinking, command and control methods are unlikely to be successful without careful attention to the cultivation, care and organization of intranet end-users and their individual and unit-level problem situations. The IT managers' role should combine traditional development and implementation project skills, with facilitation and support skills for the various intranet pioneers, coordination and integration skills for existing Web projects, standard-setting skills as developments take off (to avoid information chaos) and organizational development skills to encourage the various intranet contributors to work together in a productive way. The timing of the deployment of these skills will also be critical.

An intranet cannot be regarded as a single system or managed in a traditional paradigm, but should rather be cultivated as a mosaic of both top-down and bottom-up efforts with distributed ownership. This demands a different managerial mindset compared to many other types of IT; intranet managers must know when to let go and when to control. The complexity associated with the ubiquitous computing paradigm suggests that there are few quick intranet fixes. The technology is exceptionally attractive and promising, and the first steps in intranet implementation can be deceptively simple. However, as the case demonstrates, intranet success encompasses a complex interplay between technology and organizational practice, which take time to mutually adapt and integrate. We believe managers who recognize the inherent challenges associated with the technology and who can tailor their implementation approaches as such will be more successful in their intranet endeavors.

Acknowledgments

Thanks go to Tom McMaster and Todd Bentley for their comments. We also thank the anonymous reviewers and the editor for their useful suggestions. This work was supported in part by funding from the Danish Research Agency under the PITNIT Project – Grant number 9900102.

REFERENCES

Attewell, P. (1992). Technology diffusion and organizational learning: The case of business computing. *Organization Science*, 3(1), 1-19.

Balasubramanian, V. and Bashian, A. (1998). Document management and Web technologies: Alice marries the Mad Hatter. *Communications of the ACM*, 41(7), 107-115.

Bansler, J. P., Damsgaard, J., Scheepers, R., Havn, E., and Thommesen, J. (2000). Corporate intranet implementation: Managing emergent technologies and organizational practices. Forthcoming in *Journal of the Association of Information Systems*.

Benbasat, I., Goldstein, D. K. and Mead, M. (1987). The case research strategy in studies of information systems. *MIS Quarterly*, 11(3), 369-386.

Bernard, R. (1996). *The Corporate Intranet*. New York: John Wiley & Sons.

Bhattacherjee, A. (1998). Management of emerging technologies: Experiences and lessons learned at US West. *Information & Management*, 33, 263-272.

Bidgoli, H. (1999, Summer). An integrated model for introducing intranets. *Information Systems Management*, 78-87.

Castells, M. (1996). *The Rise of the Network Society*. Oxford: Blackwell Publishers.

Cecez-Kecmanovic, D., Moodie, D., Busuttil, A. and Plesman, F. (1999). Organizational change mediated by e-mail and intranet—an ethnographic study. *Information, Technology & People*, 12(1), 9-26.

Chellapa, R., Barua, A. and Whinston, A. B. (1997). Intranets: Looking beyond internal corporate Web servers. In Kalakota, R., and Whinston, A. B. (Eds.), *Readings in Electronic Commerce*, Reading, Massachusetts: Addison-Wesley. 311-321.

Ciborra, C. U. (Ed.) (1996). *Groupware & Teamwork*. New York: John Wiley & Sons.

Ciborra, C. U. and Hanseth, O. (1998). From tool to Gestell: Agendas for managing the information infrastructure. *Information, Technology & People*, 11(4), 305-327.

Cooper, R. B. and Zmud, R. W. (1990). Information technology implementation research: A technological diffusion approach. *Management Science*, 36(2), 123-139.

Dahlbom, B. (1996). The new informatics. *Scandinavian Journal of Information Systems*, 8(2), 29-48.

Damsgaard, J. and Scheepers, R. (1999). Power, influence and intranet implementation: A safari of South African organizations. *Information, Technology & People*, 12(4), 333-358.

Damsgaard, J. and Scheepers, R. (2000). Managing the crises in intranet implementation: A stage model. *Information Systems Journal*, 10(2), 131-149.

Davenport, T. H. and Pruzak, L. (1998). *Working Knowledge: How Organizations Manage What They Know*. Boston, Massachusetts: Harvard Business School Press.

Dennis, A. R. (1996, December). Information exchange and use in group decision making: You can lead a group to information, but you can't make it think. *MIS Quarterly*, 433-455.

Gartner Group. (1997). Meeting the intranet challenge: Technologies, organizations, processes. *Inside Gartner Group this Week*, XIII (49), 1-4.

Giddens, A. (1984). *The Constitution of Society: Outline of the Theory of Structuration*. Cambridge: Polity Press.

Goles, T. and Hirschheim, R. (Eds.) (1997). *Intranets: The Next IS Solution?* Houston, Texas: Information Systems Research Center, College of Business Administration, University of Houston.

Grudin, J. and Palen, L. (1995). Why groupware succeeds: Discretion or mandate? In *Proceedings of IRIS18, Gothenburg Studies in Informatics, Report 7* (Dahlbom, B., Kämmerer, F., Ljungberg, F., Stage, J., Sørensen, C., Eds.), 217-232.

Hills, M. (1997). *Intranet Business Strategies*. New York: John Wiley and Sons.

Hirschheim, R. A. (1986). The effect of a priori views on the social implications of computing: The case of office automation. *Computing Surveys*, 18(2), 165-195.

Isakowitz, T., Bieber, M. and Vitali, F. (1998). Web information systems. *Communications of the ACM*, 41(7), 78-80.

Jarvenpaa, S. L. and Ives, B. (1996). Introducing transformational information technologies: The case of the World Wide Web technology. *International Journal of Electronic Commerce*, 1(1), 95-126.

Jones, M. (1997). Structuration and IS. In Currie, W. L. and Galliers, R. D., (Eds.), *Re-Thinking Management Information Systems*. Oxford: Oxford University Press.

Klein, H. K. and Myers, M. D. (1999). A set of principles for conducting and evaluating interpretive field studies in information systems. *MIS Quarterly*, 23(1), 67-92.

Kling, R. (1991). Computerization and social transformations. *Science, Technology and Human Values*, 6(3), 342-367.

Kwon, T. H. and Zmud, R. W. (1987). Unifying the fragmented models of information systems implementation. In Boland, R. J., and Hirschheim, R. A., (Eds.), *Critical Issues in Information Systems Research*. New York: John Wiley and Sons, 227-251.

Lau, L. M. S. (1999). Skills for a sustainable intranet. In *Proceedings of the 7th European Conference on Information Systems*, 23-25 June, Copenhagen, Denmark. Pries-Heje, J., Ciborra, C., Kautz, K., Valor, J., Christiaanse, E., Avison, D., and Heje, C., (Eds.), 453-464.

Laudon, K. C. and Laudon, J. P. (2000). *Management Information Systems:*

Organization and Technology in the Networked Enterprise (6th ed.). Upper Saddle River, New Jersey: Prentice-Hall, Inc.

Lyytinen, K. and Damsgaard, J. (1998). *What's Wrong with the Diffusion of Innovation Theory? The Case of Networked and Complex Technologies.* Working paper, R-98-5010. Aalborg, Denmark: Department of Computer Science, Aalborg University.

Lyytinen, K., Rose, G. and Welke, R. (1998). The brave new world of development in the internetwork computing architecture (InterNCA): Or how distributed computing platforms will change systems development. *Information Systems Journal*, 8, 241-253.

Markus, M. L. (1983). Power, politics and MIS implementation. *Communications of the ACM*, 26(6), 430-444.

McNaughton, R. B., Quickenden, P., Matear, S. and Gray, B. (1999). Intranet adoption and inter-functional coordination. *Journal of Marketing Management*, 15, 387-403.

Miles, M. B. and Huberman, A. M. (1984). *Qualitative Data Analysis: A Sourcebook of New Methods.* Beverly Hills, California: Sage Publications.

Nolan, R. L. (1973). Managing the computer resource: a stage hypothesis. *Communications of the ACM*, 16(7), 399-405.

Oppliger, R. (1997). Internet security: Firewalls and beyond. *Communications of the ACM*, 40(5), 92-102.

Orlikowski, W. J. (1992). The duality of technology: Rethinking the concept of technology in organizations. *Organization Science*, 3(3), 398-427.

Orlikowski, W. J. and Gash, D.C. (1994). Technological frames: Making sense of information technology in organizations. *ACM Transactions on Information Systems*, 12(2), 174-207.

Orlikowski, W. J., Yates, J., Okamura, K. and Fujimoto, M. (1995). Shaping electronic communication: The metastructuring of technology in the context of use. *Organization Science*, 6(4), 423-444.

Patton, M. Q. (1990). *Qualitative Evaluation Methods* (2nd ed.). Newbury Park, California: Sage Publications.

Phillips, T. (1998). Members-only Web. *Management Today*, July, 70-74.

Rein, G. L., McCue, D. L. and Slein, J. A. (1997). A case for document management functions on the Web. *Communications of the ACM*, 40(9), 81-89.

Robey, D. and Newman, M. (1996). Sequential patterns in information systems development: An application of a social process model. *ACM Transactions on Information Systems*, 14(1), 30-63.

Rogers, E. M. (1995). *Diffusion of Innovations* (4th ed.). The Free Press, New York.

Romm, C. T. and Wong, J. (1998). The dynamics of establishing organizational Web sites: Some puzzling findings. *Australian Journal of Information Systems*, 5(2), 60-68.

Rose, J. (1999). Frameworks for practice—structurational theories of IS. In *Proceedings of the 7th European Conference on Information Systems,* 23-25 June,

Copenhagen, Denmark, (Pries-Heje, J., Ciborra, C., Kautz, K., Valor, J., Christiaanse, E., Avison, D., Heje, C., Eds.), 640-655.

Sabherwal, R. and Robey, D. (1993). An empirical taxonomy of implementation for processes based on sequences of events in information systems development. *Organization Science*, 4(4), 548-576.

Scheepers, R. (1999a). Key role players in the initiation and implementation of intranet technology. In Proceedings of IFIP TC8 WG 8.2, *"New Information Technologies in Organizational Processes: Field Studies and Theoretical Reflections on the Future of Work,"* St. Louis, MO, August 21-22, (Ngwenyama, O., Introna, L. D., Myers, M.D., DeGross, J. I., Eds.). Kluwer Academic Publishers, 175-195.

Scheepers, R. (1999b). *Intranet Implementation: Influences, Challenges and Role Players*. PhD thesis. R-99-5011, Department of Computer Science, Aalborg University, Denmark.

Srinivasan, A. and Davis, J. G. (1987). A reassessment of implementation process models. *Interfaces*, 17(3), 64-71.

Tornatzky, L. G. and Klein, K. J. (1982). Innovation characteristics and innovation adoption-implementation: A meta-analysis of findings. *IEEE Transactions on Engineering Management*, EM-29(1), 28-45.

Yin, R. K. (1989). *Case Study Research: Design and Methods*. Newbury Park, California: Sage Publications.

CHAPTER TWO

Service Quality
in the Virtual World:
The Case
of Extranets

Beverley Hope
Victoria University of Wellington, New Zealand

The Internet has taken globalization of the marketplace from hyperbole to present-day reality. In this marketplace, information technology can be used to create and sustain market share. One such technology is the extranet. Extranets are increasingly being used to add value through business-to-business information sharing and transaction handling in a secure environment. Yet there is limited research into perceptions of service quality in Web-based Internet environments such as extranets. In this chapter we relate the literature on services and service quality to the developing literature on extranets. Five dimensions of service quality from the physical world are applied to the virtual world of commerce. It is concluded that dimensions of quality in human-to-human interactions may also apply to human-to-computer interactions, but that the factors which contribute to each dimension may differ.

INTRODUCTION

In competitive environments organizations must take every opportunity to strengthen relationships with existing customers. Information technologies are increasingly being used for this purpose. As Abrahamson and Telford (1998) observe:

Organizations which harness the powerful new benefits of information [technology] to establish intangibles, such as service quality, should enjoy an enhanced and sustainable competitive advantage (cited in Lloyd & Boyle, 1998, p. 93).

One information technology which is increasingly being used to improve customer service is the extranet. Extranets are "permeable yet secure commerce-enabled networks, which electronically link distributed organizations over the Internet in a private forum" (OneSoft, 1998). They are IP networks which allow a company to run Web applications for customers, suppliers and trusted partners, enhancing communications, improving relationships and reducing costs (Vlosky & Fontenot, 1999). They differ from e-commerce retailing in that they are open only to selected partners and tend to involve greater information sharing on the part of the host firm.

Extranets, together with enterprise portals, are the technology of the future. Business-to-business markets are expected to account for the vast majority of e-commerce for the foreseeable future (Kalakota, Olivia & Donoth, 1999). Extranets first caught on in vertical industries and have been used to automate the supply chain (see Benjamin & Wigand, 1995). Strong use is expected in the near future from the finance and health industries (Shein & Neil, 1998). For example, in New Zealand we see strong moves into extranets by government and quasi-government agencies supplying information to producers and exporters. An early adopter was the Ministry of Agriculture and Fisheries (MAF) whose extranet supplied complex and changing regulatory information to primary producers.

Currently, there is little reported research dealing with the success of extranet systems. We have some understanding of service quality in the physical world. We have some understanding of interface issues and Web usability. But we have limited insight into customer perceptions of quality in the virtual world. In this chapter we seek to address this deficiency by reviewing the literature on services and service quality, and relating that literature to extranet systems.

BACKGROUND

Services

Commerce has come a long way since 1776 when Adam Smith distinguished between productive and unproductive labor on the basis of whether the labor produced goods (productive labor) or services (unproductive labor) (Smith, 1977). Today we live and work in an economy dominated by services. Even manufacturing firms compete to some extent on the basis of service. In the production of commodities, good products are no longer sufficient for businesses to remain competitive; service quality becomes the distinguishing characteristic (Gronroos, 1990; Mastenbroek, 1991).

But service quality has proved an elusive construct which is difficult to delimit and to measure. Four characteristics of services contribute to this difficulty: service intangibility, customer-producer inseparability, performance heterogeneity and service non-storability (Gronroos, 1990; Zeithaml, Parasuraman & Berry, 1990).

Service intangibility refers to the fact that services are performances or experiences rather than objects. This makes it difficult for consumers to assess services prior to delivery, particularly at the pure services end of the goods-services continuum. Intangibility also creates difficulties for suppliers in objectively defining service characteristics. Intangibility is often cited as the central dimension upon which others rest. In the virtual world of digitized information, intangibility dominates interactions. We might expect that the difficulties occasioned by intangibility in the physical world will apply and be magnified in the virtual world.

Customer-producer inseparability refers to the often synchronic production and consumption of services with the consequent involvement of the customer in the production process. Where the customer is involved in the production process, he or she can evaluate not only the service output but also the process and environment in which it is produced. In the physical world, this is usually where services are performed on or with *persons*, for example, hair styling or loan applications. It is less evident where services are performed on *goods*, for example, repair services. In the virtual world, there is a distancing between customer and producer, with service interaction being mediated by a computer. The 'behind-the-scene' processing separates production and consumption such that the effects of inseparability diminish or even disappear from service interactions in the virtual world.

Performance heterogeneity refers to the potential for high variation in service quality over locations, producers, customers and time. In the physical world this results from the high degree of people involvement in service delivery and the high level of discretionary effort often found in service performance (Zeithaml et al., 1985). In the virtual world, service provision is almost always centralized and frequently computer automated. Consequently, we may find greater consistency in service delivery in the virtual world such that performance heterogeneity disappears as a useful construct. Exceptions may exist where human input is required, for example, follow-ups and e-mail responses to queries, but in general automated responses from Web sites should be more homogeneous than individual responses in the physical world.

Service non-storability: Since services are experiences or performances, they often cannot be stored. The only store for pure services in the physical world is the customer queue, an unacceptable solution for quality-focused organizations. Non-storability makes production capacity planning a critical activity in the world of physical commerce (Fitzsimmons, 1990). In the virtual world, transactions are handled by computers rather than people, with many services involving manipulation of digital information or distribution of digital assets. With increased speed of processing and reusability of digital assets, we find that non-storability is less problematic in the virtual world.

The four characteristics of services have implications for quality in the physical world, notably: service quality is more difficult to evaluate than goods quality, and evaluations may be based not only on output but also on the delivery process. These implications do not necessarily hold true in the virtual world. Intangibility is often cited as the basic goods-services distinction from which other characteristics arise (Bateson, 1979). Yet in the virtual world, where intangibility is likely to be higher, problems from inseparability, heterogeneity and non-storability may actually decrease. Clearly there are differences in service provision and service quality between the physical and the virtual worlds.

Service Quality

Leading service providers see quality as a strategic tool. By delivering superior quality these companies receive benefits including increased growth through improved customer acquisition and retention (Ferguson & Zawacki, 1993; Buzzell & Gale, 1987). Studies using the PIMS (Profit Impact of Marketing Strategies) database have demonstrated a relationship among quality, market share and return on investment. Improved quality was found to lead not only to increased market share but also to increased return on investment for any given market share (Bowen & Cummings, 1990; Buzzell & Gale, 1987). Extranets are one means of adding value, thereby adding to perceptions of service quality.

Models of Service Quality

Definitions of quality have evolved over time from *fitness for use* as required by the Sale of Goods Act, through *meeting specifications* as was common in statistical process control to *meeting or exceeding customer expectations* which is the current common wisdom. These definitions reflect two aspects of quality: quality in fact and quality in perception. Quality in fact involves the meeting of explicit requirements, standards, regulations or specifications. It is a measure of the output of a process and does not question the source of the requirement. Quality in perception describes customer beliefs regarding the quality of service delivered. It is a measure of the outcome of a customer's association with the organization. Quality in fact is a necessary but not sufficient precursor of quality in perception.

In outlining a measurement model, Tenner and DeToro (1992) add a third construct, quality in production (or process). They, therefore, consider three measures: process, output and outcome. Process measures define variables of the work process including process inputs. Output measures define attributes of a completed product or service. Outcome measures define the ultimate impact of the process on the customer and take into account what the customer does with the service or product. Outcome measures are the most difficult to assess and are, therefore, frequently simplified as "customer satisfaction." Outcome measures differ from output measures in that they are more global and tend to be firm specific, whereas output measures are transaction specific.

A well-accepted model which considers process, output and outcome is the GAP model of Zeithaml et al. (1990). In this model, service quality is defined as the degree and direction of the discrepancy between expectations and perceptions of a delivered service (GAP 5). To reduce this gap the provider must close four other gaps.

Management must have an accurate perception of customer expectations (GAP 1), these expectations must be correctly translated into service quality specifications (GAP 2), and employees must produce services which meet these specifications (GAP 3). In addition, the firm must deliver everything that is promised in advertising, personal selling and other communications (GAP 4).

The significant gap in this model is GAP 5, service outcome. To understand and measure this gap, we need to have an understanding of the dimensions on which customers make their evaluations and the way in which they use these dimensions.

Dimensions of Service Quality

Sasser, Olsen and Wyckoff (1978) offer for discussion seven potential elements of quality derived from the literature on basic psychological needs. They hypothesize that service quality might consist of:

security (of the consumer and his or her property),
consistency,
attitude (in interpersonal relations or other communications),
completeness (in the array of services provided),
condition (of the service environment),
availability (in terms of time and location), and
timing (required for access to and completion of a service).

We can readily see how Internet technology and extranets in particular may serve to meet these psychological needs. A sense of *security* may be fostered by the private and secure nature of the extranet as well as by the strength of partnering which exists in the relationship. Feelings of *consistency* in communications can be fostered when pages on a site have standard layout and functionality. Perceptions of *attitude* in interpersonal relations may be improved through use of computer-generated customer profiles to present customized data and interfaces. A sense of *completeness* can be achieved if customer input is sought in determining what information and services can be supplied by the extranet. Completeness is further fostered through the information richness of multimedia implementations. In the virtual world the only control providers have over *condition* of the service environment is the Web site, that is, factors of Web usability such as simplicity, use of white space and use of color. Extranets can rate particularly highly on *availability*, with any-place, any-time being the norm. However, availability can be negatively affected by server downtime, system overload and 'page under construction' glitches. Meeting *timing* requirement requires good underlying information technology and judicious use of graphics. It is less problematic in the business-to-business environment of extranets than in the business-to-consumer environment because of the greater ability to predict load requirements. When we examine extranets from the perspective of psychological needs, we can see how they can be used to foster perceptions of quality and to manage customer relations.

The most recently cited framework of service quality dimensions is that of Parasuraman et al. (1985). These researchers used focus groups to identify potential service quality dimensions and refined them through statistical analysis of a pilot survey instrument (SERVQUAL). The resultant five dimensions were:

Reliability: The ability to perform a promised service dependably and accurately

Responsiveness: A willingness to help customers and to provide support services

Assurance: The knowledge and courtesy of employees and their ability to inspire trust and confidence

Empathy: The caring, individualized attention a firm provides its customers

Tangibles: The physical facilities, equipment and appearance of personnel

In the *human-to-human* environment investigated by Parasuraman et al. (1985), reliability was the foremost dimension used by customers in evaluating service quality, with responsiveness the next most important. Tangibles had the least influence. Given the differential impact of service characteristics in the physical and virtual worlds, we might expect the relative importance of service quality dimensions to also differ.

But how do customers use these dimensions? Sasser, Olsen and Wyckoff (1978) offer three models of how consumers make judgments. They are:

1. *One Overpowering Attribute.* One attribute basically determines the value. All other attributes receive only nominal or no consideration.
2. *Single Attribute with Threshold Minimums for Other Attributes.* An alternative must achieve at least the threshold condition for certain attributes to be considered. But the final ranking is made among the qualified candidates on the basis of a single attribute.
3. *Weighted Average of Attributes.* The alternatives are ranked on the basis of a weighted average, so that a high score on one attribute may offset a low score on another (Sasser, Olsen, and Wyckoff, 1978, p. 179).

Different attributes may attain prominence at different stages in a consumer's acquisition of a service (Bojanic, 1991). Taking this into account and considering individual differences, the wise extranet provider will endeavor to attain high marks on every attribute.

SERVICE QUALITY AND EXTRANETS

There is little literature, either practitioner or academic, that deals specifically with quality of extranet systems. Yet a major driver of extranet implementation is to develop and nurture the customer relationship (OneSoft, 1998). Extranets can foster existing relationships by enabling companies to establish and maintain one-to-one relationships at a very low cost. With extranets, firms can offer customized experiences that are dynamically generated or modified based on a customer's privileges, preferences or usage patterns. In an independent study, Lederer, Mirchandani and Sims (1998) identified the top 10 realized benefits of extranets (Table 1). The list contains several items which might impact service quality. Items 5 (improve customer relations) and 7 (provide better products and services to

Table 1: Top 10 benefits companies seek from extranet systems

1.	Enhance competitiveness or create strategic advantage
2.	Enable easier access to information
3.	Provide new products or service to customers
4.	Increase the flexibility of information requests
5.	Improve customer relations
6.	Enhance the credibility and prestige of the organization
7.	Provide better products or services to customers
8.	Increase the volume of information output
9.	Align well with stated organizational goals
10.	Enable the organization to respond more quickly to change

customers) directly target service quality. Items 2-4 are also closely related to the dimensions of service quality. Thus one-half of the top 10 benefits companies seek from extranet systems are related to service quality objectives.

How do we use extranets to achieve these benefits? What is the relationship between extranets and service quality? We can get some sense of this by considering each of the dimensions of service quality in relation to the technology and processes of Extranet implementation.

Dimensions of Service Quality Applied To the Virtual World

To relate the dimensions of service quality to extranets, we looked at some reported or claimed benefits and concerns of extranets and fitted these to the service quality dimensions defined by Parasuraman et al. (1985). We present our findings next.

Reliability: The ability to perform a promised service dependably and accurately

Using *backup systems* can help ensure the availability of the extranet and minimize downtime. Reduced downtime enhances a firm's image as a provider of reliable, dependable service. But reliability also implies accuracy. One aspect of accuracy is the capture and storage of customer data. Data capture can be enhanced in the extranet environment through automatic *data capture at input*. Removal of the need to rekey data also removes some errors. Information accuracy also implies accuracy of Web site information. Here, accuracy is enhanced through the use of *update commands* on critical information (Bort & Felix, 1997; OneSoft, 1998; Pfaffenberger, 1998) and *scheduled maintenance* of other data and links.

Responsiveness: A willingness to help customers and to provide support services

Extranets use Internet technologies for data transfer. *Bandwidth* on the

Internet is much smaller than that provided by VANs and LANs. If data transmission rates do not meet customer expectations, they may judge the firm (rather than the system) to be unresponsive (Lederer et al., 1998; Senn, 1998; Sharp, 1998). A firm may also be judged unresponsive if it fails to respond quickly to *e-mail or on-line queries* from users. In our experience, extranet processes most often fall down in *handling exceptions* rather than routine transactions. For example, extranets typically handle sales efficiently and effectively but can fall over when it comes to handling returns. Yet, 'putting it right' is the time when customers most demand responsiveness. A quality-conscious firm will need to pay particular attention to the ability of its extranet to handle the exceptions; on these its reputation may rest.

Assurance: Knowledge, courtesy and ability to inspire trust and confidence

Several authors have questioned the *security* of Internet-based transactions (Lederer et al., 1998; Senn, 1998; Sharp, 1998), while others defend extranet security levels (OneSoft, 1998; Kim, 1998). The partnership which exists in the business-to-business relationship of the extranet tends to lead to greater *trust and confidence* than is present in business-to-consumer e-commerce. However, if security precautions do not measure up to expectations trust and confidence can be lost.

The second aspect of assurance is knowledge and courtesy. How do we convey these on a Web site? One tactic is judicious and prompt use of *e-mail follow ups* to orders and enquiries. Another is *to build expertise into the system*. For example, common sense and knowledge discoveries from databases can identify common associations, allowing suppliers to offer suggestions of the type: "You ordered hinges, do you also need screws?" or better, "Screw A and Screw B are recommended for hinge type X. Do you require any?"

Empathy: The caring, individualized attention a firm provides its customers

Extranets enable companies to give customers *access to information* previously available only to employees (Kim, 1998). Allowing access to privileged and trusted customers could convey a sense of caring, individualized attention. Intelligent use of *user profiles,* based on preferences and usage patterns, can add to the perception of individualized attention. Comprehensive profiles can be developed by combining information entered by customers (e.g., on-line surveys) with information automatically captured by the system (e.g., pages visited, length of viewing). Through the use of profiles, the system can offer specialized products, customized page layouts and prearranged discounts.

Tangibles: The physical facilities, equipment and appearance of personnel

Visually pleasing *page presentations* and *ease of site navigation* can enhance a company's image and differentiate it from its competitors. Since extranets operate in a virtual environment, site and page characteristics have the most impact on the tangibles dimension in extranet-mediated service provision. A lot of work has been done in the area of *Web usability*, but it is not our intention to review that literature here. The interested reader is referred to Instone (2000), Nielsen (1993, 1995, 1999), and Spool et al. (1999) for an introduction to and exposition of Web usability.

From our analysis it appears that extranet-mediated service could exhibit all five dimensions of service quality identified in the physical world. In the next section we make some recommendations for organizations wishing to use extranets to improve their service quality.

EXTRANET QUALITY RECOMMENDATIONS

Extranet projects can be considered to have three distinct phases:
1. Planning and scoping
2. Development
   - Content
   - Technology
3. Maintenance

At each of these phases, we need to consider customer expectations of the service we intend to provide.

At the ***planning and scoping phase,*** it is important to move beyond issues of internal efficiency and cost savings to consider how we can use the proposed extranet to provide stronger alliances with our customers. To turn customers into supply chain partners, we need to work with them in developing the scope of the extranet.

At the ***development stage***, we must continue to work closely with customers in developing site content and structure. Page standards and ease of navigation assist users in developing mental models of the site. While one project team is developing content and structure, a parallel team will be acquiring and developing the required technology. Responsiveness requires that careful consideration be given to server resources, network resources and imaging standards. It is recommended that images be called on an 'as needed' basis. Reliability requires inclusion of procedures to handle site availability during peak periods and update or backup processes. Security dictates consideration of authentication and encryption issues. A further consideration during development is system scalability. No matter how careful we are in scoping and planning a site, we should anticipate some scope creep and allow for future demands and development.

The ***maintenance stage*** of an extranet project is equally as important as scoping, planning and development. Neglected sites die. Content update is a critical success factor in extranet implementation.

Our examination of the psychological elements (Sasser et al., 1978) and service quality dimensions (Parasuraman et al., 1985) suggests actions which can be taken

Table 2: Dimensions of service quality and actions in implementation

Psychological Element	Dimension	Quality Action
Availability Consistency	Reliability	Create and maintain full site backup Use update commands on critical information Perform regular, scheduled maintenance of all data Capture data at source
Timing	Responsiveness	Provide adequate server and network resources Limit use of high resolution graphics to essential tasks Develop procedures to handle exceptions Establish an email response policy
Security Completeness	Assurance	During the planning phase, pay attention to both current and potential scope of the site; ensure site scalability Communicate security features, e.g., authentication and encryption Use emails and/or online tracking systems to advise status of an order Build expertise into the system to offer advice to customers
Attitude	Empathy	Exploit user profiles to customize information and presentation of pages Provide both online and telephone support for site users Maximize access to information to foster a sense of true partnership Involve customers in content decisions
Condition	Tangibles	Use simple, easy-to-read page presentations Develop page standards to ensure consistency Use site structure to aid the formation of mental models and assist in site navigation

to improve service quality on extranets. We summarize them in Table 2, grouping them according to the dimensions of service quality (Pasrasuraman et al., 1985) and psychological needs of customers (Sasser et al., 1978).

To assure quality, be aware of the relative importance of dimensions to your customers, and their expectation levels for each dimension. In preparing to meet these expectations, examine not only the Web site but also the underlying systems, including legacy systems which may house important data for customers. Where tangible products rather than digital assets are sold or exchanged, ensure that logistical operations match the efficiency and sophistication of the extranet site. Study processes and be aware of potential fail points. Providing extranet quality involves a combination of front office (Web site), back office (systems) and production (logistics).

To monitor quality in processes, output and outcomes, customer expectations must be turned into standards and measures developed. Measuring performance indicators is the only way to understand and improve service performance. It has been observed that 'what gets measured gets done' (Trogdon, 1988). It is not the role of this chapter to detail issues in the design of data collection plans; these are left to other forums (see for example, Harrington, 1991; Hope 1997a, b; Tenner & DeToro, 1992). However, it should be noted that extranet technology can itself be used for collection and analysis of data both for one-off surveys of new features and for ongoing performance monitoring.

FUTURE TRENDS

Beginning in the late 1980s, there was a marked shift in emphasis in marketing and departments from a focus on customer acquisition to customer retention. Firms began to realize that costs of acquisition were far greater than costs of retention and that acquiring new customers often meant acquiring someone else's *bad* customers. The desire to retain existing customers led to the concept and practice of relationship management. Extranets are an information technology solution to improved relationship management. We can expect in the future an increase both in the spread of extranets and in the amount of information available on them.

Our understanding of quality in the virtual world remains limited. To gain a better understanding, we need to conduct further research into relationship management on extranets. We also need to examine the links between Web usability and functioning, and perceptions of service quality. A replication in the virtual world of the Parasuraman et al. (1985) study into service quality seems warranted. Extranets and their newer, larger offspring, Enterprise Portals, are here to stay. They will grow and develop. In competitive environments, firms which do not become part of the virtual world may no longer inhabit any world.

SUMMARY

The late 1990s have seen a growth in the number of firms establishing extranets to foster relationships with external customers. Extranets can impact the competitiveness of an organization, but little has been reported on their impact on service quality. This chapter sought to address this by relating the service quality literature to extranet systems. An examination of four key characteristics of services in the physical world revealed difference may exist between services and service quality in the physical and virtual worlds. We also showed that the dimensions of service quality identified by Parasuraman et al. (1985) could hold true for extranets.

REFERENCES

Bateson, J. E. G. (1979). Why we need service marketing. In O. C. Ferrell, S. W. Brown, and C. W. Lamb (Eds.), *Conceptual and Theoretical Developments in Marketing* (131-146). Chicago, IL: American Marketing.

Bauer, H. H., Grether, M., and Leach, M. (1999). Customer relations through the Internet. *Working paper #W23*, Mannheim University, Germany. [WWW document] last accessed 25 April 2000. URL: http://www.bwl.uni-mannheim.de/Bauer/grether/Internet_RM.PDF

Belcher, M., Place, E., and Conole, G. (2000). Quality assurance in subject gateways: Creating high quality portals on the Internet. *Quality Assurance in Education*, 8(1), 38-47.

Benjamin, R., and Wigand, R. (1995). Electronic markets and virtual value chains on the information superhighway. *Sloan Management Review*, 36(2), 62-72.

Bojanic, D. C. (1991). Quality measurement in professional services firms. *Journal of Professional Services Marketing*, 7(2), 27-36.

Bort, J., and Felix, B. (1997). *Building an Extranet: Connect Your Intranet with Vendors and Customers*. New York: John Wiley and Sons.

Bowen, D. E., and Cummings, T. G. (1990). Suppose we took services seriously. In D. E. Bowen, R. B. Chase, T. G. Cummings & Associates, *Service Management Effectiveness: Balancing Strategy, Organization and Human Resources, Operations, and Marketing*, (1-14). San Francisco, CA: Jossey-Bass Publishers.

Buzzell, R. D., and Gale, B. T. (1987). *The PIMS Principles: Linking Strategy to Performance*. New York, NY: The Free Press.

Ferguson, J. M., and Zawacki, R. A. (1993). Service quality: A critical success factor for IS organizations. *Information Strategy: The Executive's Journal*, 9(2), 24-30.

Fitzsimmons, J. A. (1990). Making continual improvement a competitive strategy for service firms. In S. W. Brown, E. Gummesson, B. Edvardsson, and B. Gustavsson (Eds.), *Service Quality: Multidisciplinary and Multinational Perspectives* (284-295). Lexington, MA: Lexington Books.

Gronroos, C. (1990). *Service Management and Marketing: Managing the Moments of Truth in Service Competition*. Lexington, MA: Lexington Books.

Harrington, H. J. (1991). *Business Process Improvement: The Breakthrough Strategy for Total Quality, Productivity, and Competitiveness*. New York, NY: McGraw-Hill.

Hope, B. G. (1997a). Data collection plans. *Proceedings of the Australasian Evaluation Society 1997 International Conference*, 285-289.

Hope, B. G. (1997b). Performance measures for ongoing quality management of services. *Proceedings of the Australasian Evaluation Society 1997 International Conference*, 290-296.

Instone, K. (2000). *Usable Web: 794 Links About Web Usability*. URL: http://www.useit.com/alertbox/9512.html. Accessed 01/05/00.

Kalakota, R., Oliva, R. A., and Donath, B. (1999). Move over, e-commerce. *Marketing Management*, 8(3), 22-32.

Kim, A. H. (1998). Intra- and extra-netting at the Boeing Company. In P. Lloyd and P. Boyle (Eds.), *Web-Weaving: Intranets, Extranets, and Strategic Alliances* (171-182). Oxford: Butterworth Heinemann.

Lederer, A. L., Mirchandani, D. A., and Sims, K. (1998). Using WISs to enhance competitiveness. *Communications of the ACM, 41*(7), 94-95.

Lloyd, P., and Boyle, P. (1998). *Web-Weaving: Intranets, Extranets, and Strategic Alliances.* Oxford: Butterworth-Heinemann

Mastenbroek, W. F. G. (1991). *Managing for Quality in the Service Sector.* Oxford, England: Basil Blackwell.

Nielson, J. (1993). *Usability Engineering.* Boston, USA: Academic Press.

Nielson, J. (1995). *Guidelines for multimedia on the Web.* URL: http://www.useit.com/alertbox/9512.html. Accessed 01/05/00.

Nielson, J. (1999). User interface directions for the Web. *Communications of the ACM, 42*(1), 65-72.

OneSoft Corporation. (1998). The extranet solution. In P. Lloyd and P. Boyle (Eds.), *Web-Weaving: Intranets, Extranets, and Strategic Alliances* (55-65). Oxford: Butterworth Heinemann.

Parasuraman, A., Zeithaml, V. A., and Berry, L. L. (1985). A conceptual model of service quality and its implications for future research. *Journal of Marketing, 49*(4), 41-50.

Pfaffenberger, B. (1998). *Building a Strategic Extranet.* Foster City, CA: IDG Books Worldwide.

Sasser, W. E., Olsen, R. P., and Wyckoff, D. D. (1978). *Management of Service Operations.* Boston, MA: Allyn & Bacon.

Senn, J. A. (1998). WISs at Federal Express. *Communications of the ACM, 41*(7), 117-118.

Sharp, D. (1998). Extranets: Borderless Internet/intranet networking. *Information Systems Management, 15*(3), 31-35.

Shein, E., and Neil, S. (1998, December 21). Eve of an extranet explosion. *PCWeek Online.* URL http://www.zdnet.com/pcweek/stories/news/0,4153,379492.00.html. Accessed 06/01/99.

Smith, A. (1977). *The Wealth of Nations.* New York, NY: Dutton (originally published, 1776).

Spool, J., Scanlon, T., Schroeder, W., Snyder, C., and DeAngelo, T. (1999). *Web Site Usability: A Designer's Guide.* San Francisco, USA: Morgan Kaufmann Publishers Inc.

Tenner, A. R., and DeToro, I. J. (1992). *Total quality management: Three steps to continuous improvement.* Reading, MA: Addison-Wesley Publishing.

Trogdon, E. N. (1988). Customer perspective as a competitive weapon. In L. Schein and M. A. Berman (Eds.), *Total Quality Performance: Highlights of a Conference* (Research Report Number 909, pp. 65-69). New York, NY: The Conference Board.

Vlosky, R., and Fontenot, R. J. (1999). Learning to love extranets. *Marketing Management, 8*(3), 33-35.

Zeithaml, V. A., Parasuraman, A., and Berry, L. L. (1985). Problems and strategies in services marketing. *Journal of Marketing*, 49(2), 33-46.

Zeithaml, V. A., Parasuraman, A., and Berry, L. L. (1990). *Delivering Service Quality: Balancing Customer Perceptions and Expectations*. New York: The Free Press.

CHAPTER THREE

Web-Based Instruction in Organizations: Impact, Advantages and Disadvantages

Katia Passerini, Mary J. Granger and Kemal Cakici
George Washington University, USA

INTRODUCTION

Many organizations are currently implementing Web-based instruction (WBI). Approaches to WBI vary according to the type of organization as well as the objectives to be accomplished. Companies interested in retraining the workforce and teaching employees new skills are mostly concerned with effective information-delivery approaches. Organizations focusing on the implementation of lifelong learning and education—such as educational institutions—are increasingly moving away from mere information-delivery approaches (posting on-line syllabi and lecture notes) to incorporating effective interaction-based approaches (utilizing discussions and virtual rooms). Both approaches to WBI are important to accomplish long-term versus short-term goals, as well as conceptualization versus task-oriented outcomes.

This chapter provides an overview of teaching methods focusing primarily on strategies adopted by educational institutions implementing WBI. The review accomplishes several objectives:

- It presents the status of WBI in academic environments and discusses its relationships with other forms of distance education.
- It highlights the paradigm shift (from objectivism to constructivism, from teacher-centered to learner-centered instruction) brought about by the use of the Internet and intranets for instructional delivery.
- It evaluates the perceived advantages and disadvantages for key WBI stakeholders (institutions, students and faculty).

- It reports faculty perceptions of the pros and cons of the World Wide Web extracted from an on-line survey conducted at a major East Coast university.
- Lastly, it supports the importance of WBI by highlighting its impact on educational institutions, as well as on other organizations.

BACKGROUND

Khan (1997) defines Web-based instruction as the delivery of instruction to a remote audience, using the Web as a medium. In this general acceptation, WBI places itself as a subset of distance education (DE), which uses a computer network (intranet, extranets or Internet) to provide the educational experience. As such, WBI represents the most recent approach to distance education and grounds its methodological approach on the learning theories and paradigms that support distance education. Some of these learning theories include:

- The open learning model (Kember, 1995) focuses on factors that affect a student's successful completion of a distance education program, such as employments, family, social commitments, etc.
- Situated learning theory (Lave, 1988) argues that learning is a function of the activity, context and culture in which it occurs. While classroom learning involves abstract and out-of-context knowledge creating, situated learning involves social interactions. Learners become part of a "community of practice" moving progressively from beginners to novice, embodying beliefs and behaviors of the community.
- Cognitive flexibility theory (Jacobson & Spiro, 1995) refers to the capability of adapting responses to changing situational demands. This capability is a function of both the way knowledge is represented (e.g., along multiple rather than single conceptual dimensions) and the processes that lead to learning. The theory places emphasis on the presentation of information from multiple perspectives. Cognitive flexibility theory is especially formulated to support the use of interactive technology, such as videodisc, hypertext and Web-based learning environments.
- Individualized or self-regulated learning theory (Hammond, 1993) holds that learning is supported through providing access to individualized information beyond the basic representations (i.e., free navigation in an open hypertext/WWW environment). Students that need additional information may obtain explanations of the same concepts from different perspectives, and from different symbol systems (Hammond, 1993).
- Multiple intelligences theory (Gardner, 1984, 1993) suggests that there are a number of distinct forms of intelligence that each individual possesses in varying degrees. Gardner identifies seven primary forms: linguistic, musical, logical-mathematical, spatial, body-kinesthetic, intrapersonal (e.g., insight, metacognition) and interpersonal (e.g., social skills). The implication for learning is that instruction should focus on the particular intelligence of each

person, which also represent individual learning modalities (Kearley, 1994) and should therefore provide access to multiple media representations.

Pushed by the capabilities and opportunities that inter-networked computers offer to knowledge sharing and learning (discussed in the concluding paragraphs), the advent of the Internet has indeed revolutionized the penetration and diffusion of distance education. Moore and Kearsley (1996) define distance education as:

> "planned learning that normally occurs in a different place from teaching and as a result requires special techniques of course design, special instructional techniques, special methods of communication by electronic and other technology, as well as organizational and administrative arrangements."

It took more than a century for distance education to gain ground from the first approaches of correspondence study, open universities, teleconferencing, computer networks and multimedia delivery to today's Web-based technologies. This evolution has been characterized by new approaches to teaching, including the adjustment of instructional materials supported by different delivery media.

Increase in network bandwidth and worldwide access to interconnected networks are enabling the Internet and the World Wide Web to become the preferred delivery system for distance education. To match this growth, the models for the development of instruction need to expand into more sophisticated approaches for instructional delivery. In order to meet the cognitive requirements of teaching in a computer-mediated environment, the impact of the technology must be considered with content knowledge and design guidelines.

The Internet has brought a new generation of distance education. Supplementary to the other models, the Internet-facilitated instruction allows for the implementation of synchronous and asynchronous interaction models and opens a new round of learning opportunities for education.

THE RECENT GROWTH AND CHANGES OF DISTANCE EDUCATION: THE ROLE OF THE INTERNET

Over the last century, distance education has evolved from communication using the printed media of correspondence education to communication involving some level of electronic communication (for the main phases and the key characteristics, see Figure 1).

Moore and Kearsley (1996) identify three main evolutionary stages of distance education:

- **The First Generation**—*Correspondence learning* was part of the opening generation of distance programs taking place at the end of the 19th and beginning of the 20th century. It involved the use of printed materials, usually customized textbooks, which contained lesson outlines and exercises. Com-

Figure 1: Development and characteristics of distance education approaches

Time	Type of distance program	Degree of interaction	Degree of flexibility	Level of learning	Primary media
Early 1900s	*Correspondence*				
	- Home study	Minimal	Moderate	Vocational	Print, video
	- Independent study	Moderate	High	Secondary and post-secondary	Print, audio, computer
1970s	***Open Universities***	Moderate	High	Post-secondary	Print, audio/visual
1980s	***Satellite television***	Low-high	Low	K-12, Post-secondary	TV/Tele-Conferences
1996-current	***Computer networks***	High	High	K-12, Post-secondary	Computers

Source: Adapted from Moore and Kearsley, 1996

pleted assignments were mailed to the instructor, who also provided feedback via mail.

- **The Second Generation**—Began in the early 1970s, with the establishment of the British Open University. The aim of open-universities was to reach off-campus students delivering instruction through radio, television, recorded audiotapes and correspondence tutoring. Audio conferencing (conducting a class using the telephone) was also part of the second generation of distance education programs.

- **The Third Generation**—Began in the 1980s with the advancement of satellite technology and the emergence of communication networks that enabled the delivery of analog and digital content to computer workstations. These networks also enabled new forms of real-time interaction with two-way videoconferencing, or one-way video and two-way audio communication. The introduction of CD-ROM products for multimedia self-paced learning was also part of this generation. Computer networks now link instructors and students, and enable electronic communication exchanges. Bulletin boards made their first appearance for group interaction at a distance, offering central repository spaces for class communication.

As noted in earlier research (Passerini and Granger, 2000), while Moore and Kearsley (1996) presented communication networks and computer-based multimedia as part of the third generation of distance education programs, current developments in telecommunication technologies, and notably the advent of the Internet, mark a new generation (**the Fourth Generation**) of distance education. It is only with the Internet that there is a substantial shift from an instructor-led approach to a real learner-centered approach.

THE INTERNET, A PARADIGM SHIFT FOR DISTANCE EDUCATION

With the diffusion of Internet technology, distance education is becoming a "closer" experience than a traditional classroom. Although physical distance is still present, the real learning "space" among students is closer. Interaction may take place more actively than in a traditional classroom (especially in large classes).

It is only with the use of the Internet, and the World Wide Web, that distance education moves away from an objectivist approach in favor of a constructivist environment. In the objectivist view of education, the grounding philosophy is the automation of repetitive tasks where the major contribution is the reduction of administrative tasks in course management. The constructivist approach to instruction uses a framework which enables learners to develop personal learning spaces in which they select their learning path, use search strategies and contribute to the "production" of learning moments (through interactions among students and instructors) as well as shape the information base relative to the course. In the new networked environment providing access to several channels of communication (student-content, student-to-student, student-to-instructor, student-to-other-hypermedia content and student-to-other-instructors), learning is a product of the interactions in the virtual classroom. Asynchronous discussions (moderated and summarized by the instructor) become the "live" textbook, where students learn from each other as well as from the instructor.

Rather than being an obstacle to interaction, "distance" becomes the seed of interaction among participants with diverse backgrounds and experiences. Therefore, it enables the realization of other learning models within the constructivist approach, such as sociocultural learning. Classrooms become boundary-less both geographically (with students taking degrees from anywhere in the world) and content-wise (with contextual access to supporting readings from any hyperlinkable site).

THE IMPORTANCE OF WEB-BASED INSTRUCTION

The popularity of Web-based instruction has rapidly increased over the past three to four years. The National Center for Education Statistics reported that over 33% of the US post-secondary institutions already offered distance education courses in 1998 (with a breakdown between public and private institution presented in Figure 2), and 20% more were planning to increase their offerings by the year 2001.

The on-line courses are popular because they offer to universities, students and instructors benefits previously not available (Morgan, 2000).

Benefits to the Universities

1. *Increased market access*—Universities with declining enrollment figures can now offer their courses to a wider market and attract students who because of

Figure 2: Percent of educational institutions offering on-line courses

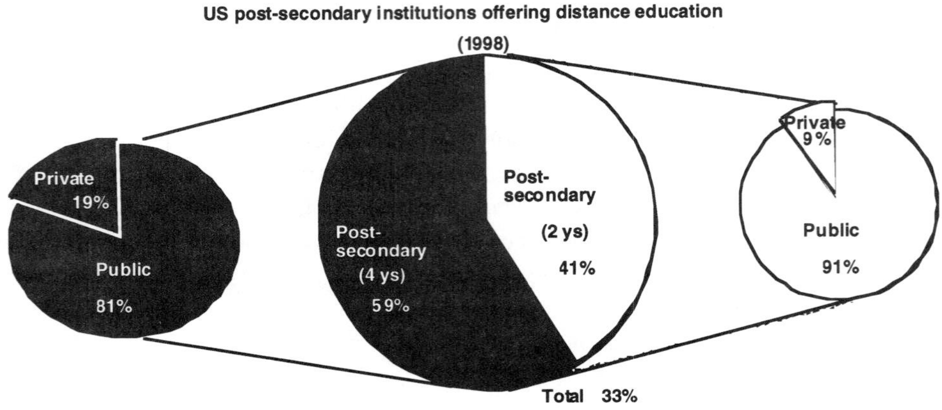

US post-secondary institutions offering distance education
(1998)

Total 33%

Source: Adapted from the National Center for Education Statistics (NCES), 1999

distance or time constraints would not have considered attending the university.

2. *Lower long-terms costs*—Universities facing increasing costs, reduced or restricted sources of funding may be able to decrease the overall cost of teaching. Inglis (1999) notes that by increasing student intake, one could achieve a greater economy of scale and reduce the overall costs per student. Zanville (1996) found that replicating courses over multiple campuses or using the same modules over multiple courses can help increase those economies of scale.

Benefits to the Students

1. *Increased participation*—On-line courses offer students who might feel lost in a large university class, or who are shy and hesitate to participate in traditional classroom settings, an opportunity for greater interaction. Some students feel more comfortable asking questions in non-face-to-face situations with an instructor or peers.

2. *Increased resources*—Through the use of hyperlinks, instructors provide students with a wealth of resources outside of the university that may help the students gain a better understanding of the materials presented and give them a greater role in their learning.

3. *Learning on their own time*—On-line courses offer the students the flexibility to learn on their own time from wherever they are. Students are able to work at their own pace and may not be as constrained by course availability issues.

4. *A global classroom*—Students from any country may register for classes at any location. This leads to greater diversity in the classroom and introduces a wealth of knowledge and experience to the class.

5. *Less expensive*—Students do not have to commute, pay for lodging or give up their jobs while they study. Downes (1998) reports that students are able to

continue working while learning, allowing them to continue their careers while obtaining college credit.

Benefits to the Instructors

The instructors' advantages and disadvantages of teaching on the Web are presented in a later paragraph. This presentation highlights pros and cons especially as perceived by faculty with WBI experience.

WEB-BASED INSTRUCTION IN EDUCATIONAL INSTITUTION: THE SUCCESS OF THE INTERNET

Educational institutions are using primarily Internets, rather than intranets, for the delivery of distance education courses. The motivation for implementing distance education is the possibility of *reaching other market segments*, beyond the geographical and regional boundaries of the university. The major target for the distance courses is, therefore, the population of users residing outside the range of local area networks, or even the wide area networks of the universities offering distance education. The Internet, widely accessible from inside as well as outside the university, represents the best vehicle for communication with distance students.

The fact that most colleges already own computer facilities fully connected to the World Wide Web has facilitated the expansion of distance education using the Internet. The 20% growth rate in less than two years, described in the previous section, witnesses an enormous interest for educational institutions to lead the Internet bandwagon. Furthermore, the rise in on-line course offerings (and the high speed of implementation) is facilitated by the flourishing of a variety of on-line course-management software packages that automate many of the most tedious as well as complex tasks of creating and maintaining a course on the Web (from security, to content creations, query and daily management of communication). Some examples are Blackboard, ClassNet, Learning Space, TopClass, Web Course in a Box and WebCT. These course management software offer a user-friendly interface that enables the realization of complete on-line courses that integrate security, chatrooms, discussion and bulletin board areas, file sharing, streaming video and audio, information presentation and search features.

Another reason for educational institutions to use the Internet rather than an intranet is related to the nature and scope of the task of educational institution: education. A complete learning experience is one that enables the learners to move beyond the borders of a bounded-information space (a self-contained course on the intranet, such as a CBT training program, for example, fits in this category).

The use of the Internet provides access to other countries, realities, cultures and information that promotes further growth of the individual, as well as the self-determination and decision of the extent of their learning experience beyond the information requirements established in the syllabus.

HOW ARE THESE TECHNOLOGIES CHANGING TEACHING?

The WBI teaching approaches can be summarized in three main categories:
1. *informational* (automated distribution of class materials) purposes;
2. *supplemental* (as an additional tool for instruction) purposes;
3. *substitutive* (as an alternative to in-class instruction) purposes.

Each WBI teaching approach presents advantages and disadvantages for course developers and instructors. The interesting aspect of Web-based instruction is that the number of advantages can be offset by the disadvantages brought about by the use of the same tool. In deciding whether or not to implement WBI, however, very few benefit/cost considerations are applied. Often, the advantages for the institutions (increased market access and economies of scale) are the key drivers of technology-based education.

In an effort to survey the perceived value of WBI on the part of those directly involved in the delivery of the distance education courses, a short on-line survey was administered to faculty members teaching on the Web at a major East Coast University. The survey consisted of 14 questions. A total of 79 faculty members responded to the survey. The mean of the responses presented in the findings tables is the average of the answers to a corresponding Likert scale question. The scale was established as follows:

Strongly Disagree	Disagree	Neither Agree nor Disagree	Agree	Strongly Agree
1.0	2.0	3.0	4.0	5.0

The responses were benchmarked against the expectations of the researchers. The results of the survey are classified by the three different teaching approaches, and the perceived advantages and disadvantages of each are reported.

The Web as an Informational Tool
Advantages:

When the Web is used as an informational tool, its grounding philosophy is an objectivist view of learning accomplishing the automation of repetitive tasks (such as notes distribution). In this form, the major contribution is the *reduction of administrative tasks* in course management. It enables faculty to utilize time more efficiently and save environmental resources. Reading materials are available on-line. The responsibility of printing class handouts is shifted to the students. Lesson plans are reviewed with more flexibility, as the instructor or teaching assistant does not have to reprint the material for every modification. Even this simple task automation is an important motivator for moving to a Web-based environment. This will in fact generate *continuous accessibility to course materials* at any time, from anywhere.

Disadvantages:

Although faculty are relieved of some administrative burdens, they take new responsibilities upon themselves. Being able to automate the distribution of class materials may mean understanding and mastering HTML editors. If instructors intend to protect their intellectual property from access beyond the classroom, security controls need to be learned as well. Administrative tasks may be reduced, but they may be replaced with new technical tasks requiring the same or greater time investments for site development and maintenance.

A drawback to the continuous accessibility to course materials is that students may feel motivated to skip classes. Instructors may need to make classroom time more appealing and an experience well beyond the presentation of the information otherwise available in the lecture notes. In a way, faculty may feel compelled to produce lecture notes and additional lecture experiences that avoid redundant information. Lecture preparation time may as well be increased by the move to a Web-based environment. This being the case, the benefits from the reduction in administrative tasks are mostly achievable only when the instructor teaches several sections of the same course, within the same academic semester.

Findings:

The results from the survey conducted show that although the perceived need for additional training is higher than the reduction of administrative tasks (with little benefits, therefore, on time allocation for other activities), faculty do not believe that they are faced with the challenge of providing more stimulus materials to increase attendance.

ADVANTAGES	Response	DISADVANTAGES	Response
Reduction of administrative tasks • Distribution of lecture notes on-line	✓ Yes *Mean=3.8*	**Faculty need for additional training** • Securing a Web site, HTML; how a Web site works and is maintained	✓ Yes *Mean=4.2*
Continuous accessibility to course materials • At any time, also for students unable to participate to a session	✓ Yes *(not tested)*	**Students may be inclined to cut classes** • Therefore faculty need to generate added value from class attendance	Neither Advantage nor disadvantage *Mean=1.8*

The Web as a Supplemental Tool

Advantages:

The Web has a more significant impact on teaching when it is used as a supplemental tool for instruction. In this role, it *enhances student-to-student and faculty-to-student communication* and matches the instructional paradigm of collaborative learning. Kubala (1998) reports that the introduction of discussion boards, chatrooms and other interactive processes increases students' motivation by fostering a sharing environment and culture. Students are more willing to interact on-line rather than in the real classroom because of the distant medium; they overcome fears of face-to-face participation and confrontation. This interaction is created by mechanisms through which students share perspectives, and instructors are more accessible to provide feedback through the learning technology.

Disadvantages:

While the use of the Web may increase the number of communication exchanges, it does not necessarily enhance them. If faculty are faced with the same set of questions via e-mail, they may prefer to address the questions in a classroom rather than writing answers to individual messages. Faculty may also need to deal with questions relative to one course at a time, rather than throughout the entire week. Students often have an expectation that e-mail questions are more urgent and need to be answered promptly. If they are not answered promptly, the students may view the instructor as unresponsive to student needs. Instead, in the traditional classroom format, the instructor was held responsible only during the class-time or during the scheduled office hours.

The number of communication exchanges is also increased with the use of the World Wide Web. However, especially when the Web is used as a supplement to classroom work, these types of discussion exchanges may *not* be crucial to learning. They may act as additional assignments, with little reflection to the quality of learning in the classroom.

Findings:

The use of the Web is perceived as an important facilitator of student-to-student and faculty-to-student communication. Communication on the Web is not perceived as an impediment to learning. Rather, the responses that stated that on-line communication enhances learning were above the mean values of the Likert scale.

The Web as a substitute tool

Advantages:

As a substitute to classroom instruction, the use of the World Wide Web enables *student-centered* rather than *instructor-led approaches*. Students become masters of their own learning by controlling the pace of instruction. Students also learn by doing, being involved in the retrieval of information on-line (text, audio and video clips) and enjoy the ability to operate (play, pause, rewind, fast-forward) these

ADVANTAGES	Response	DISADVANTAGES	Response
Enhances student-to-student communication • Students share ideas and implement collaborative work effectively	✓ Yes *Mean=3.2*	**Communication increases redundancy, not learning** • The types of communication exchanges can deal more with coordination, scheduling, rather than learning	x NO *Mean=3.6*
Enhances faculty-to-student communication • Students are not fearful to communicate and receive instant feedback from the instructor	✓ Yes *Mean=3.9*	**Overload of questions** • Faculty are compelled to answer promptly, to the same questions, with increased 'office hours' responsibility	Perception Not tested

learning materials. Experiential and situated learning are the paradigms supporting this instructional application of the Web. Additionally, learner control is increased if the instructor presents the same information in a variety of formats. The learners may choose the material that accommodates their learning styles.

Learners are also offered further opportunities for exploration. They are already connected to a networked environment that allows exploration of related materials available on the Internet. In this latter representation, the Web is an unbounded information source (Hedberg et al., 1997) and allows open navigation and user control of their learning. Information processing in a hypertext framework takes place within a constructivist approach to instruction. In this framework, users are able to develop personal learning spaces in which they select their learning path by using search strategies, contributing to the "production" of learning moments (through interactions among students and instructors) as well as the shaping of the information base relative to the course.

Disadvantages:

The student-led approach to learning, however, is based on specific assumptions: students are self-motivated, disciplined and have sufficient prior knowledge of the topic. In addition, they are able to discriminate tasks, organize schedules and choose their navigational paths through the course materials. This assumption is challenged by the age of the learners, their prior knowledge of the topic and their ability to determine their most effective learning strategy. Learners with low prior knowledge of the subject do not know what works best for them and need additional guidance. Some student-centered navigational strategies may not be as effective as intended, they may increase the cognitive load (Szabo & Kanuka, 1999), and may disorient the learner.

Findings:

Using the Web as a substitute tool for instruction is perceived as the most

ADVANTAGES	Response	DISADVANTAGES	Response
Student-centered learning • Students manage their learning, the pace of instruction and can focus their study	Neither *Mean=2.9*	**Need of guidance through the material** • Students with low prior knowledge of the topic might need further guidance or they might risk cognitive overload	✓ Yes *Mean=3.1*
Exploration and access to learning networks • In a Web environment, students are prompted to move beyond the lecture notes by hyperlink and other resources	Perception Not tested	**Lack of motivation and commitment** • The benefits of a networked learning environment are dependent on student motivation and commitment	Neither *Mean=2.3*

challenging scenario where the advantages potentially achievable are overcome (or overwhelmed) by the need for additional input and guidance.

Instructors' points of view

Faculty offered comments on their views of the advantages and disadvantages through the open-ended question included at the end of the questionnaire. While some recognized the higher learning experience of asynchronous discussions, others complained for the need of additional guidance and the amount of advanced preparation that is needed to successfully run WBI classes.

Advantages (faculty comments)

"On-line discussions best illustrate how think time or wait time positively impacts the level of discussion. Using the Web allows for some students to excel when they might not excel as clearly during an in-class session. I believe that I ask much better questions during discussions when I lead them on-line."

"I have students that are visiting at irregular intervals and for variable periods of time (medical students rotating through Radiology). The WWW and teaching on-line is very helpful in providing a stable syllabus for each student regardless of their time of entry or duration of stay."

Disadvantages (faculty comments)

"1) The time/effort needed to organize & prepackage the materials is invariably underestimated; 2) Prepackaged nature of WWW presentations unfortunately eliminates the element of spontaneity; 3) Advance preparation is crucial to success."

"I have found that the expectations of students in a Web-based environment are very high for faculty guidance and feedback. An interesting

phenomenon in a graduate course."
"Not all students have the technology to log on. Few classrooms are wired. The technology fails too often. The students use frequent failures as an excuse for not doing tasks."

Overall Considerations

Overall, the data collected on faculty perception of WBI shows that the expected disadvantages are in most cases lower than forecasted, except for the cases in which the Web is used as a substitute tool for instruction. Faculty are interested and eager to use WBI in all its forms, although the most complete applications will probably require an additional effort for guiding the students and enabling them to become fully independent learners in an open and unbounded environment.

CONCLUSIONS: IMPLICATIONS FOR ORGANIZATIONS

The positive and fast growing trends observed for educational institutions have been much slower in corporations. This slower growth is certainly due to technology equipment constraints, but mostly to the confidential and proprietary nature of the training materials (Marquardt & Kearsley, 1999). Corporations often offer the majority of their training opportunities through their internal networks (intranets), even though they often recognize the need for resorting to the Internet open-learning space and they provide easy access to external networks for each topic to be delivered. Other corporations are increasingly offering training programs for customers and, therefore, are distributing their training materials to the people outside the organization. The Microsoft On-line Institute and the IBM global education site are examples of the concurrent trends of commercial institutions towards the utilization of the Web for training. In addition, several new companies (virtual-training providers) are offering Internet-based training opportunities also available though an external interconnected network.

What are the implications and the organizational changes brought about by the use of interconnected network for learning? Marquardt and Kearsley (1999) states that the network changes the learning environment in a profound way because:

- It fosters the sharing of resources and expertise in a common 'virtual' environment.
- It enhances collaboration and idea generation among the employees (since it is much simpler, convenient, dynamic and immediate to exchange ideas).
- It promotes more informal and spontaneous interaction (solicited by the electronic communications via e-mail, conferencing, Web sites, etc.).
- It promotes time-space independent learning experiences and enables adjusting the learning moments to personal scheduling needs (and biological rhythm).

- It promotes computer literacy skills, providing an important component of the new century worker.
- It abolishes geographical boundaries and promotes the creation of virtual communities worldwide (each participant bringing a new and expanded perspective).

Therefore, interconnected networks transform the learning organization from the inside (communication and knowledge sharing among the employees) and from the outside (through the access—and the selection—of the available resources). As Marquardt and Kearsley (1999, p. 207) state: *"Networks mean that learning is no longer encapsulated by artificial limitations such as classrooms, curricula and organizational/institutional delimitations. Individuals will use networks to find other people and information sources that address their specific needs and interests. All organizations need to recognize this new circumstance and do what they can to enable their staff, students or members to be as proficient as possible in the use of the networks."*

References

Downes, S. (1998). *The Future of Online Learning.* The Economics of Online Learning. Manitoba, Canada: Brandon.

Gardner, H. (1984). *Frames of Mind.* New York: Basic Books.

Gardner, H. (1993). *Multiple Intelligences: The Theory in Practice.* New York: Basic Books

Hammond, N. (1993). Learning with hypertext: Problems, principles, and prospects. In C. McKnight, A. Dillon, and J. Richardson (Eds.), *Hypertext: A Psychological Perspective.* Chichester: Ellis Horwood, 51-69.

Hedberg, J. B. C., and Arrighi, M. (1997). Interactive multimedia and web-based learning: Similarities and differences. In B. Khan (Ed.), *Web-Based Instruction.* Englewood Cliffs, NJ: Educational Technology Publications.

Inglis, A. (1999). Is online delivery less costly than print and is it meaningful to ask? *Distance Education*, 20(2), 220-239.

Jacobson, M. J., and Spiro, R. J. (1995). Hypertext learning environments, cognitive flexibility, and the transfer of complex knowledge: An empirical investigation. *Journal of Educational Computing Research*, 12(4), 301-333.

Kember, D. (1995). *Open Learning Courses for Adults.* Englewood Cliffs, NJ: Educational Technology Publications.

Khan, B. H. (1997). *Web-based Instruction.* Englewood Cliffs, NJ: Educational Technology Publications.

Kubala, T. (1998). Addressing student needs: Teaching and learning on the Internet. *T.H.E. Journal*, 25(8) 71-74.

Lave, J. (1988). *Cognition in Practice: Mind, Mathematics and Culture in Everyday Life.* Cambridge, England: Cambridge University Press.

Marquardt, M. J., and Kearsley, G. (1999). *Technology-Based Learning.* (ASTD American Society for Training and Development). Boca Raton, FL: St. Lucie Press.

Moore, M. G., and Kearsley, G. (1996). *Distance Education: A Systems View.* Belmont, CA: Wadsworth Publishing Company.

Morgan, B. M. (2000). *Is Distance Learning Worth It? Helping to Determine the Costs of Online Courses.* Unpublished doctoral dissertation, Marshall University, USA.

Passerini, K., and Granger, M. J. (2000). A developmental model for distance learning using the Internet. *Computers & Education*, 34(1), 1-15.

Szabo, M., and Kanuka, H. (1999). Effects of violating screen design principles of balance, unity, and focus on recall learning, study time and completion rates. *Journal of Educational Multimedia and Hypermedia*, 8(1), 23-42.

Zanville, H. (1996). The promise of technology-based instruction: What we are learning. *National Center for Higher Education Management Systems News*, (13).

CHAPTER FOUR

Effect of Hypertext and Animation on Learning

Ashu Guru and Fui Hoon (Fiona) Nah
University of Nebraska-Lincoln, USA

The availability of hypertext and animation has a promising impact on education. With an increasing number of online courses and degrees offered through the Internet and a rapidly increasing enrollment in such courses, it is important to assess and understand how the use of Web-based features can affect or contribute toward learning. In this research, we propose a model to study the effect of hypertext and animation on online learning.

INTRODUCTION

Currently, the Internet dominates in the development of information and communication technology. It has taken an important role in our daily life by providing a wide range of services that include entertainment, education and business. A major advantage of the Internet is the economical and instant accessibility and availability of information resources distributed all over the globe. In the field of education, the Internet is used not only to supplement classroom teaching, but also as an increasingly popular medium for delivery of online education courses. An immense amount of research literature and Internet-based teaching modules are added to this network continually. These resources aim towards being a viable alternative for distance learning. According to a survey by the US Department of Education, a total of more than 54,000 online education courses were offered in 1998, with 1.6 million students enrolled (Lewis et al., 1999). Such online courses continue to proliferate very quickly.

Advances in Internet technology have provided users access not only to text and graphics but also digitized audio, video signals and animations as well. Two online features that have made the Internet more adaptable for education and learning are *Hypertext* and *Animation*.

"Hypertext" is the organization of information units into connected associations that the users can choose to relate at the click of a mouse. Hypertext has been found to be an effective method of training because it provides users flexibility and control over the method, speed, location and order of information access (Marshall and Shipman, 1995). In this way it caters to a wide range of users who have different goals, interests, requirements and comprehension abilities. Hypertext not only allows students the flexibility to access class information discretely in order to match their pace and personal requirements, but also furnishes students with a knowledge domain through which they can gain/retrieve information at their own pace to match their study order.

Research has shown that individuals comprehend information better with visualization than with written text. One of the simplest forms of visualization is "Animation." Animation refers to computerized simulation of processes using images to form a synthetic motion picture. In the context of learning, Pezdek and his colleague (Pezdek and Stevens, 1984; Pezdek, 1987) predict that the use of the visual mode of communication increases the grasping and retaining capability of the human mind. Animation is also expected to contribute toward learning since it appeals to the power of the human visual system (Clary, 1997). In Kehoe's (1996) review of studies on animation in education, visual aids are found to have a dramatic positive effect on learning if certain conditions ("explanative text," "sensitive tests," "explanative illustrations," "inexperienced learners") are met (Mayes, 1989). Menn (1993) evaluated the impact of different instructional media on student retention of subject matter and found that students retain almost 90% of a task if they carry out the task themselves even if only using computer simulation. The findings were confirmed by Gokhale (1996) who conducted a study to show that effective integration of computer simulation enhances the performance of students.

The Internet and its related technologies have provided us with a new dimension in education and a wider range of new teaching and learning styles. With an increasing enrollment in Web-based courses and the large amount of resources invested in designing such courses, it is important to investigate how *Hypertext* and *Animation* can influence students' interaction and motivation in such environments as well as their impact on effectiveness in learning. Using the concepts of *Flow* (Csikszentmihalyi and Csikszentmihalyi, 1988; Hoffman and Novak, 1996) and *Media Richness* (Daft and Lengel, 1984), we construct a model to explain the effect of hypertext and animation in the online learning environment.

DEFINING LEARNING

It is difficult to provide a formal definition of learning, but in simple terms learning may be expressed as the development of high order thinking and evaluation skills. Pogrow (1994) suggested that for students to be competitive, they must possess cognitive strategies that will enable them to think critically, make good decisions and solve challenging problems. In addition, effective learning stimulates students to search for solutions to problems, either working independently or in a group. They learn to utilize different resources that are available to solve a problem.

Traditionally, teachers perform one of the tasks to impart learning; they guide the students through subjective information and then evaluate the students by testing them. It may not be an overstatement when it is said that effective learning took place when a student was exposed to some information and then tested to find out that he/she has comprehended and retained the information presented very well.

RELATED EMPIRICAL RESEARCH

Various attempts have been made to evaluate and predict the effects of hypertext in human computer interactions. In a study on knowledge-based systems, Mao and Benbasat (1995) evaluated the benefits of integrating domain knowledge into the system output in the form of hypertext-based explanations. They used two "informationally equivalent" knowledge-based systems in a laboratory experiment. Both systems provided access to domain knowledge. However, only one of the two systems provided contextualized access to the knowledge from the system output through hypertext links. By providing hypertext access to the knowledge, the requested information can be retrieved within the context of the given problem and solutions. This allows users direct and contextualized access to the information as opposed to searching for the information in a different or abstract context. Mao and Benbasat presented several important conclusions regarding the interaction between the system and its users. One such conclusion is that without hypertext, users tend not to look up information that may be available elsewhere in the system even if such information is useful. In other words, a knowledge-based system may not be utilized to its fullest if access to explanatory knowledge provided elsewhere in the system is not facilitated. Mao and Benbasat claimed that access to explanatory and related knowledge present in the system is dependent on the ease of locating and accessing the information. They also suggest that hypertext efficiently integrates the domain knowledge of the task into the system which in turn enhances learning by reducing the motivational cost of learning.

In summary, Mao and Benbasat (1995) highlight three distinct features of hypertext:
   a) the users do not have to leave the primary task in order to access "further information," and hence task continuity (or flow, in the context of this research) is maintained;
   b) the appropriate domain knowledge is available with a single mouse-click; and
   c) the users are given the flexibility to search for relevant knowledge through hyperlinks.

The visual mode of communication has a significant impact on human understanding. Visual media are used in education because of their effectiveness in communication. Diagrams and video documentaries are frequently used in educational lectures. This is done to aid students in visualizing and understanding real-life systems and problems more easily.

In an experiment on visual communication, Rock and Victor (1964) found the impact of visual communication to be so strong in humans that it overpowers the decision criteria based on the other senses such as feeling or touching an object. In their experiment, Rock and Victor asked their subjects to recognize objects. The subjects could feel the objects but viewed them through a lens. They were unaware that the view through the lens reduced the scale of the object. When later asked to recognize the real objects, they made their decisions based on what they had seen rather than what they had felt. They consistently made their selection of the objects based on size and appearance that they had seen through the lens. This experiment illustrates the dominance and importance of vision (Mayes, 1989).

Other reviews and literature studies such as Loveless et al. (1970) and Menne and Menne (1972) have found audio and visual information to contribute toward facilitating human information processing.

FLOW THEORY AND CONCEPTS

Flow is the feeling or sensation of enjoyable experiences and the process of optimal experience (Csikszentmihalyi and Csikszentmihalyi, 1988). Understanding flow is important in all disciplines and systems — if a discipline or system can provide the candidates/users with a sensation of enjoyable experiences, then the users will voluntarily gain increasingly more information from the system and take a more active role in participation. In this manner the more the users enjoy and learn from the experiences, the more will be the evolution of the discipline. There have been various definitions and descriptions given to flow. One such description is (Csikszentmihalyi and Csikszentmihalyi, 1988, p. 29):

"Artists, athletes, composers, dancers, scientists and people from all walks of life, when they describe how it feels when they are doing something that is worth doing for its own sake, use terms that are interchangeable in their minutest details. This unanimity suggests that order in consciousness produces a very specific experimental state, so desirable that one wishes to replicate it as often as possible." This particular "state" is given the name "flow."

Privette and Bundrick (1987) have defined the same term as:
"… an intrinsically enjoyable experience, is similar to both peak experience and peak performance, as it shares the enjoyment of valuing of peak experience and the behavior of peak performance. Flow per se does not imply optimal joy or performance but may include either or both."

Challenges and skills are the universal preconditions of flow. For flow to occur, it is necessary to have a balance between the level of challenges faced and the level of skills possessed by an individual in a situation (Csikszentmihalyi and Csikszentmihalyi, 1988), and for flow to be sustained, these challenges should "become more complex" over time (Csikszentmihalyi, 1982). Csikszentmihalyi (1982) uses the example of a tennis player to illustrate and support the concept of flow. According to Csikszentmihalyi, a tennis player who enjoys the game will improve his/her skills through playing tennis. Now if the challenge imposed by the opponent of this player does not increase/improve, the player will get bored and eventually lose interest unless he/she finds an opponent who offers challenges that meet the improved skills of this player.

Another similar example is the case of young skateboarders who endeavor into newer and more challenging tasks and skateboard rides as their skills increase. They continued such an activity as long as they could still feel the enjoyment (i.e., by balancing the increased skills with increased challenges).

Researchers have suggested that flow is a useful construct for describing our interactions with computers (Csikszentmihalyi, 1990; Ghani 1991; Ghani and Deshpande, 1993; Webster, Trevino and Ryan, 1993). Hoffman and Novak (1996) in their work on flow proposed a Process Model of Network Navigation within a Hypermedia Computer-Mediated Environment (CME). According to them,

> "Flow is the central construct for understanding network navigation within a hypermedia CME, including movement through hypermedia links, time spent in a CME, range of hypermedia documents examined and attention paid to hypermedia documents. Flow is measurable and exists on a continuum."

Hoffman and Novak (1996) relate the list of characteristics identified by Brigish (1993) — easy to use, fun to use, fast, personalizable, comprehensive, highly visual, browsable — to the process of flow as described by Webster, Trevino and Ryan (1993). According to Hoffman and Novak, control, content and motivational characteristics influence four direct determinants of the flow state: 1) perceived congruence of skills and challenges, 2) focused attention, 3) interactivity, and 4) telepresence. Their model consists of an environment having various exit points. In this research, only perceived congruence (of skills and challenges), focused attention and interactivity are relevant. The "perceived congruence of skills and challenges" condition is the prerequisite for flow to occur. Once the congruence between skills and challenges is achieved, flow is initiated. It is important to note that in order to sustain this flow state, congruence should always be present. During the flow state, the user experiences enjoyable feelings. At the same time this environment stretches a user's capabilities in learning new skills and enhances his/her "self-esteem and personal complexity" (Hoffman and Novak, 1996). Any disparity between skills and challenges will result in the user either exiting the activity or selecting a more congruential activity (i.e., an activity where the user perceives a balance between his/her skills and the challenges offered by the system/activity). In other words, for a system or an activity to provide flow to its users, it should be flexible enough to continually match the skills of the involved users with challenges offered by the system/activity. The system or activity has to cater to the improving skills of the involved users as they continue using the system or performing the activity.

Focused attention is necessary to induce flow. Focused attention is defined as the "centering of attention on a limited stimulus field" (Csikszentmihalyi, 1977). According to Csikszentmihalyi and Csikszentmihalyi (1988), when one is in flow, "one simply does not have enough attention left to think about anything else." The concentration is so immense that the individual does not have any thoughts of being happy or being sad or in fact anything else but the activity. The following is Csikszentmihalyi and Csikszentmihalyi's (1988) description of the flow experience of a young basketball player. While playing the game, he completely concentrates on it. Everything that matters to this player is the court. The player forgets or lays aside any other thoughts and feelings of problems such as fighting with his steady girl. This is due to involvement in the activity where the mind is totally concentrated on that activity. If there is no complete involvement or concentration in an activity, then flow can never be experienced.

Interactivity is the availability of immediate feedback between entities. This exchange of information and feedback is in the form of a sensory dialogue. It is important for an activity to be interactive in order for it to induce and maintain flow. Imagine a football game where the referees do not disclose the scores or the scoreboard to the players and the spectators during the game. Further, the scores will only be disclosed once the game is over. It is no doubt that such a game would induce frustration rather than excitement among the players and the spectators. This is due to the fact there is minimal or no interactivity between the referees and the players or the spectators during the game. When no feedback on the scores is provided, it would be harder for the players or the spectators to achieve flow.

In terms of human computer interactions, interactivity can be thought of as an activity where the user requests some action to be performed and the computer responds to that request by taking the appropriate action or displaying the results to the user. An example is that of performing a search on the Web using a search engine. To carry out the search, the user will first enter the text to be searched. This text forms the input from the user to the computer. The search engine would respond to the user's request by presenting the results of the search to the user.

Telepresence is the feeling of being present in another place different from your immediate physical location. Such a feeling is achieved while interacting with a medium such as one involving virtual reality. Although telepresence is an important factor in the computer and Internet environments, we do not include it in this research due to its limited effect from "two-dimensional animation" (as opposed to "three-dimensional visualization").

Playfulness has been suggested as an important construct for understanding human-computer interactions (Webster, Trevino and Ryan, 1993). Playfulness represents enjoyable experience, feelings of fun, enthusiasm and pleasures attained by users when they interact with a system. Higher playfulness results not only in subjective experiences such as motivation to engage in computer interactions but also in long-term positive outcomes such as learning (Miller, 1973).

MEDIA RICHNESS

In order for the human brain to process and retain information it is important that the information is presented in a simple and interactive manner so that it can capture the interest of the subjects. Any mode of communication that is interactive and utilizes communication media where subjects feel to be a part of the described information will tend to have a higher impact on learning and understanding. Various studies have been conducted and theories have been put forward explaining communication media. One such theory is the media richness (Daft and Lengel, 1984). Daft and Lengel define "richness" as the "potential information carrying capacity of data." In its simple terms, the richness of a medium denotes the capacity of the medium to carry a large amount of data and convey the meaning successfully to the audience. Building upon the work by Bodensteiner (1970), Daft and Lengel (1984) rate the richness of a medium based on its *feedback capability*, *communication channel utilized*, *source* and *language*. In these criteria, *feedback capability* represents the immediacy of the system feedback. It shows the capacity of the system to provide timely information. *Communication channel utilized* can be thought of as the capability of the medium to transfer information through a variety of communication channels such as gestures, voice and tones. *Source* is the personal focus of the medium to convey the feelings. Finally, *language* is the capability of the medium to use language variety to tailor the information to increase understanding. The theory of media richness suggests that managers can improve performance by using appropriate media to transfer the information within an organization. It suggests that when a task is difficult and complex, "richer" media or a combination of different media should be used for information transfer. According to Daft and Lengel (1984), managers can use richer media to process information about complex organizational tasks and a less rich (or leaner) media for simple or straightforward tasks. They also suggest that a medium that provides immediate feedback would rate higher on the richness scale when compared to a medium that has slow feedback. Similarly a communication medium utilizing both visual and audio channel would rate high in richness. Although the media richness theory is for tasks carried out in organizational activities, we are adapting and using the concept in the Internet learning environments.

PROPOSED MODEL

The research question is: "How does the inclusion of hypertext and animation effect flow in the online educational environment and what are their implications on effectiveness of learning?" Figure 1 shows our proposed model. It considers hypertext and animation as independent variables (IVs) and effectiveness of learning as the dependent variable (DV). The two levels of mediating variables (MVs) are: 1) perceived congruence, focused attention, interactivity, media richness and playfulness; and 2) flow. The model focuses on how hypertext and animation effect perceived congruence of skills and challenges, focused attention, interactivity, media richness and playfulness, and how these five factors influence flow and subsequently effectiveness of learning. As presented in Figure 1, the determinants of flow are expected to eventually effect learning capabilities.

Our model indicates that:

A) *Hypertext increases flow by increasing the perceived congruence, focused attention, interactivity, media richness and playfulness.*

Hypertext increases the flexibility offered by the system so that it can cater to individuals who possess different levels of skill (i.e., knowledge). By providing users the flexibility to access information from various knowledge domains through the click of a mouse, the system is able to adjust its level of challenge to suit the skill level of the users. In this way, it increases the users' perceived congruence of skills and challenges. Let us consider an example of two users reading the same tutorial on Java programming. One user being a programmer would know other object-oriented languages such as C++ or Visual Basic, and the second user is a new programmer who has a very limited knowledge about object-oriented programming concepts. Further, in that tutorial there is a term "Object-Oriented Programming (OOP)." Let us also assume that this term (Object-Oriented Programming) is highlighted as a hyperlink which when clicked would take the user to a document that clearly explains OOP. It is most probable that a user who already has a clear understanding of OOP will continue to read ahead without clicking on and following the hyperlink as compared to a user who is new to OOP. The second user is likely to want to know about OOP before proceeding further in the tutorial. Analyzing the scenario, it gives support to the assumption that the Web-based educational environment is capable of providing the required level of challenge to users of different skill levels. Had it been a case where the tutorial had either explained OOP on the same document or had not included any explanation about it, it is most probable that one of the two users would have become frustrated or bored from interacting with the system either due to the system offering low challenge (for skilled programmer) or too high challenge (for unskilled programmer).

Interactivity is another key feature that these hyperlinks provide for its users. The required information is available to them (users) through the click of a button. The system responds to the user's action immediately and fetches the information rapidly, making the interaction between the system and the user very active. This immediate exchange of information deeply engrosses the attention of the users and they concentrate fully on the activity. At the same time this variety and attractiveness provide the users with enough inquisitiveness and zeal so that they can actively get involved in the system and "play" with it. Immediate feedback also makes the system richer. All these factors increase the involvement of the users and lead to increased flow.

B) *Animation increases flow by increasing the perceived congruence, focused attention, interactivity, media richness and playfulness.*

Animation helps users with visualization of phenomena. A good example to consider here will be a physics teacher explaining to the students "the phenomenon of transfer and absorption of energy by an electron." Since it is typically not easy for students to relate to such an abstract phenomenon, teachers would use various kinds of models and diagrams along with accompanied text to make it easier for the student to understand. However, even with the help of these models, it would still be difficult to convey and explain the information to the students. If the same information can be animated such that it gives the energy transfer and absorption process a "visual look," it would be much easier for the students to understand and visualize. Another example is that of dinosaurs which always have inquisitiveness for a large group of the human population. People tend to retain more information about dinosaurs after watching animations of those extinct creatures from films and documentaries. Animation leaves a greater impact and impression on the human brain. The brain stores animated images in the episodic memory along with other information presented with it. Since animation makes the phenomenon visually attractive as well as easier to understand, it makes the medium flexible in offering challenges to suit the various levels of individuals, thus increasing the perceived congruence of challenges and skills. Animations also have the capability to attract total concentration of the users and get them "immersed in the process" and achieve focused attention. Through animations, a richer content can be offered through cues such as movement and light effects, thus providing a higher media richness. Additionally, animations make the content fun to learn, thus increasing playfulness.

C) *Media richness, focused attention, interactivity, playfulness and flow lead to higher effectiveness of learning.*

Figure 1: Research model

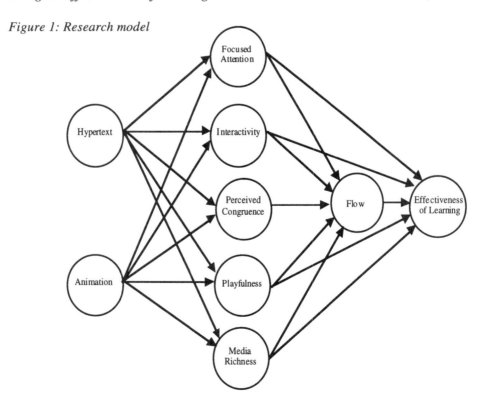

The literature provides a strong support that media richness, focused attention, interactivity, playfulness and flow contribute toward effectiveness of learning. The research done by Hoffman and Novak (1996), Miller (1973), Csikszentmihalyi and Csikszentmihalyi (1988), and Daft and Lengel (1984) form the basis of these relationships.

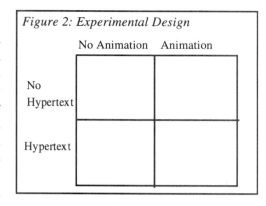

Figure 2: Experimental Design

The proposed research model needs to be tested and verified regarding the role played by the mediating variables (i.e., perceived congruence, focused attention, interactivity, media richness, playfulness and flow) in improving the effectiveness of learning.

Figure 2 presents the proposed experimental design for the study. Four versions of an Internet teaching module will be adapted for this experiment. The module will present basic principles of a subject domain and provide a glossary of terms in the domain. In the hypertext version of the module, the users will only need to click on the term to access its explanation/definition. The specific explanation will be presented in a small Internet browser pop-up window. All the information that will be available through these hypertext links will also be available as a "glossary document" elsewhere in the system. In the non-hypertext version of the module, the users will have to separately access the "glossary document" and search for the specific term to access explanations on the term. Thus, the provision of hypertext links facilitates the search process by making the explanations more "easily accessible" in the hypertext version.

In the animated version of the teaching module, animations of various processes in the subject will be presented along with the text. These animations will be in addition to the regular graphics, diagrams and photographs. In the non-animated version, the module will not contain animations of the processes. Thus, in the case of the animated version, the use of animations provides a richer mode of communicating and expressing the textual and "static graphical" information to the users.

Study data will be collected using a questionnaire and through the computer log. A test will be administered at the end of the study to assess effectiveness of learning. Structural equation modeling will be used for the statistical analysis. The data captured from the questionnaire will be used to assess the relationships in the research model.

EXPECTED CONTRIBUTION

Future research will be directed toward testing our proposed model to evaluate how Hypertext and Animation influence perceived congruence of skills and challenges, focused attention, interactivity, media richness and playfulness, and how these factors effect the flow state and subsequently, effectiveness of learning. From a practitioner's standpoint, the model will be extremely useful to educators, designers and developers of Web-based training courses. With an increased understanding of the effect of Web-based features on learning, Web designers and programmers can develop better and more effective online training modules by focusing their time and attention on incorporating features that contribute toward effectiveness of learning.

References

Brigish, A. (1993). The electronic marketplace: Evolving toward 1:1 marketing. *Electronic Marketplace Report* (formerly *Electronic Directory & Classified Report*), 7(9), 6-7.

Bodensteiner, W. D. (1970). Information channel utilization under varying research and development project conditions: An aspect of inter-organizational communication channel usages. *PhD dissertation*, The University of Texas.

Clary, J. (1997). Algorithm animation hypertext: Today's learning tools. *The Spelman Science and Mathematics Journal: An Interdisciplinary Undergraduate Journal*, 1(1), available at http://www.spelman.edu/ssmj/vol1_1/tech/clary.htm.

Csikszentmihalyi, M. (1977). *Beyond Boredom and Anxiety*, second printing. San Francisco: Jossey-Bass.

Csikszentmihalyi, M. (1982). Towards a psychology of optimal experience. In L. Wheeler (Ed.), *Review of personality and social psychology*, (2). Beverly Hills, CA: Sage.

Csikszentmihalyi, M. (1990). *Finding Flow: The Psychology of Engagement with Everyday Life*. BasicBooks, A division of HarperCollins publishers.

Csikszentmihalyi, M. and Csikszentmihalyi, I. (1988). *Optimal Experience: Psychological Studies of Flow in Consciousness*. Cambridge: Cambridge University Press.

Daft, L. R. and Lengel H. R. (1984). Information richness: a new approach to managerial behavior and organizational design. *Research in Organizational Behavior*, (6), 191-233.

Ghani, J. A. (1991). Flow in human-computer interactions: Test of a model. In J. Carey (Ed.) *Human Factors in Management Information Systems: An Organizational Perspective*. Norwood, NJ: Ablex.

Ghani J. A. and Deshpande S. P. (1993). Task characteristics and the experience of optimal flow in human-computer interaction. *Journal of Psychology*, 128(4), 381-391.

Gokhale, A. A. (1996). Effectiveness of computer simulation for enhancing higher order thinking. *Journal of Industrial Teacher Education*, 33(4), 36-46.

Hoffman D. L. and Novak, T. P. (1996). Marketing in hypermedia computer-mediated environments: Conceptual foundations. *Journal of Marketing*, 60, 50-68.

Kehoe, C. M. (1996). Algorithms and animation, available at http:// www.cs.gatech.edu/grads/k/Colleen.Kehoe/papers/lit_review/lit_review.html.

Lewis, L., Snow, K., Farris, E. and Levin, D. (1999). *Distance Education at Postsecondary Education Institutions: 1997-98*. Statistical Analysis Report, National Center for Education Statistics, available at http://nces.ed.gov/pubs2000/ 2000013.pdf.

Loveless, N. E., Brebner, J. and Hamilton, P. (1970). Bisensory presentation of information. *Psychological Bulletin*, 73(3), 161-195.

Mao, Y. J. and Benbasat, I. (1998). Contextualized access to knowledge: Theoretical perspectives and a process tracing study. *Information Systems Journal*, 8, 217-239.

Marshall, C. C. and Shipman, F. M. III. (1995). Spatial hypertext: Designing for change. *Communications of the ACM*, 38(8), 88-97.

Mayes T. J. (1989) *The M-Word: Multi-Media Interfaces and Their Role in Interactive Learning Systems*, available at http://www.icbl.hw.ac.uk/ctl/mayes/ paper4.html.

Menn, D. (1993). Multimedia in education. *PC World*, M52-M60.

Menne, J. M. and Menne, J. W. (1972), The relative efficiency of bimodal presentation as an aid to learning. *Audio Visual Communication Review*, 20, 170-180.

Miller, S. (1973). Ends, means and galumphing: Some leitmotifs of play. *American Anthropologist*, 75, 87-98.

Pezdek, K. (1987). Television comprehension as an example of applied research in cognitive psychology. In D. E. Berger, K. Pezdek and W. P. Banks (Eds.), *Applications of Cognitive Psychology: Problem Solving, Education and Computing*. Hillsdale, NJ: Lawrence Erlbaum.

Pezdek, K. and Stevens, E. (1984). Children's memory for auditory and visual information on television. *Developmental Psychology*, 20, 212-218.

Pogrow, S. (1994). Students who just don't understand. *Educational Leadership,* 52(3), 62-66.

Privette, G. and Bundrick, C. (1987). Measurement of experience: Construct and content validity of the experience questionnaire. *Perceptual and Motor Skills*, 65, 315-332.

Rock, I and Victor, J. (1964). Vision and touch: An experimentally created conflict between the two senses. *Science*, 143, 594-596.

Sandelands, L. E. and Buckner, G. C. (1989). Of art and work: Aesthetic experience and psychology of work feelings. *Research in Organizational Behavior*, 105-131.

Steuer, J. (1992). Defining virtual reality: Dimensions determining telepresence. *Journal of Communication*, 42(4), 73-93.

Webster J., Trevino, L. K. and Ryan, L. (1993). The dimensionality and correlates of flow in human computer-interactions. *Computers in Human Behavior*, 9, 411-426.

CHAPTER FIVE

Managing Value-Creation in the Digital Economy: Information Types and E-Business Models

John C. McIntosh
Bentley College, USA

Keng Siau
University of Nebraska—Lincoln, USA

INTRODUCTION

Today's economy is increasingly driven by the integration of information in many aspects of business. Greater information intensity in industries such as hospital supplies and express package delivery is causing a fundamental transformation in the way firms conduct business, the menu of competitive choices that they are faced with and the need to continuously keep ahead of competitors. Information-driven businesses appear to adopt several managerial practices to create value. These include: mass customization or the development of highly customized products for individual customers (Wind and Rangaswamy, 1999; Pine, 1993); disintermediation or the creation of direct links between producers and consumers such that traditional intermediaries such as wholesalers and retailers are removed from the value-added chain in an industry (Westland and Clark, 2000; Benjamin and Wigand, 1995); self-design of products by customers as firms allow them to design products in-house and then transmit production specifications directly to suppliers; faster response times as direct communication links between customers and suppliers enable reduced order entry and processing cycles and on-demand production (Timmers, 1998; Keen, 1993); and lower transaction costs arising from expanded use of single-source electronic sales channels (Kerridge et al., 1998; Picot and Kirchner, 1987).

This research seeks to advance understanding of information as a source of value creation in the digital economy. It therefore focuses on the nature of information itself as a resource, the effective management of which may be used to create products and services of economic value. Implicit in this assertion is the belief that the mere possession of information technology is a necessary but not sufficient condition. Hence, we focus not on the management of information technology, but on the ways that different types of information may be used to create value. The reader should note that our use of the term "products" refers to both tangible and intangible offerings. The convergence of information, physical products and services is becoming a particularly powerful driver of value creation in the form of fusion products that embody all three elements (Berryman et al., 1988; Goldman et al., 1995). Toward this end we develop a classification of information types based on the rate at which information changes and the degree to which information can be combined with other types of information to create value. We then use the classification scheme to describe the types of information that underpin four Internet business models. The reader should note that we do not purport to describe all extant business models. The Internet is a technologically dynamic, fast changing environment. It is virtually a certainty that other models will arise.

LITERATURE ON INFORMATION TYPES

Machlup (1980) suggested that information can be classified into five types: practical, intellectual, pastime, spiritual and unwanted. Although interesting, this is of very little practical use in depicting the information content of value chain activities. Holsapple and Whinston (1996) proposed two main classifications of knowledge: primary and secondary knowledge. The three primary types of knowledge are descriptive, procedural and reasoning knowledge. The three secondary types of knowledge are linguistic, assimilative and presentation knowledge. The classification scheme proposed by Holsappe and Whinston (1996) is targeted at Decision Support Systems. Though useful and applicable, it is not ideal for our research questions. An alternate classification, intended for the health care professionals, distinguishes between professional knowledge and improvement knowledge (Batalden and Stolz 1993). In psychology, Anderson (1983) distinguished between the declarative and procedural knowledge. While important for the study of human cognition, this classification is too general for our purposes.

The question of an appropriate classification scheme may be answered by adopting one already in existence or building on existing schemes to design a classification suitable for understanding the role of information as a source of competitive advantage. In this paper we pursue the latter alternative.

THEORETICAL FOUNDATION

To effectively utilize information for value creation, an organization needs to traverse a learning curve. Nolan (1979) argued that this evolution involves growth in technology and application development, changes in planning and control strategies, and changes in user involvement. He proposed a six-stage growth model: (i) initiation, (ii) contagion, (iii) control, (iv) integration, (v) data administration and (vi) maturity. No stage of the learning curve, he stressed, can be circumvented. In other words, organizations need to experience growth associated with each evolutionary stage and no stage can be skipped because associated learning processes would be lost.

Similarly, Cash and McLeod (1985) proposed a framework depicting the evolution of new information technology within organizations that provides a holistic view of the organizational change process. The phases are: (i) investment or project initiation, (ii) technology learning and adaptation, (iii) rationalization and management control, and (iv) widespread technology transfer.

As such, the classification scheme developed for this research needs to represent a pattern of growth and evolution. The information needs to progress from simple to complex and parallel organization learning.

CLASSIFICATION SCHEME

This section develops definitions of four types of information that the firm may use to create the following types of value: products with high customer appeal, reduced buyer and seller search costs, individually customized on-line experiences conducive to product purchase and opportunities for cross-selling and up-selling. Information-based competition depends partly on two features, information velocity and interoperability. Velocity refers to the rate at which information changes. Examples of high velocity information include the price of a stock or the number of packages at a logistic provider's hub at a specific point in time. High velocity information is often simple in that it tends to be quantitative and describes a single phenomenon. Low velocity information, in contrast, is often complex and changes less rapidly. Examples include the way humans interact with a particular interface or software package. Interoperability refers to the extent to which a particular type of information can be combined with other types of information to create value. Highly interoperable information, such as age and income, can be combined with a variety of other data, such as number of delinquent accounts to assess credit risk. Age and income may also be

		Velocity	
		High	Low
Interoperability	High	State Information	Procedural Information
	Low	Functional Information	Behavioral/Value Information

combined with motor vehicle registration information to identify likely marketing candidates for a low-end sports car. Information of lower interoperability, such as a description of the way photons flow through a magnetic field, can be combined with a more specialized set of information to create extremely fast optical devices. Figure 1 arrays information velocity and interoperability as dimensions of a two-by-two matrix. From this we identify four distinct types of information. Each is discussed in turn.

State Information

This is the simplest type of information. Typically descriptive in nature, state information changes rapidly (high velocity) and can be easily combined with other information to create value (high interoperability). Examples of state information include the price of a commodity on a particular day and at a specific time, the quantity or inventory level of a product and the chronology of a product or service's journey as it makes its way through the firm's value chain. General Motors' information system, for example, provides state information concerning the price of engine components from different suppliers, the number of engine assemblies in inventory and the mix of automobiles on a car carrier in the distribution system.

Procedural Information

As its name suggests, procedural information refers to the steps or protocols that are required to conduct a process or perform a service. Procedural information for a service, such as issuing a home mortgage, may be represented as the steps associated with performing a credit check, conducting a title search and issuing a payment. Procedural information tends to change relatively slowly (low velocity) and can be combined with other information to create viable business processes (high interoperability). For example, the best business practices for a particular industry may be combined with company-specific data to improve business processes. Procedural information therefore tends to be more explicit and relatively easily codifiable.

Functional Information

Functional information describes how components and/or subsystems of a tangible product interact and how these interactions give rise to the performance features that characterize a product. Functional information arises from what is commonly known as engineering knowledge (knowledge germane to the engineering discipline). As a result, it may be described as high velocity (because the stock of applied technical information changes rapidly) and low interoperability (because information is often applicable to a narrow domain). It is grounded in an understanding of the technologies that constitute a product and how variations in those technologies can affect overall system performance. Drawing on a computer analogy, functional information regarding microprocessor speed, hard drive access time and the amount of RAM in a computer permits engineers to design systems with differing performance characteristics. Unlike procedural information, functional information tends to be more complex and tacit in nature. It therefore cannot be as easily captured and represented in an organization's databases as state and procedural information.

Behavioral /Value Information

This information type is probably the most abstract and tacit. It changes relatively slowly and has low interoperability in that it can be combined with a limited set of information to create value. Behavioral/value information refers to the way in which large-scale, complex systems including humans interact under different environmental conditions and in conjunction with different stimuli. It may be used to predict the future actions of complex systems such as the trajectory of a hurricane or the layout of a Web site that is most likely to stimulate customer purchases. For example, capturing information about individual customers and buying preferences might allow the firm to create a model of consumer preference for particular product offerings and thus enable it to fine tune its marketing and sales initiatives.

INFORMATION UNDERPINNINGS OF E-BUSINESS MODELS

In this section, we take each type of information and describe how it is used in four pervasive business models on the Internet (**sites**). We do not purport that these models make exclusive use of a particular type of information. Instead, we suggest that each model's key features arise from use of a particular type of information.

Brokerage Model

Brokers create virtual marketplaces where buyers and sellers meet to engage in transactions (Rao, 1999). These transactions span the entire spectrum of e-business types: business-to-business (B2B), business-to-consumer (B2C), business-to-government (B2G), consumer-to-consumer (C2C) and consumer-to-business (C2B). Brokers create value by reducing the search costs associated with buyers finding sellers and vice-versa. The structure of the brokerage model is rather simple. Brokers typically aggregate state information regarding the types and quantities of products and services that sellers offer and make this information available to buyers. A virtual space is created where buyers and sellers can assemble. The high velocity and high interoperability of state information confers an advantage to brokers in that state information's rapid rate of change makes it difficult for buyers and sellers to remain current. The centralized space created by the broker facilitates information gathering and exchange. Travelocity.com in travel services and Fidelity's Powerstreet.com in financial services are classic examples of this model.

Vertical Trading Community

This predominantly B2B model draws on deep knowledge of the practices and procedures of specific vertical markets to create a virtual space in which buyers and sellers can engage in transactions. Firms implementing this business model often select traditional industries, such as steel, bulk chemicals and trucking, in which practices and procedures evolve at relatively low velocity. High fragmentation in these industries implies very high search costs for both buyers and sellers. Vertical trading communities take advantage of this to create highly interoperable information valued by a wide variety of users. This often takes the form of buyer and seller directories, software that matches buyers and sellers according to product or particular needs such as the purchase of nonstandard lot sizes (Palmer, 1997). Vertical trading communities also provide means for participants to access high velocity, industry-specific information such as industry news, employment ads and discussion forums. Plastics Net in industrial-grade plastics, e-Steel in steel, Procure Net in MRO sourcing (maintenance, repair and operations) and Chemical Connect in industrial chemicals exemplify the vertical trading community model.

Knowledge Repositories

A relatively new business model, knowledge repositories, draws on a deep base of topic-specific high velocity, functional information to create offerings for customers. Firms following this model tend to be very narrowly focused on a single, often technologically dynamic industry. These repositories act as clearinghouses for latest technological developments. In that respect, they are effective disseminators of functional technical knowledge. The WAP (wireless application protocol) Forum or Anywhere.com are examples of firms that specialize in creating an information space in which technical information regarding rapidly changing wireless applications, standards and tools can be exchanged.

Customized Experience

The customized experience model is most frequently used in B2C enterprises. In this model, the firm combines relatively low velocity behavioral information derived from psychological, anthropological and human factors research along with historical information concerning product preferences of individual customers to create a highly tailored on-line experience. This model creates value in the form of reduced customer search and buying costs, and the opportunity to suggest complimentary products or higher end products that the customer may not have considered. Searching and buying costs are lowered by reducing the number of product categories and page views a customer must sort through to find a desired product and by minimizing number of "clicks" required to purchase that product. Firms achieve this by combining behavioral and value information. Behavioral information regarding the way humans, in general, interact with software and customer-specific site navigation habits is combined with value information such as a customer's buying preferences to offer a one-to-one, highly tailored on-line experience.

Although the information arising from these experiences is highly context-specific and therefore of low interoperability, it nevertheless provides opportunities for cross-selling or up-selling. Amazon.com's ability to direct users to pages they visit often and to display suggestions based on their buying history exemplifies this model. It should be noted that the use of behavioral and value information to create "on the fly" customized experiences is rapidly being adopted by firms that deploy other models.

DISCUSSION

The typology presented in this chapter enriches our understanding of information and its role in the digital economy in several ways. First, it demonstrates that the potential value of information is independent of its level of complexity. In other words, information need not be complex to create value. For example, taxi companies use real-time information feeds regarding the actual arrival times and number of incoming flights to an airport to dispatch an appropriate number of taxis at the right time.

Second, the notion of interoperability allows practitioners to think of information uses beyond the boundaries of their industry or discipline. This opens the possibility for developing hybrid information products or completely reorienting a firm's strategy. The relatively new computational genomics industry applies information from computer science, structural biology and molecular genetics to create information products. Dow Corning, facing steep price competition from specialist firms that create laboratory glassware and test equipment, has recognized that it cannot survive as a firm that manufactures laboratory equipment. Dow is beginning to leverage its considerable procedural and functional knowledge of biological and pharmaceutical research to change its strategy to creating tools that reduce the time to uncover biological knowledge.

Third, the typology offers the foundation for future research to identify links between an organization's information managing competencies, the types of information it employs and business models it may pursue. For example, Procurenet.com's competencies in managing low velocity, low interoperability information associated with government procurement may not be suitable for pursuing a knowledge repository model.

This typology may also be used to stimulate other typologies to advance understanding of information-based competition. As leaps in scientific knowledge such as the Human Genome Project (HGP) create vast amounts of information and as businesses recognize opportunities to extract value from that information, there is a potential need to understand the process by which value is created from *information about information*. The evolving Genomics industry is illustrative. Organizations such as Biodatabases.com and Hyseq, Inc. act as repositories of information from proprietary DNA sequences. These firms create value by simply disseminating proprietary information to end users. Other firms, such as

Genesolutions.com and Array Genetics, Inc., recognize that much of the HGP's information is indecipherable and create value by developing specialized algorithms. These algorithms create differentiated information products by targeting results to specific domains of pharmaceutical research. Algorithms are based on state, procedural and functional knowledge of pharmaceutical research and the human genome.

CONCLUSION

Although digital technologies have existed for many years and continue to evolve at a rapid pace, contemporary organizations appear to be either reluctant or unable to apply those technologies to different types of information to create new sources of value. Indeed, many contemporary applications of information technology focus on creating operational efficiencies by deconstructing traditional value chains, retaining core activities within the firm and delegating non-core activities to external specialists (Laseter et al., 1999). While this process has led to significant procurement, production and distribution cost savings, potentially larger gains can be made by using information itself to create value. The typology presented in this paper offers a framework for systematically thinking about how information can be used to create value.

REFERENCES

Anderson, J. R. (1983). *The Architecture of Cognition*. Cambridge, MA: Harvard University Press.

Batalden, P. B., and Stoltz, P. K. (1993). A framework for the continual improvement of health care: Building and applying professional and improvement knowledge to test changes in daily work. *Journal of Quality Improvement*, 19(10).

Benjamin, R., and Wigand R. (1995). Electronic markets and virtual value chains on the information superhighway. *Sloan Management Review*, Winter, 62-71.

Berryman, K., Harrington, L., Layton-Rodin, D., and Rerolle, V. (1998). Electronic commerce: Three emerging strategies. *Mc Kinsey Quarterly,* (1), 152-159.

Cash, J., and McLeod, P. (1985). Managing the introduction of information technology in strategically dependent companies. *Journal of Management Information Systems*, 1, 5-23.

Goldman, S. L., Nagel, R. N., and Preiss, K. (1995). *Agile Competitors and Virtual Organizations: Strategies for Enriching the Customer*. New York: Van Nostrand Reinhold.

Holsapple, C. W., and Whinston, A. B. (1996). *Decision Support Systems: A Knowledge-Based Approach*. St. Paul, MN: West Publishing Company.

Keen, P. G. W. (1993). Information technology and the management of difference: A fusion map. *IBM Systems Journal*, 32(1), 17-39.

Kerridge, S., Slade, A., Kerrdige, S., and Ginty, K. (1998). Electronic procurement using virtual supply chains: An overview. *Electronic Markets,* 8(3), 28-31.

Laseter, T. M., Houston, P. W., Wright, J. L., and Park, J. Y. (1999). Amazon your industry: Extracting value from the value chain. *Mc Kinsey Quarterly,* First Quarter, 94-105.

Machlup, F. (1980). *Knowledge: Its Creation, Distribution and Economic Significance.* Princeton, NJ: Princeton University Press.

Nolan, R. L. (1979). Managing the crises in data processing. *Harvard Business Review*, March-April, 115-126.

Palmer, J. W. (1997). Retailing on the WWW: The use of electronic product catalogs. *Electronic Markets,* 7(3), 6-10.

Picot, A., and Kirchner, C. (1987). Transaction cost analysis of structural changes in the distribution system: Reflections on institutional developments in the Federal Republic of Germany. *Journal of Institutional and Theoretical Economics*, 143, 62-81.

Pine, B. J. (1993). *Mass Customization—The New Frontier in Business Competition.* Boston: Harvard Business School Press.

Rao, B. (1999). Emerging business models in on-line commerce. Working paper. Institute for Technology and Enterprise, Polytechnic University, New York.

Timmers, P. (1998). Business Models for Electronic Markets. *Electronic Markets,* 8(2), 2-8.

Westland, J. C., and Clark, T. K. (2000). *Global Electronic Commerce: Theory and Case Studies.* MIT Press, Boston, MA.

Wind, J., and Rangaswamy, A. (1999). Customerization: The second revolution in mass customization. *E-Business Research Center Working Paper #06-1999.* Smeal College of Business Administration, The Pennsylvania State University.

CHAPTER SIX

Building an Infrastructure to Manage Electronic Services

Åke Grönlund
Umeå University, Sweden

For an organization to be able to deliver electronic services efficiently and professionally requires a "service infrastructure" including organizational solutions for logistics and customer (citizen) interactions. This chapter reviews a study covering three years of efforts by nine cities in eight European countries in developing such solutions.

Generally, Web projects were seen as technical projects; though in fact issues pertaining to users and organization were most important, they were largely neglected.

We found 12 distinct "challenges," situations where the setting changed and the process was found in a stage of improvisation until new stability was achieved. The challenges fall into four categories, concerning users (4 challenges), organization (6), economy (1) and technology (1).

We found that the overall process was largely unstructured and improvised. Stabilizing factors were central government policies (national, European Union), the general technical development, market demands and a cadre of Web agents" fostered within the organizations over years of Web projects.

There was typically a missing infrastructure link, a body competent of managing the whole process of bundling services from different service providers and publishing them in a coherent fashion, providing support to service providers during the process of inventing, refining and evaluating services, improving operations and conducting the necessary but typically ignored activities of analysis of service quality and policy making.

Our conclusion is that there is a great lack of strategic leadership in the field of electronic services in local governments in Europe. This is a big problem considering the importance of that sector and the challenges it is facing.

INTRODUCTION

Over the past few years, many local and regional governments have followed companies in setting up "home pages" on the Internet. The ICMA Information Technology Surveys show that already in 1997, 90% of large US cities had Web sites, 29.2% of the small cities and 66.6% of medium sized ones (Norris, 1999). For Europe, there are no comprehensive statistics, but as one example the SUNET catalogue of Swedish municipal sites lists 227 sites, 78% of the total number of municipalities (SUNET, 2000). The figure should be 100%; a search on the Web for each of the remaining town names found a site in every case. Many cities have two sites, one "city.se" and one "city.com," the latter often including business partners. Even though the Scandinavian countries are above the European average in Internet use in general, there is no doubt that Web sites are becoming widely used in all of Europe.

Despite these indications of widespread use, expectations for advanced interactive services integrated in business procedures seem not to have been fulfilled. Investigations of adaptation of Web systems show that although generally in use in cities, the sophistication is generally not impressive. Norris (1999) found, based on surveys of actual IT use and managements' perceptions of usefulness of IT, that adaptation of "leading edge information technologies" does in fact increase, and predicts that the penetration will be more deep in the future. At present, the depth seems less than impressive overall. Scavo and Shi (1999) surveyed 145 US municipality and county government sites and found use to be less sophisticated. Citizen interaction opportunities and service delivery were rare while promotional material and bulletin boards were abundant. Norris (1997, p. 147) attributes the current shallowness for Web applications partly to their newness—depth occurs incrementally—partly to the fact that more advanced technologies are more complex, requiring time, funding and effort to become fully deployed.

This is where this chapter starts. There is a big difference between the different kinds of applications. While promotional material is static and simply published on the Web, services and citizen interaction require a *service infrastructure*. Mails must be answered correctly, goods or services delivered promptly and securely, complaints and inquiries must be answered etc. Different media—the Web, telephones, call centers, etc.—must be integrated to provide smooth service processes, both as seen from the customer side and as concerns efficiency in internal operations. This requires more advanced technology (e.g., for identification and payment) and new institutions (e.g., a multiple-media reception and delivery service). There are clearly advantages to expect from a successful employment of Web technology, both in terms of economy and of improved customer relations. As an example, the ServiceArizona project implementing Web-based transactions such as ordering personalized number plates and replacing lost ID cards resulted in cost cuts per transaction from $6.60 to $1.60, and a saving of $1.7 million per year with 15% of the transactions being done via the Web. Further, the motor vehicle department scored an 80% approval rating, way above other departments (Symonds, 2000).

This chapter examines the hurdles to successful use of the electronic medium in a local government setting based on a three-year study of electronic service projects in local governments in Europe.

The research was done in a public sector environment, but we believe the findings make sense also in other organizations to the extent that they deal with the general problem of accommodating a new technology in the organization. Certain challenges may appear more complicated in public organizations, though, for instance those that are due to organizational rigidity. In public organizations this rigidity is often supported by law, for instance in order to protect individuals' privacy, and thus it cannot easily be softened or circumnavigated.

BACKGROUND

The purposes of public sector Web information systems (WIS, but popularly often just "IT") are often boldly stated and cover economic, social and democratic topics. A typical example is the following:

"The public administration shall use IT for making *more effective operations* and provide good service to companies and citizens. More *rational work routines*, more *effective organization* and *cooperation in the public agencies* shall *improve services* and at the same time *reduce costs* ... IT shall be employed to *develop contacts and interplay* among the public, businesses and the public administration. Citizens' and businesses' public sector *contacts* shall be made *simpler* and more *open.*" (Gov. Bill No 1995/96:125; Toppledarforum, 1998. My italicization and translation.)

Goals such as these are inscribed in central government IT strategies in many countries. At the local level, however, strategies are often lacking, or outdated (Håkansson, 1996; Hansson & Johansson, 1997). This is a problem, because much of the development is in the hands of local authorities. The goals in the above quote clearly require changes in the way government works, but so far this does not seem to have happened. Seneviratne (1999) finds, based on a literature review, that despite its potential, "information technologies have not been associated with organizational transformation in the public sector" (p. 49).

It seems technology is under-used, and strategies are lacking at the local level, but why is that so? Why has Web use not become more deeply integrated with operations? Is it just a matter of time, or are there other obstacles? Since use of the Web has been on the agenda for more than five years, there is a history of attempts to organize electronic services to study. The technology is there, yet more advanced services in local government are rare. This chapter investigates what happens during the process of developing electronic services, what hurdles are there and how to get past those?

Since more advanced systems are rare, there is not much literature to tell us. Case stories abound (see for instance the listing by IDPM, 1998), but they usually only describe ongoing projects with little analysis or comparison. As for research, it typically falls into one of two categories. One is about exploratory sites working under nontypical conditions, like the Blacksburg Electronic Village studies (Virginia Tech, 1998) and Tsagarousianou et al.'s (1998) research on use and users of sites motivated by a strong community element. In such cases, there are typically a lot of "project effects" which make results less applicable to everyday settings; sites are set up with extraordinary resources, they involve subsidies to providers and/or users, they target special, advanced, audiences, they get a lot of extra attention by universities and media, etc. In the other category, single special issues of a technical character are covered: fraud prevention, integrity of data in electronic document exchange, public access to official records, etc.

While both kinds of research are important, they only give fragmentary insights. Very little can be found about evaluations of comprehensive strategies for using Web Information Systems (WIS) for achieving the bold purposes exemplified above: improvements of everyday government interactions with citizens and businesses. After all, government strategies must be about finding general ways of relating to WIS as a medium for the everyday operations. This means it is important to understand the Web, and the use of it, from a general point of view; how should government relate to IT as a strategic medium? How can development methods be found, that is, how can early experiences be shared, evaluated, related to societal goals and debated so as to make the transition to the electronic medium as smooth as possible? Some claim the development so far has happened much ad hoc (Greeves, 1998). Strategy documents of the kind cited above abound, but knowledge about implementation beyond things like guidelines for home page design are largely lacking.

For a city to provide services electronically is in many ways a much more complex task than it is for a company. A city is the hub of many processes; it regulates use of natural resources as well as social organization, it runs businesses such as housing companies and power companies, it is a political organization managing public debates, and it is an important player in local culture and local business. Products are diverse, often intertwined and involve exertion of authority and doing business as well as democratic aspects of citizen influence, equality, universal access and so on. Often, the "services" are mandatory for citizens, and seen as trouble rather than as a service. Since local government handles many services which each often has little traffic, there is a strong need for a local infrastructure making the most of common solutions in terms of both logistics and technical solutions. Such solutions will also typically have to include local SMEs, which often make up an important part of a city's business contacts.

Before reporting our findings, we shall briefly discuss the theoretical framework used, and the discussion of how IT adaptation in organizations take place.

BUILDING INFRASTRUCTURE; "IMPLEMENTATION," "DRIFTING," "INSCRIPTION" OR WHAT?

An electronic service infrastructure involves basic physical infrastructure (wires and computers) as well as software and organizational institutions and routines. Here, we deal with the two latter: cities concerned with building Web services, including production of "pages," scripts and databases, adaptation of existing services for delivery in the new medium and definition of new services so as to make more efficient use of the medium.

Many see technology deployment in an organization as a rather straightforward matter of "implementing decisions" (Broadbent & Waill, 1997) or a process of diffusion (Levitt & March, 1988; Rogers, 1962). A contrasting view is that of Ciborra (1997); in this view technology "drifts"; during the "implementation" numerous decisions of different scope are made, by many actors, that make the original "grand plan" obsolete. Drifting is attributed to both the flexibility of technology to allow many interpretations and social processes. New appropriations of the technology are made along the road, which makes the outcome considerably different from the intended. Ciborra goes so far as to say that the outcome is "almost out of anybody's control" (Ciborra 1997, p. 76). Others make more modest claims, saying that these reappropriations are in fact not so free and unpredictable, but structured by the "ongoing effort to keep the (gradually metamorphosed) infrastructure alive" (Monteiro & Hepsö, 1998, p. 270).

According to Latour (1996), "for technology, every day is a working day" (p. 86); over time different actors get in touch with the technology and try to have its use their way. Technology adaptation in the view of Actor Network Theory (ANT) is thus not a matter of diffusion, but of *translation*; which includes "all the negotiations, intrigues, calculations, acts of persuasion and violence" (Callon & Latour, 1981, p. 279) that will over time result in that "claims become well-established facts and prototypes are turned into routinely used pieces of equipment" (Latour 1987, p. 132).

This view is one where "drifting" occurs, and events down the road form technology and use patterns (which is the same in ANT parlance; "technology is society made durable" [Latour, 1991], that is, technology also includes institutional arrangements). Technology is "inscribed" (with views of actors) rather than "implemented."

This discussion of how technology is "implemented," "inscribed" or "drifts" relates to where the long-term plans for the new infrastructure are laid out. From that point of departure, the problem concerns how to make things happen the way they were intended to. The public sector environment introduces some extra challenges. As we saw in the Background, there is generally a lack of grand plans at the local level. One reason for this is that local governments in the countries we studied have relatively large room to maneuver, there are generally rather weak links between central government IT plans and local actions. Other reasons include the ongoing development of Web technologies and increases in user demands and access.

We thus face a situation with both grand plans, a flexible "line of command" and an unstable setting where implementation of these plans seems hazardous in the lack of safe predictions. The field seems open for entrepreneurs, and the IT field is full of them. Let us go on to see what can happen.

ANT—Shaping Technology by Negotiation

In contrast to the visions of electronic government briefly sketched in the Background section, which imply a straightforward process where strategy is formed on the basis of the visions, and used to formulate action plans and to guide implementation, we saw a rather diversified process. In this chapter, I therefore retrospectively analyze our material using the terminology of actor-network theory, ANT (Latour, 1999; Wiebe &Law, 1994), since I find that framework well designed to describe such a meandering development. I will use some of the concepts of ANT to describe the trajectory of electronic services projects as we have seen it. Let me first introduce briefly these terms.

According to Actor-Network Theory (ANT), the creation of *facts* comes about during processes of *negotiation* (any kind of action) among *actants* (human or non-human actors). Facts are not *found*, they are introduced into a social context as *claims*, which are *translated* by enrollment and *inscriptions* of networks of actants. Over time a growing network of actants are involved as claims get strengthened and

Figure 1: IT "implementation" as ongoing negotiation loops (from Holmström, 2000)

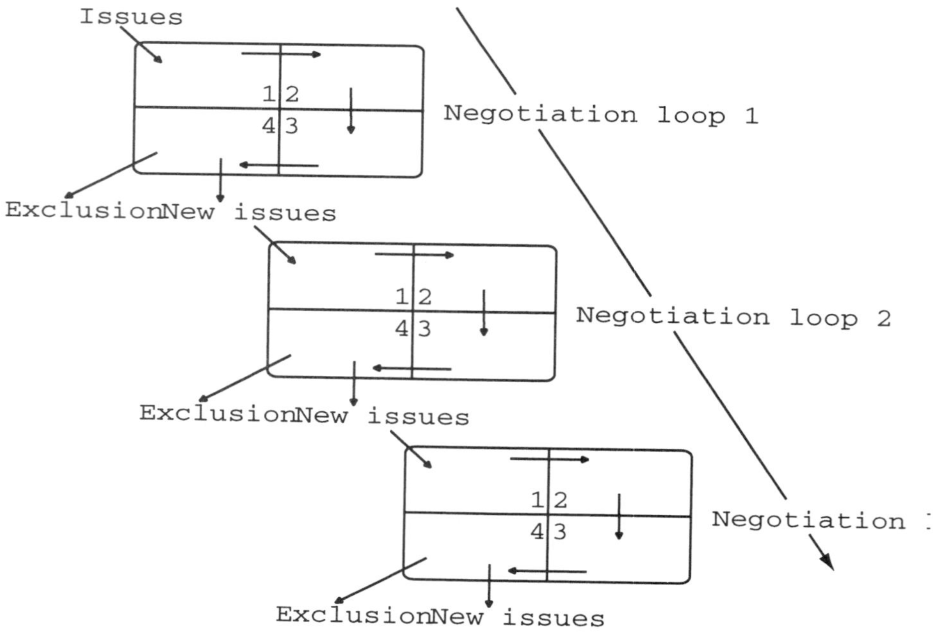

weakened (McMaster, Vidgen & Wastell, 1999). Actants are heterogeneous; the strength of the network relies on the strength of the actors' aligned interests.

(In the following, numbers refer to Figure 1.) During the negotiation process, a *claim*, a candidate fact, pertaining to an issue gains support or gets excluded. Introduction of a claim brings *perplexity* (1) to the network (or organization) where it is introduced. Following is a period of *negotiation* or *consultation* (2) where the claim is considered by the actors in view of other claims and existing facts. On the agenda is the claim's place in the *hierarchy* of things (3). If accepted, the claim becomes institutionalized (4): a *fact*. This new fact becomes part of the new social setting into which new claims will be introduced. If not accepted, it gets rejected; in order to be reconsidered, it will have to go through the process once again (McMaster et al., 1999).

Although networks evolve constantly, at times the development is "frozen" (4). This might be at a time when a product is developed. Bijker (1997) describes how various versions of the bicycle, attracting different social groups, were developed during the later half of the 1800s to end up with the "safety bicycle" (which, among other things, didn't so easily tip over forward when braking). But the label "safety bicycle" is not just the name of a certain product. It is also the name of the *meaning* a social group (actors) ascribe to it. Thus there were social groups wanting a safe bicycle, but there was also show-offs (males) more interested in making an impression (on women) than in safe transportation from point A to point B, thus promoting the development of what Bijker calls the "Macho bicycle" (which had a larger front wheel, was less stable and harder to mount).

Thus, at certain instances in the development, technology is *inscribed* with certain meanings—certain things are actually developed, others are not (a bicycle can't have a big front wheel and a small one at the same time). Such a moment in the development can be called a *freeze frame* (McMaster, et al, 1999).

In the following, I describe the development of electronic services, or rather of an infrastructure for managing electronic services. I do that in a very simplified way by sketching the development by the following terms:

The *setting* is the assembly of humans and nonhuman actors that act during a certain period of time. The three negotiation loops in Figure 1 each represent a particular setting—each one different from the previous since new facts have been accepted.

The *actants* are the human and non-human actors.

An *inscription* is the way technology is designed to promote socially desired actions and prevent non-desired ones. Examples include the alarm in cars that sounds when the engine is running and the seat belt is not fastened (Latour, 1997, in Bijker & Law, 1997) or the heavy weights attached to hotel keys forcing clients to remember to return the key (Akrich & Latour, 1997). In the below description, some inscriptions are rather clear, whereas others are still at the stage of being a *claim*, that is, some actor's suggestion for an inscription. This is because much of the development I describe is happening as we speak, especially the latter challenges.

Technology is "society made durable" (Latour, 1991), it includes institutional arrangements and social conventions as well as artifacts.

Interpretive flexibility means technology can be seen as different things by different actors. The safety bicycle and the macho bicycle, as Bijker names them, were at a certain point in time not different products but representations of different actors different views of the (same) bicycle. Similarly, at some stages described below, there were different actors definitely having different views of what the technology "is," that is, they have different *claims* for how technology should be inscribed.

In the following, I describe very briefly the "freeze frames" of the development we saw in the nine cities. Each of them represents a completed step in the development in terms of activities and goals in the cities (often termed "projects" and formally organized as a such). In that way they represent stable networks (shared views of the technology). Seen in retrospect, they were, of course, not stable at all. They were only steps toward the goal of arriving at a stable electronic services infrastructure providing for proficient electronic service management.

"Stability" means that people in the organization feel a problem encountered is solved. It usually is, but the problem is that the challenges ahead are not yet foreseen, so in fact the solution often contains the seed to problems during the next stage of development.

I have divided the development into what I call "challenges." I do not claim that they necessarily follow in exactly this order (which a term like "stages" might imply). What marks a challenge is that the organizations in fact felt faced with new, unexpected situations; one stage of stability has been reached, then—all of a sudden - the scene changes radically. Sometimes, the new decisions required were made without much controversy, but often they required much thought and discussion, and the issues took a long time to be settled.

Method

This chapter summarizes a three-year empirical study of the efforts of nine European cities in eight countries striving toward developing electronic services within the Infosond project,[1] running from January 1996 to March 1999. The empirical material is presented in more detail in the final report from the project (Grönlund, 1998) and in a popular book for managers and project leaders (Grönlund & Forsgren, 1999; Grönlund, 2000).

A large number of cases were collected mainly in two ways: (1) Project leaders in the nine cities were interviewed at several occasions over the three years (they met every two months). Interviews were sometimes semistructured, sometimes unstructured. Sometimes we just were present in their meetings and listened to their discussions. This gave us second-hand information about different projects in the cities and first-hand information about strategies, visions, progress reports and considerations among the project leaders. (2). We also gathered some first-hand information from the implemented systems by evaluating them. We did a usability study of selected systems in 1997 (Grönlund, 1997) and studies of use, management and economic evaluation in 1998 (Schijvenaars, 1998). Both studies covered all project cities. We also studied project reports, minutes from meetings and documents from the cities, like infrastructure plans and regulations.

In Spring of 1998, we set up a project review group, involving four people from the cities: two represented organizations running telematic services for cities, two represented cities directly. During a four-day seminar in April 1998, the group arrived at a model of the development process over the past years. The result, which drew on the cases and the experiences of the practitioners and the researchers, was the "dozen challenges model," briefly presented below.

Over the following six months, we wrote a report. Cases from the cities were detailed and used as illustrations to the model. The project group met two more times for two-day seminars where the emerging text was thoroughly discussed. On three occasions during the process, the contents of the report were presented to a wider audience of project leaders and decision makers in the cities—the model, the description of the challenges and the use of the cases. This was done to ensure people understood our model and agreed with our interpretations, and that we had used their cases appropriately.

Findings

We identified the following 12 challenges on the road toward electronic service provision:

1: "Start-up...of what?" (Initial motivations differ from final)
2: "Thousands of pages..." (Institutionalization of production)
3: Messy appearance (Graphical design, Web organization)
4: Parallel systems (How to phase out old routines?)
5: Choice of future technical platform (What *is* this thing we're building?)
6: Cross-departmental integration of data resources
7: Staff motivation
8: Poor usability
9: Where is the payoff? (How to measure costs and benefits?)
10: From monopoly to service provider (The organization faces a role change)
11: Where are the users? ("There is not much use yet—when will it come?")
12: "Administrative tribal struggles" (Threats to social groups and their domains)

In the following, I briefly describe the settings, who were the main actors, what were the main conflicts, what were the claims and the resulting inscriptions, if any.

Challenge 1: Start-up...of what?

Setting: Cities typically enter the Internet with unclear motivations. They are there largely because others are there. Of course goals are specified, but these goals are usually short term and, at best, only remotely related to better services or more efficient logistics in service production. Examples of early goals include providing jobs to unemployed (creating Web pages), establishing a Web presence, keeping up with neighbor cities, etc.

Systems are typically initially set up by some enthusiast(s) and funded by project money, which means they do not automatically outlive the project. Typically, projects promise lavishly, get a lot of press and interfere in the work of others, making not only friends. After some time, if a project is successful, there appears a need to integrate it in other IT and organizational projects going on. This typically does not happen easily.

As a consequence of the lack of goals, it is hard to focus and provide good contents. A typical Web project starts off with the Chief Information Officer (CIO), or the equivalent thereof in the organization, publishing things like the company brochure on the Web. (S)he does that alone with technical support from someone: a consultant, a project group rallied up from a local university media education programme or from a programme for unemployed, or from the computer department.

Once this is done, the debate on the purpose of the Web system starts (until this stage, only the CIO has given it a thought). Why should we be on the Web? The CIO comes up with a number of reasons, typically pointing in a number of directions, not always compatible and often requiring organizational change at business departments. At this point, it becomes clear to several people in the organization what the Web system will cost, if they go along with the CIO's suggestions. So they start to think, "why should we?"

In this phase, there is just a small group of actors:

- The Web itself, creating a climate in which people feel they must act to adopt the technology. This inspires external funding, from the European Union or national governments. This inspires local managers to support entrepreneurs.
- An entrepreneur, acting as a catalyst for this unleashed wish by managing to rustle up some resources from external sources and making a tasty proposal to local mangers based on local institutional conditions.

Legitimacy of the project is found in places at best vaguely related to the overall goal of "managing electronic services" or "electronic government." People who are needed to formulate such an overall goal are typically not involved, or are involved in a way that in effect conceals that goal. Thus, success or failure of the project is at this stage measured against the "wrong" goals.

There is an important inscription, however. This is "our Web is a totem." It is important for self-esteem, for making clear to all that "we're here, too." Other goals that are mentioned are most often just means to get some important actors on board.

Challenge 2: Thousands of pages ... institutionalization of Web production

Setting: When the initial Web project is over, a Web site is established, but there is typically no special budget allocated to further Web-related work. Initially, work is typically carried out as a marginal low-cost activity by students, people hired with unemployment support or other types of cheap labor. The task of maintaining all the pages quickly overwhelms the small team of active staff. As a result, the task of overseeing the accuracy of the information pertaining to that department is delegated to business departments.

An additional problem is that Web technology develops, and cities have to keep up. Further, demands for information and services increase, and there appears to be a need for automation and integration with existing computer systems.

Production may be organized in a centralized or a distributed fashion. The choice is not so easy. Quite obviously, there is always a need both for delegation of work and coordination, but the decision on which way to go can typically not be decided freely. There are traditions, and there may be changes of direction ensuing from political decisions that entail some actions and prohibit others.

At this stage, tradition typically conquers innovation. There is typically not yet a network of people in the organization with the goal of "professional electronic services operation," but there are several networks with departmental interests. These networks are invoked at this stage, and engage in discussions on how to share the burden of production of the new services (note the negative tone; it is not "engage in conquering the new medium"). Thus, the organization of production is negotiated on a "something for everyone" basis, not in terms of efficient logistics or improved services.

An illustration:

In 1995, the City Council of Stockholm decided to divide the city into 24 districts. The stated reason was increasing local democracy. Therefore, a local city council was established in each district. A few political decisions were delegated, but the main idea was to provide service locally. In each district, one or more "citizen offices" were set up. This office was to provide local information and services, but also locally adapted information and services originating from other sources.

The citizen offices were given some room to maneuver, but there was also a decision made that information should be provided in a uniform way at all offices.

From the point of view of providing services, the reform meant two things. First, a number of local entrepreneurs with ambitions (social, technical, political, business, etc.) appeared. Second, the need for a coordination committee mediating between the different local entrepreneurs became apparent. This, however, did not happen immediately.

In 1997, it became apparent that the districts were taking different directions regarding their Web use. Some districts developed a relatively high profile, developing also external services aiming directly to citizens. At the other end of a spectrum of views, some maintained that face-to-face service at the desk, possibly aided by an internal IT system, was the only way to go.

The activities of the local entrepreneurs, let loose by the borough reform, meant that the common "City of Stockholm Approach" was at risk. The reform had not intended to decentralize strategic decisions, but to maintain the city as a unit; all citizen offices were to be able to inform about every district. To work in practice, this called for a common profile. This meant a coordination committee mediating between the different local entrepreneurs, and disseminating best practices, was needed. Such a committee was set up in 1997. This did not, however, happen by itself as the result of everyday operations. The crystallizing factor was a EU project, which had among its goals to create a uniform navigation system from the citizens' point of view. This uniform system required information providers across the city to provide information in a common way, and to have a common understanding of citizens' requirements.

The coordination committee met problems of two distinct kinds. First, among the local champions, there were different opinions about "citizen needs." There was also some envy, because some districts were clearly ahead of others in terms of the sophistication of their Web systems. Second, there was an abundance of consultants involved. The Information Office had hired a consultant for designing the "City Web," which was to be the entrance to Stockholm and the "main menu" on top of the district ones. This consultant company was originally in the public relations business, but had moved into Web design (as many such companies did at that time). But when it came to coordination of the Web system, there were other consultants involved. There was one, to which the computer department had outsourced the maintenance of the city's servers. There was another, which had built a "comprehensive information concept" for one city district, and wanted to propagate it across the city. Both of the two latter also claimed to have service development concepts. Because issues of design, organization and adaptation of the existing computer system were involved, there was a need for cooperation among the consultants. This turned out to be difficult, since all of them had aspirations on all parts, but had very different competence and visions. The risk of having too many cooks mess up the soup was apparent. As the city's IT manager put it: "We need to find invoicable interfaces among the consultants" (Jundin, 1997).

In conclusion, in this phase we see a number of actors entering the scene;
- Local entrepreneurs promoting departmental interests.
- Central bureaucrats and politicians striving for control. This is often the CIO, but it may anyone who is in the position of assuming a coordinator role.
- Technical consultants promoting their products, which have different focuses and overlapping scope. These may be employed by any of the other two actors, and by more than one. Thus products implementing different views may occur in different parts of the organization, potentially making the organization process very complicated.

The inscription during this stage is, "Our Web is a brochure." It is there to inform people about our whereabouts. To maintain it we need proper organization so we don't do double work. This is a fairly strong inscription; there are no competing antiprograms (conflicting ideas) on that point, only about demarcation of territories.

Challenge 3: Messy appearance

Setting: As systems grow big and there are multiple information providers, responsibility for information provision and maintenance must be delegated. This results in each department wanting to do things its own way. Thus arises a coordination problem: top management wants the organization to appear in a coherent and stylish form on the Web, following a corporate profile. This interferes with work already done, as well with different ambitions at different departments.

In this phase, again, there typically arises a conflict between:

- Departmental interests in service quality, customer contacts, and perceived business mission.
- Top management's strive for uniformity and rational production overall.
- Technical consultants may interfere in the negotiation process in the same way as in the previous challenge, by supporting some department(s) or with central management with a product implementing certain.

Often, a "graphic profile committee" is set up to resolve the conflict. Sometimes—rarely—independent evaluation is involved. This often happens when some external project (for instance EU funding for some user-oriented service) so requires, only occasionally by own initiative.

At this stage, there are several claims. While the Web is still a brochure, views on how it should be employed diverge. Top management now tends to see it as "our face to the world," emphasizing uniformity, elegance etc. Business departments tend to see it as "our business tool," emphasizing functionality. This is conflict-prone. Functionality may include publishing a vast amount of data, specialized terms, etc., whereas elegance and uniformity will not benefit from this.

Challenge 4: Parallel systems

Setting: By now, the graphic profile committee has made the system look nice. Contents are produced efficiently, and at least some people use the services. But all manual operations are still in place and run like before. The Web system has not replaced anything. Thus arises the first cost crisis: "Why is there no process reengineering? The banks introduced automated teller machines, and this made less people go into the offices. The result was substantial cuts at the offices. Why does this not happen with our municipal electronic services?"

Reengineering does not just happen. Determined measures have to be taken, since the preserving forces in an organization are typically stronger than those striving for innovation. A problem appearing here is the scope of reengineering; Process? Department? Organization? At this stage, again, networks at a department level are invoked to preserve status quo, or to have any global changes their way. The actors during this stage are:

- Preservation networks try to preserve work roles, privileges. These networks may include managers, staff and consultants engaged in local/departmental development different from a centrally prescribed one. Or they may be staff at a department opposing reform plans by local management, possibly supported by some consultant.
- Reform forces. These may be central management or local management, either possibly supported by some technical and/or management consultant.

There are typically different inscriptions resulting from this stage, if any. Not many have yet seriously gone through this stage. The focus of the struggle is not clear. It mixes traditional preservation reflexes ("I like to keep my job") with centralization/decentralization power conflicts. In local government agencies, an important factor is a fear to create gulfs between haves and have-nots by downsizing manual procedures.

Challenge 5: Choice of future technical platform

Setting: Debates over choices regarding technical platforms and tools abound.

Actors: The IT department, different consultants, different business departments, EU projects.

Conflicts: (1) There are technology-related choices to make in order to reduce the risk of having to make drastic changes in the future – what database, what Web platform, etc. Still vivid in this debate is the controversy between proponents of the Web and of proprietary systems, like kiosk systems.

(2) External funding often comes with a more offensive agenda than that of the IT department. While the former is often directed toward use and service reinvention, the latter is typically defensively focusing on security, standardization and maintenance. For instance, until quite recently, many cities' IT strategies did not include Web technologies.

(3) System metaphors. Different business departments typically employ consultants from different trades: Web design/PR, databases, infrastructure, business solutions, etc. These all claim to be in the "IT" business, but they have very different working metaphors for what they build – a library, a database, a newspaper, a brochure, a traffic system, etc. When different departments which have walked the World Wide Web road some time with different consultants at some point have to merge their IT activities, clashes in world views occur. By then, the views typically have been implemented in software to a considerable extent, which makes shifts expensive and complicated.

It is typically not until this phase that IT infrastructure strategies are discussed with Web services as an ingredient.

Attempts to inscribe prescribed actions, or prohibitive means, into the technology are strong during this phase. The IT department typically sees "standards" and "security" as keywords. Business departments want powerful tools for their business, keywords being "expansion" or "consolidation." EU projects are often even more avant garde, a keyword often being "innovation." This conflict is typically not resolved, since the medium is under development—improvements can currently be seen in all these directions.

Challenge 6: Cross-departmental integration of data resources

Setting: Cities that have come this far are likely to have produced working services in several departments. As services grow, service producers often find that it would be useful to have access to some data possessed by other city departments. For instance, the tourist information could be better presented by using maps. Maps can be manufactured anew, but they often already exist in the form of GIS systems, owned by the city planning office or the like. Or the tourist information systems want to expand into also providing booking services. The city may have computerized booking services for sports facilities, for instance, but those are not owned by the tourist office.

There appears to be a need for cooperation, or at least ways of sharing or co-using each other's data. How can this be achieved? The answer in practice depends a lot on what legacy systems there are, but also on how far the different departments have come toward electronic service provision. Those who have come far are likely to want to pursue their way of doing (which is often by old technology). Those who have not come so far are typically more likely to try new ideas. Neither is willing to become subordinate to the other.

In many cases, problems of this kind are created by organizational innovations like departmental reforms and internal trade regulations that make cross-departmental use of resources expensive to the individual department.

As we have seen, until now, departmental networks have had a strong influence over the development, and by now, considerable investments have been made. At this stage, typically another committee has to be set up to negotiate use of "common but divided" resources. There has to be substantial knowledge and visions in the technological field in this committee; pure mediation may well lead to old technology prevailing and/or the committee becoming a forum for inter-departmental struggles.

The actors at this stage are:
- Inter-departmental networks, trying to organize co-use of resources.
- Old technology, which is often a big obstacle to the above by being expensive or impossible to modify.
- Institutional arrangements, which sometimes act to prevent co-use of resources, for instance internal trade regulations may make co-use expensive.
- Departmental networks, often trying to resist changes, certainly always strongly striving toward making such go their way.

Challenge 7: Staff motivation

Setting: When Web services entailing changes in old routines are suggested, the staff involved realizes that this will affect their role as service providers. Some see genuine decrease in their income. Even more people are afraid of becoming redundant. Others simply fear losing some of their authority by not being the only ones in possession of a certain type of information. Some see extra work coming down the road without a matching increase in benefits. This challenge is only met when a serious discussion of the professionals' role in the new, more technology-equipped organization is undertaken with those involved.

Actors and claims:
- Management, trying to implement process changes by means of IT. To them, the Web is an opportunity for a new business model.
- Staff, trying to preserve their role. To them, the Web is a threat.

Challenge 8: Poor usability

Setting: Although more and more cities set up their own Web site it is an open secret that many local government Web information systems are little used. A closer look at the log files of systems reveals that it is most often only the front page that is frequently visited. Pages deeper down the hierarchy often have few hits, if any. As the front page is usually a cover page and the more detailed information is typically found deeper down in the system, it is not a very daring conclusion to say that many government Web systems are not used in the way they are intended.

Web systems development typically starts with a "push" approach: "We have this information, let's get it out to people." Few worry about whether or not there is a demand for it. At some stage, service providers have to learn about their users. Who are the people that will use the services? What knowledge do they have, what do they *not* have? In what situations do they use your system? What do they look for? How do they look? These are examples of questions a service provider needs to answer in order to be able to design services properly. For each particular service, there may certainly be special conditions, but there are a few general facts that make a difference in every case. A problem in the public sector is that these issues have a hard time finding an arena where they get attention.

Actors:

- Users, who often have problems using the system. They want a tool for doing some business, and they want to inscribe in this tool some properties. These are typically not articulated, because...
- Web service producers in the public sector are usually ignorant of user problems—usability studies are very rare!—or unable to address them, because of lack of resources, expertise, focus on user problems or other.

Challenge 9: Where is the payoff?

Setting: Electronic services can be delivered over many different channels. Business on the Internet is a much hyped phenomenon that—still—often falls short of expectations for private and public service providers alike. Mostly "return on investment" will have to be expected in strategic terms rather than direct cash flow.

There may be several reasons for downright failure: that there are not enough users of a given service with access to the Internet; that the users do not find the service; that you cannot have a service that costs money on the Internet, because the whole concept teaches users to expect all Internet content to be free and so forth.

But even if services do get used, most Internet service providers find the economic assessment of their services a daunting task. The number of uncertain factors involved defies traditional financial analysis. It is helpful to look at the problem first from a variety of different angles.

Many different kinds of payoff may be expected: better served citizens, strategic advantages, better market/citizen communication, improved corporate profile, lower costs due to more self-service and other. Eventually, also cities reach a stage where these issues have to be brought forward.

Actors:

- The economy department wants some figures on the development: What has IT cost, and what has it paid back? What is the return on our investment?
- Business departments want to be modern and find new opportunities; innovation.

Depending on organizational arrangements, this conflict may occur within one department or between departments and central management.

Challenge 10: From monopoly to service provider

Setting: City organizations and staff are used to work in a monopoly environment. They are not used to thinking about what users look for, how they look and so on. The Internet culture, totally different in this respect, as well as deregulation in several fields, including telecommunications, leading to competition with other service providers, have begun to foster a change of attitude.

This challenge is only resolved when the city finds its role, its market niche. Different cities may assume different roles; not every city must necessarily provide every possible service. For instance, rural towns often play a more important role in supporting local small business than major cities in prosperous regions do. Only when the role of the city is found can the appropriate roles of the individuals in the organization be properly designed.

Actors are mainly:

- Preserving forces, such as staff or a department wanting to maintain a position.
- Internal change drivers, such as a department trying to increase its domains.
- Competing forces, such as private companies finding a niche where they can utilize public information to enhance their own business.
- The Web itself: Web shops/sites are becoming a standard way of doing business (banking, shopping, finding info, newsletters, etc.), thus forcing public organizations to adopt to new forms.

While the first three are mainly involved in territorial struggles, the fourth is inscribing a "Web mode" of doing things into technology.

Challenge 11: Where are the users?

Setting: Many ask themselves about their Web systems: "There is not much use yet—when will it come?"

In our study, we saw that the "media chain" in which the organizations under study worked was missing a crucial link. The development in Web business is toward concentration and exclusion; a few global companies are gaining ground, not the least due to the policy of many Internet providers to grant exclusive contracts. Small companies working on a local or regional basis are largely excluded. For promoting local and regional Web business, and for building the often envisioned "local agora," there needs to be an interesting mix of local content; the services have to be packaged in an interesting way by a service provider. The problem in the environments we studied—which are typical for Europe—is that cities are not concentrating on finding and packaging local content, one of the crucial catalysts for getting people on-line. So far, there is not the equivalent of a book publisher or television or film distributor for emerging on-line services, not with a local/regional focus and ambition. The small company or organization that wants to go on the Web will have to go alone, which is more often than not beyond its capacity.

Actors:

- (Other) Web portals, which provide focal points on the Web, places to start, places to go to find things, creating lots of traffic, thus justifying new investments. Portals try to establish agoras. This inscription effort is quite strong; portal technology does exist, as do established portals. These are often global, but encroach on the territory of a city by picking out pieces where profit can be found, such as entertainment and sales of products where local small-scale competition have problems keeping up, such as books.
- Cities, which have problems organizing portals, since they cannot create popular ones without engaging in public-private partnerships (PPPs), against which there is resistance for ideological, legal and practical reasons. Cities often end up in this situation because they want to preserve their uniqueness. This is, however, a rather weak inscription effort in a time of increased globalization and competition.
- Departments within cities, which often resist changes; they can often not engage in PPPs on their own, and they are often too small for providing momentum alone.

Challenge 12: Administrative tribal struggles

Setting: Man has only recently emerged from a tribal existence. Loyalty to your clan was the leading guarantee of human survival for thousands of years. This legacy sits deep within our subconscious, and is the source of much of the excitement, but also antagonism, at work.

One of the principal problems of the modern society is the difficulty of identifying a tribe to belong to. We feel many sympathies and loyalties, and thereby identify ourselves with many different "tribes" of like-minded people. However, it is not uncommon that our various tribes end up in conflict among themselves. In such a situation, our loyalties are torn, and we are forced to take sides, often against our will. Any significant perturbation in the working environment is likely to provoke a tribal crisis—and there are few other potentially as controversial perturbations as the process of replacing manual service patterns by telematic ones.

The stated goals and business practices of many professional organizations are widely disparate. Municipalities may openly wish to serve their members efficiently and well, always seeking ways of improving their service, and cutting unnecessary costs. As a professional community, however, city officials wish not to rationalize away city jobs. Cities—especially those where the economy is not so viable—are reluctant to shed off jobs, because that would decrease state subsidy to the city, as well as its relative economic importance in a region. Shedding jobs would also aggravate a city's financial position, by pushing former employees into the ranks of the unemployed.

In such a situation, members of the corresponding "professional clans" are torn between loyalty to their explicit professional mission and that to their professional community.

Introducing electronic services amounts to changing established service patterns. The professional staff influenced by such a perturbation will be divided by their tribal loyalty. If the tribal chief or council concludes that such services will do more harm than benefit to the tribal community, the service will prove cumbersome and awkward to use, and definitely too immature to be seriously considered for operational adoption.

The main actors here are of course the communities of practice which often go to work unnoticed, creating their own agendas, not necessarily corresponding to that of a department or a city.

Summary: Actors, claims and inscriptions

Our findings can be summarized by actors, claims and inscriptions as follows:

While there are claims at every stage, it is only in the first few challenges that a clear inscription can be distinguished. I believe this is partly evidence of the unsettled state of affairs in the public sector. In business settings, there would often

Challenge 1: "Start-up...of what?"

Actors	Acts how?	Claims	Inscription
The Web	Creates a climate: we must adopt this technology. Inspires funding from EU, national governments. Inspires local managers to support entrepreneurs		A Web page is a totem for corporate identity
Entrepreneur	Catalyst for the above factors: gets things rolling	A Web page is a totem for corporate identity	

Challenge 2: "Thousands of pages..."

Actors	Acts how?	Claims	Inscription
CIO (similar)	Organizes production of Web pages, distributes tasks	Our Web system is a brochure	Our Web system is a brochure
Local entrepreneurs	Try to promote departmental ideals/business models	Our Web system is a brochure	
Technical consultants	Promote special (different) products to different departments	A Web system is a brochure	

Challenge 3: Messy appearance

Actors	Acts how?	Claims	Inscription
CIO (similar)	Organizes Web design, sets corporate graphical standards	Our Web is our face to the world	Depends on local context
Local entrepreneurs	Try to promote departmental ideals/business models	Our Web is our business	
Technical consultants	Promote special (different) products to different departments	(Products can support either of the above)	

Challenge 4: Parallel systems

Actors	Acts how?	Claims	Inscription
Preservation networks	Try to preserve work roles, privileges, etc.	The system is a threat	Not clear. Struggles may
Reform forces	Try to reengineer procedures	The system is an opportunity	be on a center vs. department basis, staff vs. management or internal at a department

Challenge 5: Choice of future technical platform

Actors	Acts how?	Claims	Inscription
IT department	Defensive: tries to preserve uniformity, compatibility and security	Standards	Depends on local context
Consultants	Come from different areas: PR/Web design, databases, business solutions, infrastructure, etc. ...with different, often incompatible, working metaphors	Various, depending on products	
Business departments	Try to expand their role, often in direct conflict with IT dept.; they may develop own technical solutions	Expansion, consolidation	
EU projects	Come with more offensive agendas than IT dept. Often employed by business departments to enhance usability, promote certain business ideas or other	Innovation	

Challenge 6: Cross-departmental integration of data resources

Actors	Acts how?	Claims	Inscription
Inter-departmental networks	Try to organize co-use of resources	Reengineering	Depends on local context and technical development
Old technology	Often big obstacle to the above by being expensive or impossible to modify		
Institutional arrangements	Sometimes act to prevent co-use of resources, for instance internal trade regulations may make co-use expensive	Economic optimization based on exist-ing organization	
Departmental networks	Often trying to resist changes, certainly always strongly striving towards making such go their way		

Challenge 7: Staff motivation

Actors	Acts how?	Claims	Inscription
Management	Try to implement process changes by means of IT	The Web is an opportunity for a new business model	Depends on local context
Staff	Try to preserve their role	The Web is a threat	

Challenge 8: Poor usability

Actors	Acts how?	Claims	Inscription
Users	Have problems using system	The Web is a tool for solving problems	Depends on local context & further tech-nical develop-ment
Web service producers (management and staff)	Usually ignorant of user pro-blems or unable to address them	The Web is an outlet for our information	

Challenge 9: Where is the payoff?

Actors	Acts how?	Claims	Inscription
Economy dept.	Wants some figures on the dev-elopment: What has IT cost, and what has it paid back	Return on in-vestment must be calculated	Depends on local context
Business depts.	Want to be modern and find new opportunities	Innovation	

Challenge 10: From monopoly to service provider

Actors	Acts how?	Claims	Inscription
Staff	Try to preserve their role	Technology is *our* tool	Depends on local context
Local depts.	Some try to preserve their role; some try to increase their role	Technology is *our* tool	
Competing organizations	Public sector information appears on commercial sites	This is our business, too	
The Web	Web shops/sites are becoming a standard way of doing business (banking, shopping, finding info, newsletters, etc.), thus forcing public organizations to adopt to new forms	The Web mode of operations: interactivity, on-demand service, etc.	

Challenge 11: Where are the users? ("There is not much use yet – when will it come?")

Actors	Acts how?	Claims	Inscription
Portals	Provide focal points on the Web, places to start, places to go to find things, creating lots of traffic, thus justifying new investments	Building virtual agoras	Depends on local context and further technical development. The support for virtual agoras is strong—technology exists—while city uniqueness is typically a weaker claim
Cities	Have problems organizing portals, since they cannot create popular ones without engaging in public-private partnerships, against which there is resistance for ideological, legal and practical reasons	Preserving their uniqueness	
Departments	Often resist changes; can't engage in PPPs on their own, too small for providing momentum alone		

Challenge 12: "Administrative tribal struggles"

Challenge	Actors	Acts how?	Claims	Inscription
12	Communities of practice	Create their own agendas, not necessarily corresponding to that of a department or a city	This is our technology	Depends on local context

be less uncertainty about some of the challenges, for instance usability, and generally fewer parties with claims, at least so long as we look at the development within one single company.

To some extent, the uninscribed development stages are evidence of a new technology at a formative stage. Web technology is generally past the stages of being a totem and brochure, but issues of how to use the technology in an organizational and a business perspective is still generally unclear.

SOLUTIONS AND RECOMMENDATIONS

In this section, I will first summarize our findings by describing the "trajectory" of the projects we have studied and the types of challenges we have seen. I will then go on to discuss our proposed solution, the creation of an "electronic service management champion unit" and establishment of creative partnerships, typically public-private, to tackle the complexity of the challenges involved.

Trajectory of electronic services

Having described the 12 challenges, we shall now look at what happened to the projects over the whole period. Figure 2 illustrates the trajectory of electronic services projects as described above, which has the following main features:

- Top management has not been involved actively and in a clear manner.
- No persistent focus, but several partial and incompatible ones.
- External funding, leading to diverse goals.

On the other hand, there were some factors that served to promote Web development:

- An increasing number of services have been developed.
- Committed staff, who have often participated actively in developing services.
- Demand pull for services.

This means the development has led to good technical and psychological preconditions for developing services, but a lack of leadership. We shall now turn to this issue, which I think is the most important for being able to justify further investment.

Four types of challenges

As we have seen above, a number of challenges occur on the road toward offering electronic services. I do not claim that in every organization each of

Figure 2: The trajectory of electronic service projects; dominant actors during different challenges. Note that some challenges are missing. This is because no dominant actor was found. For instance, in Challenge 8, most often no actor in organizations have dealt with the problems seriously. In challenge 12, the major actor is a non-formal one challenging the formal actors from an under-cover position.

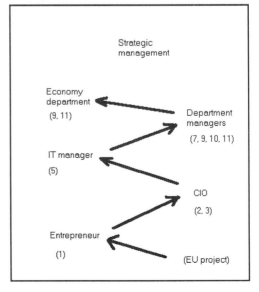

them escalates to the level of what people perceive as a crisis. Neither do I claim that the challenges necessarily appear in this order (although in the cases we have studied they in fact seem to do). As an example, late starters may be better off than those who started in the early Web days of around 1994, because there are now better tools available for construction and administration of Web sites, and some of the challenges may therefore be more easily avoided, for instance, the "thousand pages" one. On the other hand, late starters will not be able to benefit from the bonanza of the early Internet years, and will more quickly have to show results, that is, tackle the latter challenges, like the "Where are the users?" and the "Where is the payoff?" ones.

Still, the challenges require the organization attempting electronic service delivery to make judicious choices for each of them, based on adapting emerging technology and experiences from use elsewhere to the local situation.

Summarizing the nature of the challenges, we can see that they fall into four categories:

- *Users*; Number 3 (understanding what design suits users best), number 8 (usability), number 10 (understanding needs of service users), number 11 (where are the users?).
- *Organization*; Number 1 (strategy), number 2 (organization of procedures), number 3, partly (organizing a common design), number 4 (cutting down on old services as electronic ones expand), number 6 (organize for smooth sharing of resources among departments), number 7 (staff motivation), number 12 (tribes).
- *Economy*; Number 9 (developing models for assessment of electronic services).
- *Technology*; Number 5 (future technical platform).

Looking at the classification of challenges into the four main topics—users, organization, economy and technology—we can see that of the challenges identified, 10 out of 12 belong to the area of users and usability of electronic services and the ensuing organizational problems that arise when trying to serve users. It is therefore fair to say that the issues of use and usability are the most prominent and the organizational come second, because they to a large extent follow from the former. Third place is occupied by economic challenges. Technological problems rank as the least prominent source of problems (the two latter cause one challenge each, but the one about economic assessment is harder to resolve).

Given this situation, it is curious that so often the IT department is put in charge of electronic services projects. The organization that embarks on the road toward offering comprehensive electronic services will have to prepare for overcoming all of the 12 challenges. This means there are four fields that have to be addressed simultaneously, and in a way that makes developments in all areas go well together. This is a problem in any city. Typically, neither expertise in, nor responsibility for, all these areas can be found in one single city department; all topics must be dealt with in an organization-wide manner, starting at the top managerial level.

However, as we have seen above, top management has typically not yet taken serious part in the developments. So far, departmentalization is the word, except, possibly, for technical standards.

In order to succeed in developing public electronic services, there is a need for not only bundling services from different service providers and publishing them in a coherent fashion, but also providing value-added services and support to service providers during the process of inventing, refining and evaluating services, and improving operations. We use the concept Electronic Services Management (ESM) to mean being aware of the dozen challenges, and making strategies and solving problems that come up in ways that not just aim at overcoming one challenge at the time, but has the focus on overcoming them all without too many steps back having to be taken during the process.

Before elaborating on the ESM concept, let us look at the recent development on the Internet, where we will find more that supports our arguments.

Service infrastructure—Digital communities and local communities

Recent developments on the Internet have emphasized the role of *portals*. Portals are gateways to Web-based services that people use. Most of us start our Web roaming by logging on to some home page first that is common to many people, before moving on to searching for something else. Both our first home page, and the search engine home page, act as portals. Advertisers are using this opportunity to try and sell us some new products or services. Browsers today come with a pre-programmed start page, the manufacturer's own portal. Business portals today offer important infrastructure components such as payments and logistics to facilitate setting up shops.

People use many portals, depending on their interests. Local interest is very central to people's daily lives, and any Web site that links to many local services can be a very powerful portal, but local portals are still rare. This is a problem for many, not the least all the small and medium enterprises who do business primarily on a local/regional basis.

A portal can also be much more than just a mall. It may be a virtual meeting point of a *community* of people. A meeting point must facilitate collective discussion, as well as exchange of private messages. It must contain archives and interactive services for its members, regardless of whether the latter are formally identified or not.

In the case of local communities, local interest provides for a good defining structure of a community. However, since the content providers for such a local portal are organizations that target the same group of individual users with very different kinds of approaches and attitudes, a local electronic service provider must fulfill a range of roles outside the Web site. Examples of such roles are:

- Achieving good public-private partnerships in setting up and providing content to a local portal.

- Setting an example to local businesses on how to put services on the Internet, thereby helping them modernize their business models.
- Attracting individual users and potential content providers to the portal by offering them concrete financial incentives when doing so.

A city, as a dominant actor in its geographical area, is often in a good position to adopt a leading role in creating a local digital community around a local portal.

Services where a broad range of local activities is needed are, for example, cross-organizational telematic care and education processes. In both cases, many different local and sometimes non-local actors need to agree on a common information exchange and transmission process. A good agreement will result in both savings in cost and improvement in service quality to users. A city may be the unique local organization in a position to create a platform for such negotiations.

Another advantage that public portals may have is an emphasis on universal access, covering all social classes of people. A good portal should be very easy and intuitive to use. It may include free e-mail and messaging services, picture archival and other services, so implemented that users do not need to own a computer to use them.

It may well be that for various reasons, such as availability of interest, investment resources or technical skills and equipment, a city may end up yielding the role of a local electronic service manager to another organization. Suitable candidates may be local newspapers with a Web edition, Internet service providers, sometimes even national or international portals. The city should, however, see to it that a local electronic service provider does emerge from somewhere in the reasonably near future, in order to get also its own electronic services used by the citizens.

There are many challenges to setting up local portals involving local authorities, including the following:

- *Volume*: attracting enough visitors to motivate investment. For a local authority, this will typically require arranging partnerships.
- *Integrating media* to produce efficient service processes (Web, telephone, physical meetings, etc.) and create the necessary service infrastructure institutions (reception, logistic functions, payment systems, wailing wall, etc.).
- *Maintaining competence* in several areas: Web design, process reengineering, marketing, technology, etc.
- *Attaining a mandate* to influence reorganization of procedures (management attention and commitment).
- *Endurance* over the relatively long period of time which is necessary to become proficient and attractive.
- *Accountability* (somehow accounting for values and costs in the operations).

Our findings suggest that instead of going alone, a city should seek creative partnerships. The short To Do-list is:

- Set up an ESM champion unit.
- Envision your appropriate role in a "portal" environment.

- Enroll partners to complement your role, activities and competence.
- Script attractive roles for them all.

Managing electronic services

The "ESM champion unit" should be an entity that provides a general framework for publishing electronic services, which are produced by others: service providers. There is a relatively well-defined role for such a unit, but organizational implementations may vary; it may be a company, an organizational unit or a responsibility within some existing organizational unit.

A champion unit is necessary in a local government perspective because individual service providers are often not big enough to carry on the whole way through all the challenges. As we have seen above, there are a lot of issues that will have to be dealt with. Many of those issues need an organization of some scale to be dealt with professionally and efficiently. There are a number of things the unit must have competence in so as to increase the quality, reach and profitability of services under its roof, including the following:

- It must have, and constantly update, a clear view of customers and users.
- It must serve as a value-adding link between service providers and their customers, by for instance providing general value-added services (such that can be used across services, search tools, user studies, market surveys, format conversion for different media, etc.).
- It must understand how to make work processes more efficient and assist its service providers in doing so.
- It must have technical, organizational and marketing expertise.
- It must contribute to achieving advantages of scale by bundling several services together using a common concept for service delivery.
- In contrast to the global electronic service publishers, it should be a local and/ or regional concept, publishing services in a way that promotes local/regional competitiveness as well as small and medium enterprises and cooperation and creative partnerships, public-private ones or other.
- It must be able to cope with the rapid technological changes on the Internet.
- It must engage in more than only actions in the electronic medium, for instance promotion in other media.
- It must in marketing as well as in services take into account the different ways of doing what stems from the multicultural societies of Europe.
- It must concentrate on effective publishing and strive for reshaping of any underlying processes when necessary.
- It can promote services in a more powerful way than information providers can do themselves, because of economies of scale.
- Because of scale, it can invest in software tools, statistics-analyses, design-issues, user studies and other things necessary for the business.
- It must have direct contact with the end-users in order to get a clear overview of what is still missing in offering a bouquet of services and help-devices.

- It should be a speaking partner to providers of hardware, software and infrastructure.
- It must not have overhead information providers have so as to be able to offer services at competitive prices.

Electronic services management, then, is not just a concept for a city to produce Web systems. It is a more general business concept aiming at helping the many small (mostly) service providers in cities and small businesses into the Information Age. In the next section we shall dwell for a while on this aspect of it.

A SPECULATIVE LOOK AHEAD—CITIES AND THE LOCAL INFORMATION SOCIETY

Electronic service management in the public sector is not just a matter for the individual city or region involved. There is a wider political issue pertaining to the sector as a whole; how the many small companies that work mainly locally or regionally can find ways into use of the electronic medium.

Cities are a focal point in people's lives as well as a key public sector organization. Cities are responsible for a large share of the most important services needed by the citizens, such as education, health care and social services. Although the role of cities differ in different countries, their importance is considerable everywhere.

Information and telecommunication technologies are changing the conditions for many services and business activities. Such changes produce both threats and opportunities to national and regional economies, as well as public services. Some important examples of such changes are the following:

- With the advent of the Internet, cities have a new way of accessing a rapidly growing percentage of their citizens. Cities can both improve their services to citizens, and make them economically more efficient, by using Internet technologies, but adopting an electronic service model is by no means simple. Stable working patterns in the use of the electronic medium are difficult to find for any city department, and yet many departments are solving the same technical and organizational problems each at the same time. Not only is this wasteful, but it also results in divergent Web practices in different city departments. It is very difficult for citizens to navigate through the Web of different Web sites of even a single city. Moreover, the best electronic services are often cross-departmental in city administration.
- Sales of nonperishable goods on the Internet are quickly becoming a transnational business. Many on-line service providers get their revenue from granting exclusive sales rights of goods and services to a single company. Examples of such agreements are those granted by America Online to a single bookstore or to a single music shop worldwide. There are, in fact, arguments to say that the Internet is one of the most centralizing technologies ever. The

current "portal struggle" is one example. Over past years we have seen Web search engines becoming ever more overloaded with commercial advertisements. Currently, many have stepped up the struggle by providing portals, which go far beyond company information and an effective search engine. Companies engaging in the business are not only the browser manufacturers Netscape and Microsoft and the companies specializing in searching on the Net, Excite and Yahoo, but also the magazine group Ziff-Davies, dedicated companies such as Intuit and CMPnet, and security company Network Associates. The portals are intended as starting points for visiting the Net. Competition leads portal managers to provide bonuses to users, such as the option to create personal home pages and free e-mail addresses. Portals have different focuses: branch focus (like Intuit's SME portal, or Telia's Swedish School Net), special interest (like ZDNet's focus on computers and Internet) or local focuses. Competition is tough, often leading to active promotion activities; one example is Netscape's lottery where users can win TVs or DVD players—if they go there regularly and check.

If most on-line communities that people spend time in are global, local businesses will be effectively excluded from doing business on the Internet. Advertising revenue on the Internet is already more concentrated on only a few sites than in any other medium. Such virtual communities have no local identity, and cities have no role in them.

- In many Western countries, the population is getting older. An increasing number of old people means an increasing need for social and health care. Yet the basis of tax revenue, from which public health and social services are funded, keeps diminishing. Local governments must find more efficient ways of looking after the elderly than keeping them in hospitals. Electronic technology will help in this, allowing for information, emergency procedures and communication to proceed efficiently even from home.

Developments, such as the ones described above, deserve the serious attention of cities in countries where the electronic medium is by now quickly becoming a standard service delivery channel.

CONCLUSION

In our study we found 12 distinct challenges, situations when the setting changes and the process is found in a stage of improvisation until new (temporary) stability is achieved. We saw that:

- The Web appeared as a "cuckoo in the nest," intruding in ever more activities and introducing new demands on them as new actors came up with new claims.
- This generally came as a surprise, both from a top management perspective and for people involved in projects.
- There was typically a missing link in the organizations' infrastructure, which made them less capable to deal with electronic services in a comprehensive

manner. Generally, Web projects were seen as technical projects; though in fact issues pertaining to users and organization were most important, they were largely neglected. The missing link was a body competent of managing the whole process of bundling services from different service providers and publishing them in a coherent fashion, providing support to service providers during the process of inventing, refining and evaluating services, improving logistics, and conducting the necessary but typically ignored activities of analysis of the quality of services and policy making.

One might ask, how could the process at all go on despite these challenges and the unstructured nature of the process? All along, there were a couple of stabilizing factors. Arguably most important were the general technical development and the market demands: The Web has continued to grow and improve technically, and people today demand Web services also from government. In all the studied countries, there were also national government policies of the type cited in the introduction accompanying, and supporting, this development.

Second, in every city there were several EU-funded projects where electronic services and the Web were understood as the way to go. These projects influenced cities by their goals and activities, but also, and more permanently, because they over time fostered a cadre of "Web agents" in the cities, people with international contacts and visions of technology use for service improvements.

Other important driving forces were of course the actors that came into action at different stages. While not always contributing in an apparent way to the distant goal of the organization as a whole becoming a proficient and efficient manager of electronic services, they certainly provided momentum at certain points in time.

Another note is that issues pertaining to users and organization are most important, far more so than technical issues. Of the challenges identified, 10 out of 12 (all except nos. 5 and 9) belong to the area of users and usability of services and the ensuing organizational problems that arise when trying to serve users. Against this observation, it is curious to notice that most often electronic services are developed under the leadership of the city IT department, whose main expertise is technology.

Why were projects pursued as technical projects and not as service projects? Why were no ESM champion entities set up? In this chapter we have discussed the development in terms of the actors involved at different stages of the development, how these actors influenced the ways technology was viewed. We have seen that these views changed a lot over the years, and that the changes were not planned. They evolved as new actors entered the scene. There was never an overall tactical plan that outlined "the road toward proficient electronic service management," just plans for "implementing a Web system," "making our system usable," "making users satisfied," etc. The cities acted reactively, often with considerable success, but typically not proactively.

Returning to the issue I raised in the beginning, whether infrastructure was "implemented" or "drifted" due to events down the road, we saw that there certainly was a lot of "drifting" if we see the different "challenges" in relation to the overall goal of becoming proficient in electronic service management. But that goal appeared only late in the process, if at all. If we look at each stage of development, the drifting was not appalling. Certainly there were conflicts; and certainly departmental interests, or even those of individual actors, made a great difference. But in most places solutions to the problems encountered at a particular challenge were found that were digestible for all parties. The development went in a relatively controlled way, but in many different directions.

Our conclusion is that there is a great lack of strategy in the field of electronic services in local governments in Europe. This is a big problem considering the importance of that sector and the challenges it is facing; increased competition, not the least from globally operating companies, private initiatives, increased costs due to more demands, an aging population and the necessity to incorporate Web technology in the operations.

Our proposed solution for local government starts with:

- Setting up an "ESM champion unit" for the purposes of focus on electronic services, competence, top management attention, commitment and accountability.
- Arranging strategic partnerships for the purposes of endurance, competence, attractiveness and volume of traffic.

The electronic services trade in Europe's public sector is a cottage industry. It needs to be modernized. The solution is not more home pages but an institutionalized service perspective.

Acknowledgements

Thanks are due to the Infosond project review group which had long, interesting and pleasant discussions over a year's time about the issues discussed here, the challenges, cases from different cities, etc.: Tuomo Kauranne (Oy CR-Net Ltd), Frank Hartkamp (then City of Rotterdam, currently Novem BV), Olov Forsgren (Mid Sweden University), Huberta Kritzenberger (City of Nuremberg) and Robert DeBeukelaer (Telepolis Antwerp).

References

Akrich, M., and Latour, B. (1997). A summary of a convenient vocabulary for the semiotics of human and nonhuman assemblies. In Bijker, W. E., and Law, J. (1994). *Shaping Technology/Building Society. Studies in Sociotechnical Change.* Cambridge, MA: MIT Press.

Bijker, W. E., and Law, J. (1994). *Shaping Technology/Building Society. Studies in Sociotechnical Change.* Cambridge, MA: MIT Press.

Broadbent, M., and Waill, P. (1997). Management by maxim: How business and IT managers can create IT infrastructure. *Sloan Management Review.*

Callon, M., and Latour, B. (1981). *Unscrewing the big Leviathan: How actors macro-structure reality and how sociologists help them to do so.* In Knorr-Cetina,

K., and Cicourel, A. V. (Eds.), Advances in social theory and methodology. London: Routledge and Kegan Paul.

Ciborra, C. (1997). De profundis? Deconstructing the concept of strategic alignment. *Scandinavian Journal of Information Systems*, 9(1), 67-81.

Garson, G. D. (1999). *Information Technology and Computer Applications in Public Administration: Issues and Trends*. Hershey, PA: Idea Group Publishing.

Greeves, R. (1998). *The Penultimate Mile: Local and State Governments Collaborating to Serve Citizens Through Information Technology*. http://www.excelgov.org/techcon/sldoc/index.htm.

Grönlund, Å. (1997). *Report on Usability and Estimated Usefulness*. Infosond Deliverable D8. Antwerp: Informatikcentrum. http://www.infosond.org.

Grönlund, Å. (1998). *Make IT Happen—A Tale of a Dozen Crises. A Cookbook for the Organization Endeavouring the Journey from the First Home Page to Professional Telematic Service Publishing*. Infosond project, Report D10. Antwerp: InformatikCentrum.

Grönlund, Å., and Forsgren, O. (1999). *Portalbyggarens Klokbok*. B1999:2. Stockholm: NUTEK.

Grönlund, Å. (2000). *Managing Electronic Services—A Public Sector Perspective*. London: Springer Verlag.

Hansson, L., and Johansson, M. (1997). *Den Kommunala IT Strategin i Västerbotten (Municipal IT Strategies in Västerbotten)*. Umeå University, Department of Informatics, Report SPC 97.55

Holmström, J. (2000). *Information System and Organization as Multipurpose Network*. Umeå University, Department of Informatics. Doctoral dissertation.

Håkansson, S. (1996). *Svenska kommuners IT Strategier (IT Strategies in Swedish Cities)*. Stockholm: Näringsdepartementet, Struktursekretariatet.

IDPM. (1998). *Government and Public Sector Pages*. Institute for Development Policy and Management, University of Manchester. http://www.man.ac.uk/idpm/devtlinx.htm#itgov.

Jundin, P. (1997). Personal communication, October 10, 1997.

Latour, B. (1987). *Science in Action: How to Follow Scientists and Engineers Through Society*. Cambridge, MA: Harvard University Press.

Latour, B. (1996). *Aramis or the Love of Technology*. Cambridge, MA: Harvard University Press.

Latour, B. (1999). *Pandora's Hope. Essays on the Reality of Science Studies*. Cambridge, MA: Harvard University Press.

Levitt, M., and March, J. G. (1988). *Organizational Learning*. Annual Review of Sociology.

McMaster, T., Vidgen, R. T., and Wastell, D. G. (1998). Networks of association and due process in IS development.. In T. J. Larsen, L. Levine and J. I. DeGross, *Information Systems: Current Issues and Future Changes*. Proceedings of ICIS 1998, Helsinki, Finland. IFIP, Laxenburg, Austria.

Monteiro, E., and Hepsö, V. (1998). *Diffusion of Infrastructure: Mobilization and Improvisation*. In T. Larsen, L. Levine, J. I. DeGross (Eds.), Information

Systems: Current Issues and Future Changes, 255-274. IFIP, Laxenburg, Austria.

Norris, D. F. (1999). *Leading Edge Information Technologies and Their Adaption: Lessons from U.S. Cities.* In Garson, G. D. (1999). Information Technology and Computer Applications in Public Administration: Issues and Trends. Hershey, PA: Idea Group Publishing.

Rogers, E. M. (1962). *Diffusion of Innovations.* New York: Free Press.

Scavo, C., and Shi, Y. (1999). *World Wide Web Site Design and Use in Public Management.* In Garson, G. D. (1999). Information Technology and Computer Applications in Public Administration: Issues and Trends. Hershey, PA: Idea Group Publishing.

Schijvenaars, T. (1998). *Report on Economic Evaluation and System Use.* Infosond Deliverable D8. Antwerp: Informatikcentrum. http://www.infosond.org.

Seneviratne, S. J. (1999). *Information Technology and Organizational Change in the Public Sector.* In Garson, G. D. (1999). Information Technology and Computer Applications in Public Administration: Issues and Trends. Hershey, PA: Idea Group Publishing.

SUNET. (2000). The Swedish University NETwork, list of Swedish Municipal Web Sites, http://www.sunet.se/sweden/government_municipalities-sv.html

Symonds, M. (2000). The next revolution *The Economist*, June 24.

Toppledarforum. (1998). *Regeringens Proposition 1995/96:125 Åtgärder för Att Bredda och Utveckla Användningen av Informationsteknik. (Government proposition 1995/96:125. Measures for broadening and developing use of information technology.)* http://toppled.nutek.se/itprop.html.

Tsagarousianou, R., Tambini, D., and Bryan, C. (1998). *Cyberdemocracy: Technology, Cities and Civic Networks.* London: Routledge.

Virginia Tech. (1998). *Blacksburg Electronic Village Research.* Virginia Polytechnic Institute and State University, http://www.bev.net/research. Visited 1999-09-28.

Endnotes

1 INFOrmation and Services ON Demand, Fourth Framework Telematics Applications Programme, Project UR 1017.

CHAPTER SEVEN

Macroeconomic Implications of Virtual Shopping: A Theoretical Approach

I. Hakan Yetkiner and Csilla Horváth
University of Groningen, The Netherlands

Recently, parallel to developments in the communication technology, on-line shopping has become increasingly popular for many products, like books, CDs, software and computers. Most analysts conjecture that the future will witness a wider basket of products and a higher trade volume via the Internet. This chapter investigates the economic implications of Internet shopping in a Ricardian equilibrium framework. First, it shows the necessary and sufficient condition for the shift to Internet shopping. Next, it indicates that macroeconomic variables like consumption and income rise when this shift takes place. Thus, this shows that the economic implications of Internet shopping will be higher than the current experience, and Internet shopping will become an important element of the 'new economy' when the bulky part of the shopping is done via the Internet.

INTRODUCTION

Trade via the Internet has far-reaching economic implications as it provides a fundamentally new way of conducting transactions. This arises from the fact that it shrinks the physical and economic distance between traders. Physical distance disappears because buyers can 'go' anywhere for shopping at almost zero cost in terms of time. Economic distance shrinks because buyers are able to reach sellers directly without the need for intermediaries. In this chapter we focus on the business-to-consumer aspect of trade via the Internet. We call commerce between consumers and producers (businesses) through the Internet *virtual shopping*. In computer terminology, virtual is used to denote memory created by software but physically not present in the hardware. Analogously, the Internet technology lets consumers go shopping without being present in the shop physically.[1]

The main characteristic of the new technology is that it uses digital information. Therefore the first wave of expansion of Internet-based commerce is observed in trading "zeros and ones," such as e-mail, text, graphics, etc. For example, subscribing to the Country Profiles Database of the Economist Intelligence Unit and receiving data *on-line* falls into this category.[2] However, it is technically not possible to deliver many products in zeros and ones, such as computers or detergents. Therefore, it is not surprising to predict that business-to-consumer Internet transactions *will* shift to nondigitizable goods and services in the future. This shift will support further growth of virtual shopping and necessarily result in a new delivery technology.

In this study, we take Internet shopping to mean a new way of shopping for consumers in all aspects, that is, including the delivery of goods and services purchased via the Internet. On-line shopping currently uses the conventional delivery system, by and large. We conjecture that as virtual shopping expands, the current postal delivery system will become incapable of handling the delivery of goods and services and a new delivery system, that fulfills the requirements of on-line shopping, will emerge.[3] A good example to the emerging new delivery system is the 'adjustment' of United Parcel Service (UPS) of America Inc., "an icon of the old economy with fleets of trucks driven mainly by men in brown uniforms," to a gleaming symbol of the digital age. UPS has become one of the major distribution companies in the Internet economy in the United States, and this adjustment makes it such a prominent player in the Internet that people are using its performance as a proxy for the Internet and Internet commerce. Analysts also expect that delivery technology will adapt itself to the requirements of the new economy in the near future.[4]

The volume of Internet shopping is still negligible in total trade. Nevertheless, all business analysts predict a growth in on-line retail sales. There are many indicators of the expansion of Internet trade. First, the size of the Web grows exponentially. While experts disagree on which metric is the best for sizing the Web, everyone agrees that it is growing phenomenally. Web sites show up at a rate of more than 4,400 per day resulting in 3.6 million sites in 1999. The number of Web pages, perhaps the best gauge of the expansion of Internet, has also skyrocketed in 1999. NEC Research reports around 1.5 billion Web pages, an 88% increase from 1998. IDC expects this number to hit 8 billion in 2002, exceeding the world's population.[5] Second, parallel to the growth of Internet usage, the volume of on-line trade expands exponentially. Forrester, a Research Company, predicts that electronic commerce will reach $200 billion in 2000 across the globe. International Data Corporation (IDC) forecasts the dollar volume of business-to-consumer sales to reach 50.7 billion for 2000. Forrester Press Release (2000) projects an exponential rise in on-line retail sales for Europe. The company forecasts that on-line retail sales in Europe will grow 98% annually over the next five years, soaring from 2.9 billion Euro in 1999 to 175 billion Euro in 2005. Projected U.S. on-line retail sales also show phenomenal growth. The main indicators of the expansion of U.S. Internet retail shopping are presented in Table 1.

Table 1: US on-line retail sales and on-line consumer projections

	1998	1999	2000	2001	2002	2003
Total U.S. Online Retail Sales ($Billions)	7.8	18.1	33.0	52.2	76.3	108.0
_Total Convenience($Billions)[a]	2.8	5.6	9.7	15.2	22.7	32.3
_Total Researched ($Billions)[b]	4.4	11.0	20.0	31.0	43.0	56.2
_Total Replenishment ($Billions)[c]	0.7	1.6	3.3	6.0	10.7	19.4
U.S. Households Shopping Online (Millions)	8.7	13.1	17.7	23.1	30.3	40.3
U.S. Households Online (Millions)	28.6	33.5	38.3	43.5	48.6	52.8

Note: From the Forrester Report (1998). The sum of subtitles may not add up to aggregate due to rounding errors.
[a]Convenience goods are software, books, music, tickets, etc. [b]Researched goods are leisure travel, electronics and housewares. [c]Replenishment goods are food and beverage, health and beauty products.

Table 1 and the Forrester Report (1998) indicate that more people shop, more retailers sell and more categories become available in the coming years in the U.S. on-line retail sales market.

Internet shopping is facing some more obstacles, apart from lacking a new delivery system, that limit its expansion in all aspects. Briefly summarizing, two main areas can be listed. First, user (consumer) trust in electronic transactions has to be built.[6] Second, regulatory uncertainty in the new electronic environment has to be minimized. These impediments support the 'traditional' consumer behavior, the pro-real shopping behavior. We assume that these obstacles will be eliminated through time due to improvements in technology, legal structure, education level, etc., and this will ease building a voluminous trade through the Internet. Consumer sales today are dominated by services and intangibles like travelling and ticketing services, software, entertainment and financial services. On the goods side, few highly standardized commodities, like books, CDs and computers can be mentioned. When above-mentioned obstacles are overcome, the business-to-consumer sales via the Internet will replace real shopping significantly.

The main aim of this study is to show the macroeconomic implications of virtual shopping. Starting from micro-foundations, we build a static model in Ricardian equilibrium framework. First, we investigate the traditional way of in-store shopping, which we call 'real' shopping in this study. This study assumes that in-store shopping is characterized by physical appearance of customers in stores. Brown (1989), analyzing the store-shopping behavior of consumers, finds that store location and the associated travel costs play an important role in store selection. Bell, Teck-Hua and Tang (1998) show empirical evidence for households having linear disutility over the total shopping cost that includes travel distances. Bakos (1997) and Alba et al. (1997) argue that 'electronic marketplaces' will lower the buyers' cost to acquire information about seller prices and product offerings, which leads to a reduction of inefficiencies caused by buyer search costs. Palmer (2000) argues that in-store shopping may cause the shopper to spend more time in the shopping process, owing to the fact that it contains a rich level of information for the shopper, like face-to-face interaction with the opportunity for iterative questions and personalized responses. We sum up these findings by assuming that time cost is the differentiating aspect of real shopping. More specifically, this study assumes that each unit of real shopping, which is represented by consumption, requires the consumer to spend some time on shopping.

Second, we examine the new way of shopping, namely virtual shopping. The major benefit of the Internet marketplaces for consumers is the time gained due to being freed from going to a physical store for shopping. Obviously, on-line shoppers also spend some time on shopping via the Internet. For two reasons we ignore these direct time costs. Firstly, relatively speaking, the time cost of on-line shopping is substantially less than the time spent by real shoppers.[7] Secondly, the cost of on-line shopping is primarily attributed to connection costs. Subsequently, it is not the 'raw' time cost but the income cost of the use of on-line connections that matters. Connection cost is related to the amount of on-line shopping, represented by consumption, by definition. Consequently, when we compare two shopping technologies, consumers on one hand gain time and on the other hand incur income loss. This constitutes the main tradeoff between real shopping and Internet shopping. In reality, data also supports this argument.[8]

Third, by comparing the welfare effects of the two different shopping behaviors, we derive a necessary and sufficient condition for shifting to virtual shopping. Wigand (1997) argues that the rise of Internet marketplace in retail sales involves not new retail spending, but a switch of customers from shops to on-line sales. This switching behavior is captured in our necessary and sufficient condition. Next, we investigate the macroeconomic implications of the expansion of virtual shopping. We find that when the bulky part of business-to-consumer trade shifts to the Internet, the economy will realize higher consumption and income, and a higher labor supply in aggregate. In all, the expansion of the Internet economy will surpass current predictions due to a boom in business-to-consumer transactions conducted via the Internet, and the economic implications of this expansion will be significant. Fifth, we make an introductory attempt of policy analysis. More specifically, we investigate under which conditions on-line consumers may tolerate being taxed. The interesting feature of this section is the introduction of a new tax, namely, on-line investment tax, which is hardly discussed in the Internet literature. Finally, we consider briefly managerial implications of switching to Internet shopping.

The next section models real shopping. The third section models Internet shopping. The fourth section presents the welfare analysis. The fifth section considers macroeconomic implications of Internet shopping. One interesting finding is that aggregate consumption and labor supply increases when the bulky part of retail shopping goes on-line. The sixth section provides an introduction to the policy implications of Internet shopping. The seventh section discusses challenges faced by traditional retailers when they decide to shift to some form of on-line retailing. The last section concludes the chapter.

REAL SHOPPING

Suppose there exists a large number of identical individuals. Furthermore, assume that firms use only labor to produce a composite good. Prices (normalized to one) and wages are determined in the markets for goods and labor and therefore taken as given. There is no capital (hence no saving) and no uncertainty.

Suppose that the production function is:

$$Q = x \bullet n \bullet N \qquad (1)$$

where Q is aggregate output, x is the productivity parameter, n the amount of time spent on working by each worker (individual) and N the number of workers. Under the assumption of constant returns to scale, market equilibrium is obtained such that real wages w / p are equal to productivity x. An individual with real wage x earns real income y:

$$y = x \bullet n \qquad (2)$$

where income is measured in real units.

Suppose that households can consume only by doing some shopping. This necessarily requires, in the 'real' world, the physical appearance of a household on the market and therefore will cost some time. We shall call this real shopping. Let us label consumption via real shopping as real consumption, c_r. Since there are no savings, real consumption c_r equals real income (given in equation 2).

Assume that the representative household's utility function $u(c,l)$ is strictly concave in consumption c and leisure l. We suppose a Cobb-Douglas type of utility function:

$$U_r = \theta \log(c_r) + (1 - \theta) \log(l_r) \qquad (3)$$

where subscript r stands for real shopping. A rational household has to decide how to allocate time among leisure l_r, working n_r and shopping n_l. A unit of time is allocated as follows:

$$n_r + n_l + l_r = 1 \qquad (4)$$

A very simple assumption about the time spent on shopping is that there exists a constant linear relationship between the amount of consumption and the time spent on shopping. We argue that households rarely make 'odd-size' purchases compared to the time spent on shopping. Therefore, as a first approximation, it is realistic to assume that

$$n_1 = \delta c_r \qquad (5)$$

where $\delta > 0$ is a parameter. The solution of the model yields $n_r^* = \theta/(1+\delta x)$, $l_r^* = 1-\theta$, $n_l^* = (\theta \delta x)/(1+\delta x)$, and $y_r^* = c_r^* = (x\theta)/(1+\delta x)$. This part of our analysis investigates how households allocate their time between working, leisure and shopping when consumers take into consideration a time cost of shopping in their time-budget constraint. We show that a representative consumer allocates her time among these three in constant proportions.

In order to consume, people need to shop. Before the introduction of the Internet technology consumers were required to appear physically in the market. However, after the introduction of the Internet technology, consumers are given the opportunity to shop virtually and therefore not to appear physically on the market, which obviously saves shopping time. The next section shows how the representative household's allocation problem changes when time cost of shopping drops, i.e., virtual shopping becomes fully operational.

BACK TO THE FUTURE: VIRTUAL SHOPPING

"You're about to pour the last ounce of milk into your late-night bowl of cereal. Oops—looks like there'll be none left for your morning coffee! All the stores are closed. What's a hungry night owl to do? Pour away! By 6 a.m., a new gallon will be on your doorstep, thanks to a microchip sensor embedded in the milk carton and transmitted to an Internet device on your kitchen counter" (LaPlante, 1999).

One of the latest battles in cyberspace is in refrigerator technology. Look at the "intelligent" refrigerator that Frigidaire Home Products debuted recently.[9] Equipped with a microprocessor, touch screen, bar-code scanner and communications port, the refrigerator allows consumers to automate their grocery shopping. Whenever someone is low on a given product, he can simply swipe the carton past the refrigerator's bar-code scanner, which adds that item to a list. When the consumer is ready, the list can be transmitted to the local grocer. The groceries will either be delivered to the consumer's door or packaged for pickup. The fridge can be connected to the Internet via a standard phone line or an Ethernet network.

The refrigerator example, which even eliminates the computer, represents perfectly what we mean by virtual shopping. The distance between the seller and the consumer disappears and in addition to this, the consumer does not worry about the delivery of the goods and services ordered. In other words, compared to real shopping, the time cost arising from the distance between the consumer and the seller disappears.[10] In one respect, we go "back to the future" and imagine a world such that shopping through the Internet is as easy as swiping a carton through a bar-code scanner or voicing the name of the product to the computer (or may be to any home appliance). We further imagine a (virtual) market that covers almost all products for virtual shopping. Now suppose that a representative agent purchases virtually and therefore shopping time drops out as a decision variable. Accordingly, utility function is defined as

$$U_v = \theta \log(c_v) + (1-\theta)\log(l_v) \qquad (6)$$

where subscript v represents virtual shopping. A unit of time is allocated between working and leisure

$$n_v + l_v = 1 \qquad (7)$$

However, in order to 'run' virtual shopping, the representative household has to incur some costs. These costs are of two types. First and foremost, the household has to incur variable costs that we call connection costs in this study.[11] Second, some fixed costs like buying a computer with an Internet connection are incurred. However, we exclude these costs in our analysis for two reasons. Firstly, consumers do not purchase a computer or a refrigerator to undertake solely Internet shopping, that is, their main functions are different. For example, most home computers are used for education, leisure (entertainment) and even for business. Secondly, adding fixed costs does not change the results qualitatively and we prefer to keep the model as simple as possible. Obviously, in case of virtual shopping, real income is spent on two items: consumption and variable costs. For simplicity, let us suppose that total variable costs are a linear function of total consumption:

$$Total\ costs = \alpha_1 c_v \tag{8}$$

where $0 < \alpha_1 < 1$ represents the cost incurred per unit of real consumption via the Internet.[12] According to equation (8), total connection costs rise as the amount of shopping, represented by consumption, increases. Accordingly, the maximization problem becomes

$$Max\quad U_v = \theta \log(c_v) + (1-\theta)\log(l_v)$$
$$s.t.\quad n_v + l_v = 1 \tag{9}$$
$$c_v + \alpha_1 c_v = n_v x$$

Then, the optimal values of variables become $n_v{}^* = \theta$, $l_v{}^* = 1 - \theta$, and $c_v{}^* = \theta \cdot x/(1+\alpha_1)$, $y_v{}^* = \theta \cdot x$, respectively. The representative consumer allocates her time between working and leisure in the constant proportions θ and $1-\theta$, respectively. These values should be interpreted with caution. The results are sensitive to the type of utility function. Normally, we expect the household to allocate extra time in such a way that both leisure and working time rise.[13] However, the basic interpretation does not change, though in the virtual shopping case, the consumer incurs some (variable) costs from her income, the time cost of shopping disappears, and the representative household uses this extra time to work more (n_v is larger than n_r) and to earn more (y_v is larger than y_r). Which shopping technology makes the representative consumer better off? The next section investigates this issue.

WELFARE ANALYSIS

In this section, we investigate the circumstances under which it may be optimal for a representative consumer to shift to virtual shopping given the model above. We derive the necessary and sufficient condition for shifting to virtual shopping. We begin by evaluating economic welfare under real shopping. Suppose that the representative consumer chooses to remain with real shopping technology. The representative agent's real income, which is equal to real consumption c_r, is given by real wage, x, times the amount of time worked. The representative agent allocates her time between working, leisure and shopping in the constant proportions $\theta/(1+\delta x)$, $1-\theta$, and $\theta\delta x/(1+\delta x)$, respectively. Hence, from equation (3), the representative consumer's utility may be expressed as

$$U_r = \theta \log\left(\frac{\theta x}{1 + \delta x}\right) + (1 - \theta)\log(1 - \theta) \tag{10}$$

Consider now the alternative "regime," namely virtual shopping. The representative consumer allocates her time between work and leisure in constant proportions θ and $1-\theta$, respectively. The representative agent's real consumption is lower than her real income due to the fact that she incurs some (variable) costs linear to the amount of shopping via the Internet. From equation (6), the representative consumer's utility is

$$U_v = \theta \log\left(\frac{\theta x}{1 + \alpha_1}\right) + (1 - \theta)\log(1 - \theta) \tag{11}$$

Internet shopping will improve welfare relative to real shopping if and only if $1 + \alpha_1 < 1 + \delta x$, which implies

$$\alpha_1 < \delta x \tag{12}$$

What is δ? It is the opportunity cost of one unit of real income in terms of time, that is, how much time the representative consumer is ready to give up in order to save one more unit of real income (by doing shopping via physically appearing in the market). Remember that real wage is equal to the productivity parameter, x. Thus, the right hand side of equation (12) is the loss of real income due to incurring costs in terms of time. The left-hand side, on the other hand, is income loss per unit consumption due to shopping via the Internet. Thus, the consumer is better off shopping via the Internet if and only if the cost of virtual shopping is lower than the opportunity cost of real shopping.

The opportunity cost of real income in terms of time δ is a function of many variables like real wage, average distance to the market, skill and education levels, consumer attitude, etc. Most of these factors are 'internal' in the sense that they are specific to individuals. An interesting result appears for a specific value of δ. Suppose for the moment that the representative consumer takes into consideration her real wages alone in forming the value of δ, and suppose specifically the representative consumer takes $\delta = 1/x$. Then, the right hand side of equation (12) becomes unity. In this case the consumer is always better off by shifting to virtual shopping due to the fact that $\alpha_1 < 1$ by definition. The loss of income due to shopping via the Internet is also a function of many variables like Internet infrastructure, unit cost of electricity, the power of computer, the speed of modem, etc., which are 'external' to the representative consumer, by and large. In all, the switching condition reflects that people with higher income value their time higher. Subsequently, they are more willing to implement the new type of shopping. Our argument is also supported empirically. For example, the Forrester Report (1998) states that while households earning more than $50,000 a year make up only 36% of the total U.S. population, they account for 47% of total consumer spending and 74% of spending on-line.[14]

We state above that the condition given in equation (12) is a function of many 'internal' and 'external' variables. We argue that our results can be extrapolated into long run by adding a 'time-dimension' to the switching condition in equation (12). By this, we mean that, practically, the condition found in (12) will be satisfied at different times for each consumer in an economy. The intuition is as follows: since there are many internal and external factors, we may argue that each person will evaluate the condition given in equation (12) and decide accordingly where to shop. In that sense, those who 'pass' the condition will shift to Internet shopping. Obviously, the current trend is in favor of Internet shopping, that is, many variables ranging from computer technology to Internet education support the shift to virtual shopping. Here we discuss some of them in detail to confirm our intuition. First, computer skills have been continuously increasing. Computers (and the Internet) have already become part of the education in many countries and especially in developed economies.[15] In the new millennium, especially in developed economies, major part of the economically active labor force will not need to extend any additional effort (in terms of education) to learn how to use the Internet. Second, technological changes, which are very rapid in the computer industry, ease Internet shopping in many ways. Third, governments see the Internet as a tool that serves to accelerate and diffuse more widely changes that are already under way in an economy, such as deregulation or the establishment of links between businesses. Furthermore, trade via the Internet, by definition, is the main tool of further globalization and integration of economies and therefore receives big support from governments. A good example is US government, which takes a leading role in promoting e-commerce.[16] Obviously, these three reasons are comprehensive but not exhaustive. In conclusion, we believe that it is intuitive to argue that the current trends will give rise to more and more consumers to prefer Internet shopping to real shopping through time. Based on this premise, we shall reinterpret our results to hold in the long run, though our model is framed in a static world.

MACROECONOMIC IMPLICATIONS OF VIRTUAL SHOPPING

In this section we investigate the macroeconomic implications of the shift to virtual shopping. As the necessary and sufficient condition is a function of internal and external variables, each consumer will shift to virtual shopping as soon as her condition is satisfied. In that context, we postulate that aggregate consumption will follow the path illustrated by Figure 1 (not necessarily in linear shape).

The economy can be considered to be on its long-run path C_r (the aggregate real consumption until t_o) before the introduction of the Internet technology. After the introduction of virtual shopping, the consumers whose switching condition, given in equation (12), is satisfied shift to virtual shopping. Thus, aggregate consumption begins to rise. At some point like t_1, real shopping is expected to approach its lowest 'stable' level C_r^*, and the virtual shopping its highest level C_v^*. Analogous to dynamic analysis, we may call these values the respective 'steady-state' values,

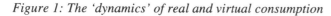

Figure 1: The 'dynamics' of real and virtual consumption

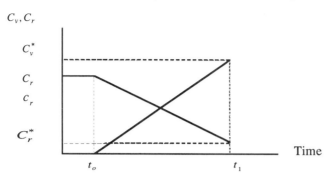

where virtual and real shopping levels remain unchanged. At time t_1, C_r^* may stay positive because some consumers may prefer to continue real shopping. We have to note here that C_v^* is not necessarily above C_r. To see this, let us suppose that N_v is the number of 'virtual' consumers/workers and N_r is the number of 'real' shoppers. At time t_0 aggregate consumption is $C_r = N \cdot c_r$, where N is the total number of consumers. At time t_1 aggregate virtual consumption will be $C_v^* = N_v \cdot c_v^*$. Obviously, we cannot compare C_r and C_v^* because $N > N_v$ and $c_r < c_v^*$. Yet, it is easy to see that $0 < C_r < C_v^* + C_r^*$ due to the fact that virtual consumption is always higher than real consumption for those who shifted to virtual shopping. Thus, aggregate consumption is higher in the Internet economy.

When Internet shopping becomes fully operational, two other important results appear. The aggregate real income and output, $Q^* = Q_v^* + Q_r^*$, and the aggregate labor supply, $N_v n_v^* + N_r n_r^*$, increase given the Cobb-Douglas utility function. Workers allocate the extra time they generate due to switching to Internet shopping between work and leisure (in the Cobb-Douglas type utility function leisure stays intact, which is a case-specific result), which increases aggregate output and income proportional to the change in the amount of time worked. Thus, the effects of virtual shopping exceed the current premature business-to-consumer trade realization and contribute significantly to the emergence and performance of the new economy in the (near) future. We argue that the future will witness more lively discussions on the virtual shopping issue in the field of economics (at the theoretical level), of government (policy level) and of business (at practical level). The next two sections offer introductions at the policy level and the management level.

SOME POLICY ANALYSES

The nice feature of our model is that it is extendable in many aspects due to the fact that it is set up in a theoretical framework. In Section 5 we show that the permeation of Internet shopping leads to higher aggregate income, as well as to higher aggregate consumption inducing growth in the economy during transition. The report of the U.S. Department of Commerce (1999) argues that without sufficient investment into network technologies, nations may find themselves behind in an increasingly wired (and may be wireless) world. In the US, the country in infrastructure investment besides promoting Internet shopping in other ways. Several private sector organizations are linked to government projects supporting the Internet infrastructure, such as electronic Commerce Committee, CommerceNet and the Electronic Messaging Association. In fact, in 1995-97 expenditures on Internet-related infrastructure reached $40 billion.

In Section 4 we argue that the condition to switch to Internet shopping from real shopping will be satisfied for each individual according to certain internal and external variables. Naturally, one major external variable is the quality of the Internet infrastructure, which directly determines the cost of connection to the Internet. We believe that the success of Internet shopping depends on consumers' access to Internet shopping without network delays (for example, due to congestion) and without other restrictions on access as well as (lower) connection costs. In essence, the former highly determines the latter. The efficiency of underlying infrastructure (by all means) is important in this respect.

The infrastructure requirements for on-line shopping are changing rapidly with new technological developments and widening of Internet shopping. As the demand for virtual shopping grows, it stimulates higher demand for better infrastructure. Slowness in meeting demand for 'better' network infrastructure may create reluctance of potential on-line shoppers to shift to virtual shopping and thus retards the growth of Internet shopping (and Internet economy).[17] Hence, policy makers have to ensure continuous improvement of infrastructure to support virtual shopping and Internet economy. Given the current fashion of balanced budget policy among policy-makers, the most obvious way of funding these infrastructure investments is to collect some taxes from the on-line shoppers (in our framework). We call these taxes on-line-investment taxes in this study.

Are on-line consumers in favor of on-line-investment tax or not? The answer is obvious and intuitive: if on-line-investment taxes improve network infrastructure sufficiently, then the consumer may end up better off in the end. In order to show this result, we need to modify our model. Let us introduce a government into our model, collecting taxes and investing tax revenues in improving network infrastructure. Assume that an investment tax is imposed on the representative on-line consumer in the form of

$$t = \tau c_v \tag{13}$$

where t is per capita investment tax and τ is investment tax per consumption unit and taken as given. According to equation (13), investment taxes are proportional to shopping via the Internet. Let us suppose that all tax revenues are used for improvement in network infrastructure. In our model, the efficiency of infrastructure is hidden in the connection costs, α_i real units per unit of on-line shopping. Improvements in infrastructure via new investments must appear as a reduction in connection costs.[18] We assume that the relationship between tax revenues and connection costs can be represented by

$$\alpha_0 = \alpha_1 - \xi\tau \tag{14}$$

where α_0 is the connection cost and ξ is the infrastructure technology parameter. The second part of equation (14) on the right hand side represents the improvement in infrastructure, which leads to a reduction in connection costs. The crucial property of equation (14) is that the infrastructure is assumed to be a private good rather than a public good.[19] Investment taxes paid per head produce a linear improvement in infrastructure, which leads to a decline in connection costs according to our formulation. It may be argued that a linear infrastructure improvement is not realistic. We agree that an efficiency production function with decreasing returns to scale is preferable. Nevertheless the public good character of infrastructure investments is also obvious and therefore we approximated these investments in a linear fashion.

The solution of the model yields the optimum consumption level

$$c_v^* = \frac{\theta \cdot x}{(1 + \alpha_1) + \tau(1 - \xi)} \tag{15}$$

while optimum values of other variables remain the same due to the special utility function we use. Is the representative agent better off? The answer lies in the value of the infrastructure technology parameter. If one real unit of tax produces more than one real unit of decrease in connection costs, then the consumer is better off paying on-line investment taxes. Thus, we conclude that consumers may be more ready to pay on-line taxes than some people think given that governments will use these tax revenues for the benefit of on-line consumers.

Another issue concerning policy-makers is the bit tax. The bit tax issue is about whether local or federal governments should impose tax on Internet traffic (on-line sales in our case) owing to the fact that borderless trade causes some governments or states to lose part of their tax revenues. The counter-argument is that Internet trade is still fragile and therefore, to tax it now may seriously damage its growth.[20] Bit tax is welfare reducing, given our framework. Nonetheless, our model shows that per capita consumption as well as per capita income will increase when on-line shopping becomes the major way of shopping. This fact implies that some of the tax revenue losses incurred by governments and states may be compensated due to increases in consumption and income. However, it is obvious that there will be reallocation of tax revenues among state and federal governments within a country. Governments and states located in areas that are centers of Internet trade will realize a rise in tax revenues, while governments located in regions that specialize in real shopping will lose their tax bases. The same trend may be observed across countries, and especially in those regions that formed regional blocks like the European Union (EU) or North American Free Trade Agreement (NAFTA). Within each region, centers of Internet economy will gain and others will lose. We believe that the increase in Internet trade across borders necessitates greater need for mutual cooperation and international tax enforcement, namely countries need to develop a tax framework together that protects the tax base but avoids hindering the development of virtual shopping.[21] This part of our analysis also shows that on-line consumption (as part of trade via the Internet) has far-reaching implications for policy-makers, too.

MANAGERIAL IMPLICATIONS OF SWITCHING TO INTERNET SHOPPING: SOME CHALLENGES

In previous sections, we found the switching condition from real shopping to virtual shopping, discussed the reasons why this condition favors a shift from real shopping to virtual shopping and projected that the demand for Internet shopping would significantly increase at the cost of real shopping in the future. The increased preference for Internet shopping will lead to growing pressure of competition coming from on-line retailers. This fact, together with the development of on-line technologies and increasing government interest in the Internet, makes it imperative for brick-and-mortars to seriously consider switching to the Internet. The transition of brick-and-mortars to, say, click-and-mortar businesses meets with several managerial difficulties. [22] These may include the entire reshaping of the traditional retail outlet environment, resolving channel conflicts, developing a flexible delivery system, reducing margins to compete with pure-play Internet retailers (e-tailers), recreating consumer services, etc. In this section, we discuss the managerial implications that arise when brick-and-mortar retailers decide to start on-line business. [23] It is beyond the scope of this work to analyze all the implications in full detail. Therefore, we shall limit ourselves to some of the most prominent challenges and leave discussing other implications to future study.

"If a company is to survive, it will have to have some sort of electronic commerce solution," says Martha Wahoski, the director of electronic commerce for the Computing Technology Industry Association (CompTIA). Walsh and Godfrey (2000) go further and argue that if traditional retailers do not respond to current developments, they are in danger of becoming extinct soon. Many brick-and-mortars are aware of the threat and all try to take precautionary measures against losing their markets. Walsh and Godfrey (2000) and Dutta and Segev (1999), for example, have enumerated diverse responses.[24]

We may order these responses on a continuum ranging from conventional retailing to pure-play on-line retailing (e-tailing). Each retailer takes a position on this continuum according to the unique characteristics of the company, sector, competitive environment, etc. We discuss some of them. First, the company may decide to close down all of its conventional operations and become an Internet-only business. A good example is Egghead, a computer and software retailer. The Menlo Park, California, discount computer retailer was well known for its 200-plus brick-and-mortar locations built between 1984 and 1997. While falling revenue forced the company to shut all those doors in 1998, the business became a well-known pure-play Internet retailer in the name of Egghead.com. Another possibility for the retailer is to offer all or part of its merchandize on-line (click-and-mortars). Barnes&Noble.com and Toys"R"Us.com are two examples for this common way of response. Third, the conventional retail store may assign on-line retailing to a subsidiary. One advantage of a subsidiary company is that it gains benefits from its established parent, while the parent company can continue to focus on the core business. Fourth, the retailer may use an integrated 'combination' of its traditional and on-line services. A very good example is SaksFifthAvenue.com, which is a static storefront where customers can only request catalogs and get store locations. Another example is Dress Barn's decision to tie their (static) Web site to their store locations by planning to use Web kiosks in the future. The kiosks would let customers order products that are out of stock in the store, or purchase a product in a color not available in the store. Finally, the traditional retailer may merge with a pure on-line retailer. This response is especially suitable for those brick-and-mortars that do not want to do on-line business alone. For example, Chase Manhattan Bank, Bank of America and Microsoft agreed to form a new dot-com for financial services. These reactions have different managerial implications as they require different ways of coordination, distinct types of physical assets, operational systems, provide different opportunities in customer service, etc.

The challenges to brick-and-mortars that decide to go on-line are various. We conjecture that these challenges can be examined under two headings parallel to the two phases brick-and-mortars experience in transforming their (part of) business into some form of on-line retailing. The first phase is the transformation of (part of) the business from traditional retail outlet environment to cyberspace environment (the transition period).[25] To this end, let us compare the characteristics of the two extreme environments in the continuum. Hereby we list a few of the differences. While brick-and-mortars usually have several physical stores, e-tailers may have one centralized warehouse. This allows e-tailers, for example, to carry fewer stocks in inventory, offer a greater variety of merchandise and serve a larger geographic region. While the location of the stores is essential for real retailers, e-tailers can be located in areas with low real estate costs. Brick-and-mortars need wide aisles lined with expensive fixtures and multiple checkout counters that on-line businesses do not require. In the case of brick-and-mortars, order and delivery are usually instant; electronic retailing generally requires some time delay between the order and the delivery. This gives flexibility to e-tailers to handle the orders (e.g., e-tailer may have them shipped directly from manufacturers).

The second phase of the transformation concerns the support of daily operations. Obviously, daily operations will also depend on the type of on-line 'presence' chosen.[26] One of the distinguishing characteristics of on-line retail sales is global competition, as distance and location does not matter in the cyber-world. Hence, besides other managerial challenges, the main task of managers will be to survive in a tougher competition coming from anywhere. This necessarily requires the retailer to maintain an established relationship with its customers. Managers must use the Internet not only as a marketplace but also as a tool in order to survive in cyberspace.

First, the use of the Internet provides a rich set of data. This data may range from personal information to tracks of the customer's navigation path, allowing retailers (managers) to gather information about their customers. The increasingly accessible data provides the opportunity to improve the understanding of consumer interests and preferences. But quick processing and interpretation of such an amount of data may easily become a problem if the management is not ready for it. For example, when Toyota decided to create its Web site, company leaders underestimated the volume of e-mails they would receive from people who suddenly had a direct line to speak with the company. Second, click-and-mortars must develop a close relationship with their customers due to seven-days-a-week and 24-hours-a-day accessibility, relevancy and virtual dialogues. Since the retailer knows exactly the profile of any specific consumer, she can target each consumer with perfect relevancy. For example, a consumer known to be attracted to a certain style of music may receive a message when a new CD in this style is launched. Or a virtual character can be created, which replaces a salesperson in providing help for customers in their purchasing decisions via dialogues.

Third, using the Internet, retailers can provide a high level of added value to their customers. For example, consumers can customize retailers' Web pages according to their needs and interests. Or, consumers can easily interact with retailers (feedback). This means both a challenge and an opportunity for the management. A constant failure of maintaining a high level of added value may create dissatisfied customers.

Fourth, developing and keeping up customer loyalty is the real challenge for on-line retailers. Developing consumer loyalty has always been a great challenge and brings further difficulties for an e-business.[27] As in cyberspace consumers have the opportunity to switch to any competing retailer at zero cost (push-effect), retailers are increasingly left to the mercy of customers. Thus, managers must be alert and be able to maintain consumer loyalty in a dynamic market via perfecting their on-line operations including a well-developed customer service and customer relationship.

We have mentioned several challenges that brick-and-mortars must consider in order to run a successful on-line business. Experience has shown that the transition and maintenance of on-line business is not trivial. Due to tough competition, many conventional retailers have suddenly found themselves in the on-line jungle. Some of them had great success. Barnes and Noble.com, for example, has transformed its business from a brick-and-mortar to a click-and-mortar successfully. But the success is not at all for sure. Due to the increased pressure, there is no time to fully prepare, so companies have to learn by doing. This requires continuous revision of their measures and flexibility to reconsider and readjust their strategies. Take, for example, Staples.com, an office supplier. After operating on-line for 18 months, the managers understood that a big revision was needed. They improved on-line customer service, installed two new search tools, added several small business services and improved purchasing management. They also created a centralized one-stop rebate center in response to complaints that tracking down forms and information around the site was difficult. Many other click-and-mortars are also working feverishly to enhance the customer experience.

Causal observation, supported by predictions of retail specialists, suggests that the traditional retail industry will inevitably experience transition to on-line retailing. Nevertheless, experience has shown that this transition is painful and success is not guaranteed. However, one thing is clear; those who fail to initiate the transition will sooner or later disappear from the market. And the extent to which retailers deciding to shift can make use of the unique opportunities provided by the Internet itself determines their success.

CONCLUSION AND FUTURE RESEARCH

The 1990s witnessed the breakthrough of Internet technology. The Net has quickly spread over all aspects of life ranging from entertainment to education. Recently, it brought an alternative to conventional retail technology. In this paper we compare the old and new ways of shopping. We base our analysis on consumer theory. Comparing the results of conventional and Internet shopping, we obtain the switching condition for a representative consumer to shift from the former to the latter: when the real cost of virtual shopping becomes lower than the respective cost of real shopping, the representative consumer shifts to virtual shopping. Then, we project our results to the aggregate. We indicate that consumption, income and labor supply rise when the majority of the consumers shift to Internet shopping. Thus, we show that the economic implications of Internet shopping will exceed current expectations in business-to-consumer trade in specific and Internet trade in general. This result points to the efficiency gains that the new way of trade provides for consumers (and other traders). It is worth noting that this efficiency-gain arises if the time of the consumer is valuable. This may explain why consumers living in the most developed economies were the first users of the new economy.

There are many other issues not discussed in this study. First and foremost, we do not analyze the supply side. Second, we build our model in a closed-economy framework. One of the implications of the Internet technology is its contribution to globalization. Perhaps extension of the model to a two-country framework will highlight other sources of efficiency gains, such as specialization. Third, we construct our model in a static framework. Its extension to a dynamic model can better emphasize the transitional dynamics of the shift from real shopping to virtual shopping on the one hand, and growth effects of virtual shopping on the other hand. All these issues and probably many others are possible areas of future study.

REFERENCES

Alba, J., Lynch, J. G., Weitz, B., Janiszewski, C., Lutz, R., Sawyer, A., and Wood, S. (1997). Interactive home shopping: Consumer, retailer and manufacturer incentives to participate in electronic marketplaces. *Journal of Marketing*, 61, 38-53.

Bakos, J. Y. (1997). Reducing buyer search costs: Implications for electronic marketplaces. *Management Science*, 43, 1676-1692.

Bell, D. R., Teck-Hua H., and Tang, C. S. (1998). Determining where to shop: Fixed and variable costs of shopping. *Journal of Marketing Research*, 35, 352-369.

Brown, S. (1989). Retail location theory: The legacy of Harold Hotelling. *Journal of Retailing*, 65, 450-70.

Dick, A. S., and Basu, K. (1994). Customer loyalty: Toward an integrated conceptual framework. *Journal of Academy of Marketing Science*, 22, 99-113.

Dutta, S., and Segev, A. (1999). Business transformation on the Internet. *European Management Journal*, 17, 466-476.

Dutta, S., Kwan, S., and Segev, A. (1998). Business transformation in electronic commerce: A study of sectoral and regional trends. *European Management Journal*, 16, 540-551.

Forrester Report. (1998). Retail's growth spiral. Retrieved April 3, 2000, from the World Wide Web: http://www.nrf.com/ecommerce/ecommerce.htm.

Forrester Press Release. (2000). European on-line retail will soar to 175 billion Euros by 2005. Retrieved April 23, 2000, from the World Wide Web: http://www.forrester.com/ER/Press/Release/0,1769,266,FF.htm.

Goolsbee, A. (1998). In a world without borders: The impact of taxes on Internet commerce. NBER Working Paper, No. 6863.

Goolsbee, A. (1999). Internet commerce, tax sensitivity and the generation gap. Retrieved March 14, 2000, from the World Wide Web: http://gsbadg.uchicago.edu/internet.htm.

Goolsbee, A., and Zittrain J. (1999). Evaluating the costs and benefits of taxing Internet commerce. Retrieved March 14, 2000, from the World Wide Web: http://gsbadg.uchicago.edu/internet.htm.

Jarvenpaa, S. L., Tractinsky, N., and Vitale M. (2000). Consumer trust in an Internet store. *Information Technology and Management*, 1, 45-71.

Katsushima, T. (1998). Internet and electronic commerce-the new frontier. *Intertax*, 26, 86-87.

LaPlante, A. (1999). Battle for the fridge. CNN News (April 9), Retrieved April 12, 1999 from the World Wide Web: http://www.cnn.com.

Mottl, J. N. (2000). The brick-and-mortars fight back. *Internetweek*, 818, 51-53.

OECD (2000). Electronic commerce: Initial survey of liberalisation and facilitation measures. Retrieved February 22, 2000, from the World Wide Web: http://www.oecd.org/ech/index_2.htm.

Oliver, R. L. (1999). Whence consumer loyalty. *Journal of Marketing*, 63, 33-44.

Palmer, J. W. (2000). Electronic commerce in retailing: Convenience, search costs, delivery and price across retail formats. *Information Technology and Management*, 1, 25-43.

Roberts, L. G. (2000). Beyond Moore's law: Internet growth trends. *Computer: A Publication of the IEEE Computer Group*, 33, 117-19.

Schwartz, E. (2000). Brick-and-mortars take the e-commerce plunge. *InfoWorld*, 22, 40-43.

U.S. Department of Commerce. (1998). The emerging digital economy I. Retrieved June 12, 1999, from the World Wide Web: http://www.ecommerce.gov/emerging.htm.

U.S. Department of Commerce. (1999). The emerging digital economy II. Retrieved June 12, 1999 from the World Wide Web: http://www.ecommerce.gov/ede/.

Varian, H. R. (1999). Market structure in the network age. Retrieved April 10, 2000, from the World Wide Web: http://www.sims.berkeley.edu/~hal/Papers/doc/doc.htm.

Walsh, J., and Godfrey, S. (2000). The Internet: A new era in customer service. *European Management Journal*, 18, 85-92.

Wigand, R. T. (1997). Electronic commerce: Definition, theory and context. *The Information Society*, 13, 1-16.

APPENDIX: THE SOLUTION
FOR CES-TYPE UTILITY FUNCTION

Let us suppose that the utility function is CES-type:

$$U = \left(c^{1-\sigma} + l^{1-\sigma}\right)^{\frac{1}{1-\sigma}} \tag{A.1}$$

where the elasticity of substitution is $1/\sigma$. In case of real shopping, the representative agent's maximization problem is

$$
\begin{aligned}
&Max \quad U_r = \left(c_r^{1-\sigma} + l_r^{1-\sigma}\right)^{\frac{1}{1-\sigma}} \\
&s.t. \quad n_r + n_1 + l_r = 1 \\
&\qquad\quad n_1 = \delta c_r \\
&\qquad\quad c_r = x n_r
\end{aligned}
\tag{A.2}
$$

After necessary substitutions and after taking logarithmic transformation of the utility, we end up with the following 'reduced form' of maximization problem

$$Max \ \ln[U_r] = \frac{1}{1-\sigma} \ln\left[c_r^{1-\sigma} + \left(\frac{x - (1+\delta x)c_r}{x} \right)^{1-\sigma} \right] \tag{A.3}$$

First order condition with respect to real consumption yields

$$c_r = \frac{x^{\frac{1}{\sigma}}}{(1+\delta x)^{\frac{1}{\sigma}} + (1+\delta x)x^{\frac{1}{\sigma}-1}}. \tag{A.4}$$

Equilibrium values of other unknowns are given in Table A.1 below.

In the case of virtual shopping, the representative agent's maximization problem is

$$Max \quad U_v = \left(c_v^{1-\sigma} + l_v^{1-\sigma}\right)^{\frac{1}{1-\sigma}}$$

$$s.t \quad n_v + l_v = 1 \tag{A.5}$$

$$c_v = xn_v - \alpha_1 \cdot c_v$$

which is reduced to

$$Max \ \ln[U_v] = \frac{1}{1-\sigma} \ln\left[c_v^{1-\sigma} + \left(\frac{x - (1+\alpha_1)c_v}{x}\right)^{1-\sigma}\right] \tag{A.6}$$

First order condition with respect to virtual consumption yields

$$c_v = \frac{x^{\frac{1}{\sigma}}}{(1+\alpha_1)^{\frac{1}{\sigma}} + (1+\alpha_1)x^{\frac{1}{\sigma}-1}} \tag{A.7}$$

Table A.1 also presents equilibrium values of variables in the case of virtual shopping.

The critical element in analysis is to compare the welfare of the representative

Table A.1: Equilibrium values of variables in the case of CES utility function

	REAL SHOPPING	VIRTUAL SHOPPING
n^{*}	$n_r = \dfrac{x^{\frac{1}{\sigma}-1}}{(1+\delta x)^{\frac{1}{\sigma}} + (1+\delta x)x^{\frac{1}{\sigma}-1}}$	$n_v = \dfrac{x^{\frac{1}{\sigma}-1}}{(1+\alpha_1)^{\frac{1}{\sigma}-1} + x^{\frac{1}{\sigma}-1}}$
n_1^{*}	$n_1 = \dfrac{\delta x^{\frac{1}{\sigma}}}{(1+\delta x)^{\frac{1}{\sigma}} + (1+\delta x)x^{\frac{1}{\sigma}-1}}$	N/A.
l^{*}	$l_r = \dfrac{(1+\delta x)^{\frac{1}{\sigma}}}{(1+\delta x)^{\frac{1}{\sigma}} + (1+\delta x)x^{\frac{1}{\sigma}-1}}$	$l_v = \dfrac{(1+\alpha_1)^{\frac{1}{\sigma}-1}}{(1+\alpha_1)^{\frac{1}{\sigma}-1} + x^{\frac{1}{\sigma}-1}}$
y^{*}	$y_r = \dfrac{x^{\frac{1}{\sigma}}}{(1+\delta x)^{\frac{1}{\sigma}} + (1+\delta x)x^{\frac{1}{\sigma}-1}}$	$y_v = \dfrac{x^{\frac{1}{\sigma}}}{(1+\alpha_1)^{\frac{1}{\sigma}-1} + x^{\frac{1}{\sigma}-1}}$

agent in both cases. To this aim, first, calculate welfare (take equation [A.1]) in the case of virtual shopping. After necessary substitutions, the utility function becomes

$$U_v = \left[c_v^{1-\sigma} \left(1 + \left(\frac{1}{c_v} - \frac{(1+\alpha_1)}{x} \right)^{1-\sigma} \right) \right]^{\frac{1}{1-\sigma}}$$

(A.8)

Note that c_v can be written as

$$c_v = \frac{x}{(1+\alpha_1)^{\frac{1}{\sigma}} x^{1-\frac{1}{\sigma}} + (1+\alpha_1)}$$

(A.9)

and thus U_v becomes

$$U_v = \left[c_v^{1-\sigma} \left(1 + \left(\frac{(1+\alpha_1)^{\frac{1}{\sigma}} x^{1-\frac{1}{\sigma}} + (1+\alpha_1)}{x} - \frac{(1+\alpha_1)}{x} \right)^{1-\sigma} \right) \right]^{\frac{1}{1-\sigma}} \Rightarrow$$

$$U_v = \left[c_v^{1-\sigma} \left(1 + (1+\alpha_1)^{\frac{1-\sigma}{\sigma}} x^{-\frac{1-\sigma}{\sigma}} \right) \right]^{\frac{1}{1-\sigma}}$$

(A.10)

Note that

$$1 + (1+\alpha_1)^{\frac{1-\sigma}{\sigma}} x^{-\frac{1-\sigma}{\sigma}} = \frac{x}{(1+\alpha_1)c_v}$$

(A.11)

from (A.9). Then, substituting (A.11) into (A.10) gives

$$U_v = \left(c_v \right)^{-\sigma/(1-\sigma)} \left(\frac{x}{(1+\alpha_1)} \right)^{\frac{1}{1-\sigma}}$$

(A.12)

Similarly, we get

$$U_r = \left(c_r \right)^{\frac{-\sigma}{1-\sigma}} \left(\frac{x}{(1+\delta x)} \right)^{\frac{1}{1-\sigma}}$$

(A.13)

in case of real shopping. It is easy to see that the consumer is better off by shifting to Internet shopping if and only if

$$-\frac{\sigma}{1-\sigma} \ln[c_v] - \frac{1}{1-\sigma} \ln[1+\alpha_1] > -\frac{\sigma}{1-\sigma} \ln[c_r] - \frac{1}{1-\sigma} \ln[1+\delta x]$$
(A.14)

This condition implies that

$$\ln[\frac{c_v}{c_r}] > \frac{1}{\sigma}\ln[\frac{1+\delta x}{1+\alpha_1}]$$ (A.15)

Substituting back respective values of c_v and c_r and some simple algebra yields that

$$\alpha_1 < \delta x$$ (A.16)

This is the condition we get also for Cobb-Douglas type utility function.

ENDNOTES

1 Throughout this work, we use virtual shopping, on-line shopping and Internet shopping interchangeably.

2 Varian (1999) offers to use the term "information good" to refer to a good that can be distributed in digital form.

3 For example, suppose that a book is purchased via the Internet. The transaction has two parts. While the ordering and the payment can be made via the Internet, the completion of the transaction, that is the delivery of the book, can be done through the conventional postal system. In that respect, purchasing a book via the Internet is mainly a hybrid of the new and the old ways of trade.

4 See, for example, the Forrester Report (1998, p.13), making the same prediction.

5 A general overview of Internet Economy can be found in the reports of the U.S. Department of Commerce (1998, 1999).

6 For example, 80% of companies say that security is the leading barrier to expand e-commerce links with customers and suppliers. See Jarvenpaa, Tractinsky and Vitale (2000) on the importance of consumer trust on Internet shopping. In this chapter, the authors show that the size and reputation of an Internet merchant are important to form customer trust. Credit card security of on-line transactions is another aspect of consumer trust. We consider especially the latter as pure technical constraint that will be overcome.

7 Nielsen NetRatings shows that the average at-home Internet use is approximately two-and-a-half-hours per week for a Japanese and three hours for an American. Let us suppose that half of this time is spent on virtual shopping. Compared to in-store shopping, the time spent is quite small.

8 See the discussion in Section 4.

9 Another example is a new venture between appliance maker Electrolux and L.M. Ericsson Telephone that aims to deliver wired appliances for use in networked homes.

10 Evidently, the consumer spends some time searching the Internet for the products she looks for. But, relatively speaking, it reduces to ignorable amounts. Rather, the income cost of this time becomes important.

11 By connection cost we mean all types of variable costs. For example, in the case of computer connection, the representative consumer uses some electricity and telephone. According to a survey by Nielsen NetRatings, most home surfers

are still using slow modems to connect to the Net. Fully 47% of Web users have modems with speeds of 33.6Kbps or slower, and 93% connect at 56Kbps or less. It is worth it to mention that a 56Kbps is 25 times slower than a high-speed T1 line.

12   It is hard to imagine that connection cost of unit on-line shopping is higher than the cost of unit consumption.

13   See Appendix for results of CES-type utility function.

14   On the contrary, households that earn less than $25,000 per year (constituting 34% of the population) account only for 6% of on-line retail sales.

15   For example, in the UK, Internet access is highest among 18-24 year-olds. Of these, 37% are regular users, accessing the Internet at least once a week. This figure is expected to increase to close to 100% when the Internet becomes fully available in schools. Trends in the access to Internet at schools support this. In France, for example, by the end of 1998, the number of schools connected to the Internet had increased remarkably: for ordinary secondary schools from less than 40% to 85%; from 1% to over 10% for primary schools. And free Internet access is to be available from schools, cultural centers, national employment agencies and libraries.

16   For example, the Telecommunication Act of 1996 encourages the rapid deployment of advanced telecommunications capabilities for all Americans. The New Millennium Classrooms Act, introduced in 1999, gives tax credits to those that donate computers to schools and disadvantaged communities. There are several examples of government support of the Internet in other countries as well. In May 1999, the Canadian Radio-television and Telecommunications Commission (CRTC) announced its decision to leave new media services and the Internet unregulated. The Performance and Management Unit of the British Cabinet Office released a report in September 1999 that sets out the government's strategy for enhancing the UK as a favorable environment for the development of Internet shopping. See the OECD report (2000) for further examples.

17   Roberts (2000) states that to keep pace with the Internet's expansion, for example, the maximum speed of core rooters and switchers must increase at the same rate, which means that performance improvements are required at a rate faster than 18-month doubling of semiconductor performance.

18   For example, tax revenues can be used to replace coaxial cables for ones that have higher capacity or to increase the maximum speed of core rooters and switchers.

19   We assumed away public good property of government investment for three reasons. First, connection costs are partly consumer-specific and therefore results might have been biased had we included openly public character of these investments. Second, the linearity in the infrastructure efficiency improvement part of equation (14) partly captures the public good character of government investments. Third, we prefer to keep the model as simple as possible. Note that Equation (14) would be $\alpha_0 = \alpha_1 - \xi \tau N$ had we assigned public good character to the government investment.

20   Goolsbee (1998) provides an empirical study about the potential effects of local taxes on Internet commerce. He finds that tax differences are significant stimuli for people to switch to on-line shopping. He states that applying existing sales tax to the commerce via the Internet will reduce the number of on-line buyers by us much as 24%. See also Goolsbee and Zittrain (1999) and Goolsbee (1999).

21   Recognizing this, governments have in fact begun the task of analysis and policy formulation. In November 1996, the United States Treasury Department initiated a discussion. Later, the Australian Taxation Office and the Japanese Ministry of International Trade and Industry contributed, among others. In response to the need for international consensus, the OECD has started to issue international guidelines for the taxation of electronic commerce. For further details see Katsushima (1998).

22   Retailers that are founded and that operate solely on-line (e-tailers) also face several managerial problems. However, this is not the main concern of this section. Obviously, some challenges faced by brick-and-mortar retailers do overlap with those of e-tailers. Moreover, we do not discuss advantages to brick-and-mortars at on-line startups.

23   See, for example, Alba et al. (1997), Mottl (2000) and Schwartz (2000).

24   It should be noted that the latter paper's coverage is any business including retailing. See also Dutta, Kwan and Segev (1998) for a study of sectoral and regional trends in business transformation in electronic commerce.

25   See, for example, Mottl (2000) for actual stories of transition.

26   Here we restrict ourselves to the analysis of brick-and-mortars for illustration purposes.

27   See, for example, Dick and Basu (1994) and Oliver (1999) for detailed discussion of the issue in real retailing environment.

Author Note

We are grateful to Peter Kooreman and Marco Haan for helpful comments and suggestions on an earlier draft. We alone are responsible for any errors.

CHAPTER EIGHT

M-Commerce: Mobile Electronic Commerce

Raymond R. Panko
University of Hawaii, USA

In the next few years, we are likely to see dramatically improved wireless communication technologies and small handheld access devices (HADs) such as Internet-enabled cellphones and personal digital assistants (PDAs). These converging trends open new possibilities for electronic commerce. These new possibilities often are discussed under the banner of m-commerce or mobile electronic commerce. This chapter looks at device trends, wireless communication trends, potential applications and potential problems in m-commerce.

INTRODUCTION

When people visit e-commerce sites or intranet servers today, they normally use desktop computers or notebook computers. Both machines are very large. Someone once suggested that the desktop computer received its name because it takes up your entire desktop. Notebook computers are smaller but still give travelers "jet lug." Neither has the convenience of a wallet or a purse.

Another problem for e-commerce and intranets is that most users need a wired connection, whether it is a telephone line, a digital subscriber line (DSL), a cable television system or a LAN. Although notebooks are physically portable, connecting them to networks is another matter. Notebook users usually have to find a telephone jack to connect to the Internet. When consumers want to buy and when intranet users want to reach their servers, they often have no way of doing so.

Handheld Access Devices (HADs)

Things are likely to change dramatically in the future, thanks to a trend known as m-commerce or mobile electronic commerce. This new form of e-commerce has two major thrusts. The first is the creation of new handheld access devices (HADs) that will be much smaller and simpler than today's PCs.

Today, the charge toward truly portable devices is being led by intelligent cellphones and by slightly larger personal digital assistants (PDAs) such as the Palm Pilot. However, in the future we will also see devices with new form factors (shapes and sizes). We will have clipboard HADs, HADs using our televisions as displays, wristwatch and bracelet HADs, wallet HADs, wearable HADs with eye screens and even automobile HADs with heads-up displays resembling those in fighter jets.

Future access devices, furthermore, should not be judged by the processing limitations of today's cellphones and PDAs. Moore's Law, which suggests that processing power for a given price doubles every 12 to 24 months, means that even HADs the sizes of cellphones and PDAs soon will be as powerful as today's desktop PCs.

At the same time, very fast processing speeds, large memories and bright displays require a great deal of electrical power. HAD designs will always have to balance capabilities against battery life. Still, as the speed of low-power components continues to increase, even HADs with considerable battery lives will reach the levels of today's desktop computers fairly soon.

One way to leverage the processing power of HADs is to use them as thin clients, putting most processing power on application servers. However, thin clients can place heavy burdens on network transmission systems. As discussed below, speed is growing but high-speed service is likely to be expensive, and radio frequency spectrum will continue to be somewhat limited, making its use for thin client support a policy issue.

Wireless Access

The other major thrust of m-commerce is wireless access, so that users will not need a physical access line to reach an e-commerce site or an intranet server. Internet access for cellphones and PDAs is already here, but speeds are limited, costs are high and there are incompatible competing services. Tomorrow's wireless access networks will be faster, more affordable and hopefully more standardized.

The Future Is Now

Although the idea of wireless devices that can connect us to e-commerce and intranets anytime and anywhere may sound futuristic, it is not. Cellphones are already very widespread. In 2000, the number cellphones in Japan exceeded the number of fixed telephones (Reuters, 2000). Cellphones will also pass the number of wired phones in other countries soon, especially in Europe. The Cahners In-Stat Group predicts that there will be a billion wireless phone users in 2002. Gartner believes that this number will be reached in 2003.

In addition, cellphones will be widely used for Internet access. Part of the reason for cellular's popularity in Japan is NTT's DoCoMo i-mode system for always-on Internet access. The Yankee group predicts that 30% of all cellphones sold in the US in 2000 will be Internet-capable. According to the International Data Corporation, almost *all* new cellphones will be Internet-capable in 2001, and by the end of 2002, there will be many more wireless devices accessing the Internet than wired PCs. Gartner believes that of the one billion wireless phones it forecasts for 2003, 600 million will be Web-enabled.

Quite simply, the cellular industry is fully committed to implementing Internet access in their phones, and this enormous mass of Internet-ready devices should drive content providers to serve the needs of these limited but very numerous devices.

Objectives

The first objective of this chapter is to explore how m-commerce may change e-commerce and intranets in the future. We will present examples of how m-commerce may change the very ways we see e-commerce and intranets.

The second objective is to explore the problems that m-commerce will have to overcome if it is to be successful. We will discuss potential issues in three areas: wireless networking, the user interface, security and fears about radiation.

The third objective is to discuss where ubiquitous computing may go over the next few years.

NEW POSSIBILITIES

Let us begin with a thought tour of how wireless handheld access devices (HADs) may change e-commerce and intranets.

General Web Access

Both e-commerce and intranets depend heavily on the World Wide Web. Obviously, Web access is nicest if you have a screen with a great deal of "real estate" for showing text and images. However, both cellphone and PDA access have shown that it is possible to get meaningful Web information on very small screens.

Web access is perfect for simple but valuable and often-accessed information, such as weather forecasts, sports scores and stock prices. It is also suitable for making purchases online, such as ordering a pizza on your way home. Within corporations, Web access may link HAD users to internal sites for making purchases, looking up information and other purposes.

Telephony

Today, cellular telephones are already widespread. Although there is a strong trend toward adding Web access and other tools to cellphones, it is also possible to upgrade all HADs (including PDAs) to provide telephone service. Telephony alone can justify a price of $100-$200.

Within our homes, our HAD could act as a cordless telephone connected to our home telephone line. We would not have to pay cellular charges while at home. At work, a wireless PBX could link us to the corporate site telephone network so that we could also use our HADs at work without cellular charges. Of course, once we leave our home or office building, our HAD would be a regular cellphone, and we would have to pay cellular charges.

Third-generation cellular systems (discussed later) are likely to offer videoconferencing as well as traditional voice service. It will be interesting to see if this becomes popular despite the failure of video telephone services in the past even when these services were offered for free. Of course, subscribers may simply want to receive television programs over the Internet the same way they now receive Internet radio stations.

Other General Tools
Electronic mail.

After Web service, the most popular Internet application is electronic mail. Some cellphones and PDAs already offer e-mail delivery. This includes both full Internet e-mail and the more limited short message service (SMS) resembling paging. Receiving e-mail is easy, but its usefulness is restricted by the small size of HAD screens. Sending messages can be a serious problem because of keyboarding difficulties.

Instant messaging services.

Instant messaging services inform you when someone on your "buddy list" is using the Internet. This knowledge allows you to send an instant message to the other person. They receive a notification sound and a notification icon to tell them that your message has arrived.

Instant messaging services also provide other services. For instance, you may be able to send the other party a file of any type, such as a word processing document or a spreadsheet file.

Location services.

Global Positioning System (GPS) receivers are now small enough to place in handheld computers. However, GPS receivers are still reasonably expensive for use in the highly price-sensitive HAD market. Cellphone companies in the United States, under FCC mandate, will soon be able to find the user's location within 400 feet, which is less precise than GPS but does not require a GPS receiver. In either case, location information will allow your HAD to display text directions to where you wish to go and perhaps even to display a map.

Radio/player services.

Today, many people carry radios and audio CD players with them. Multifunction handheld access devices could also act as radios. In fact, they could act as Internet radios, connecting to multicast streaming radio channels with particular types of music. Even streaming video will be possible as wireless speeds increase. Your handheld access device could also be a portable digital music player, playing

MP3 files and other music files stored digitally in your handheld device or retrieved on demand from your home or office library.

Games.

Handheld devices can act as stand-alone game machines. However, on the Internet, multi-person games allow you to interact with several of your closest friends and kill them (or engage in some other type of contest). Games on HADs will allow you to play multi-person games whenever you wish. In addition, you will be able to download both single-person and multi-person games on demand.

Interacting with M-Commerce Sites

For electronic sites, obviously we need Web access. We also need other things if the shopping experience is to go smoothly.

Electronic wallets.

One problem with today's e-commerce is the need to enter certain information each time you want to make a purchase, such as your name, your mailing address and your credit card information. New electronic wallet standards will allow you to store such information on your HAD and expose whatever information you wish to a specific Web site to reduce the number of keystrokes you need to make when placing orders.

Micropayment systems.

Credit card payments are fine for larger purchases. However, for small purchases of a few pennies, the overhead of paying transaction charges is prohibitive. Micropayment systems will allow small payments to be made with little transaction overhead. Micropayment software can be built into the HAD or downloaded as needed. In Europe, cellphones can be used already to make some vending machine purchases.

Interacting with Devices

We normally think of users as interacting with distant electronic commerce resources and corporate servers. However, we may find that m-commerce greatly improves our shopping experience when we enter traditional brick-and-mortar stores and when we interact with corporate resources that are within a few feet of us.

Nanoservers.

Web servers traditionally have been desktop PCs and larger computers. However, miniaturized Web server hardware and short-range radio transmission are becoming inexpensive. A Web server can be built for fewer than $5 today. Just as HADs give us access everywhere, tiny nanoservers may bring identity to everything.

A grocery shopping trip.

Suppose we look up recipes on the Internet and wish to try them. We would create an automatic shopping list and download the list to our HAD.

When we got to the store, an m-commerce nanoserver at the store entrance would read our shopping list and tell us as we walk down each isle which items we need to pick up on that isle. It could even alert us to special promotions on our items.

Now suppose that we come to the deli section. A local nanoserver could provide specialized information on that section, including items on sale, nutritional information, food preparation tips and so forth. We could read these on our HAD and even download this information for copying to our home PC for later reading.

At the cash register, our HAD would act as our credit or debit card. We could even check our account balance before and after checkout.

Even individual items will eventually get nanoservers or at least simple responders that allow us to query them and get back basic information. In the store, this information could be a universal product code for checkout, a downloadable coupon or promotional information to encourage people to buy the item.

For the home, product nanoservers could allow our "pantry server" to check constantly on the items it has in stock, including expiration dates. In addition, each item can give its own preparation instructions, as well as a coupon to encourage repeat buying.

Self-guided tours.

In many museums and cities, there are places of interest. Nanoservers in these locations could present information on our HAD as we pass by, giving us a self-guided tour. The tour could include voice, animation and even video for a richer presentation.

Come-hithers.

One can envision many other cases in which a store or item will advertise itself to attract attention. For instance, if we walk by a restaurant, a complete menu may be available for our HAD. Announcements could even tell us about special promotions and offer downloadable coupons.

Car diagnostics.

If our car is malfunctioning, our HAD might be able to download diagnostics data and even a diagnostics program. If we could not diagnose the problem ourselves, we could upload the data to the manufacturer for assessment.

Locks.

Within our corporate premises, our HAD could announce our presence as we approach, unlocking doors to which we have access before we reach them. It could even turn on lights in rooms as we approach.

Remote control.

Finally, our HADs could become what has arguably become the most important and fought-over device in many homes, the remote control for our television and VCR. With its intelligence, our HAD could download a full program schedule for rapid searching and even software so that we could program our VCR with a good user interface. We could perhaps even get the exact current time from the Internet to set the time on our VCR to something other than 12:00.

WIRELESS TRANSMISSION ISSUES

Although the future of handheld access devices is promising, they raise a number of issues that will need to be addressed before HADs can become widespread. For instance, it is obvious that HADs will require a wireless infrastructure to allow them to talk to the outside world.

Problems of Radio Transmission

Propagation problems.

Ubiquitous computing proponents talk about how liberating it will be to move from wires to radio. However, wire is a very good transmission medium. If you inject voltage changes into a copper wire pair or inject a light signal into an optical fiber, propagation after signal injection will be highly predictable.

In contrast, radio signals have some unpleasant propagation tendencies. If there is an object between you and the radio source, you may find yourself in a shadow zone in which you cannot receive its signal. In addition, signals bounce off objects, so you may find yourself with multipath interference, in which straight signals and bounced signals arrive at slightly different times and so interfere with one another.

Signal propagation problems depend heavily on frequency. As frequencies increase, for example, there tend to be more problems with shadow zones. In addition, rain attenuation can become a serious problem at higher frequencies. At the same time, the number of possible channels increases rapidly as frequency increases because of the way that frequency bands are defined.

For mobile users, there is a "golden band" of frequencies ranging from UHF frequencies (300 MHz to 3 GHz) to about 10 gigahertz. Within this golden band, there are quite a few possible channels and relatively good propagation characteristics. Around the world, there is a tendency to move non-mobile services out of the golden band, into higher frequency bands where propagation is more complex but where there are fairly good technical solutions for propagation problems between fixed transmitters and receivers.

Radio attenuation and cellular service.

With an omnidirectional (all-directional) antenna, such as those on cellphones, when a station transmits, a wave spreads out as a sphere around the antenna. The power of the transmission is spread over this sphere. As distance increases, the area of the sphere increases rapidly, and the signal strength at any position falls proportionally. Consequently, radio transmission follows an inverse cube rule in which power falls as the cube of the distance. For instance, if Station A is 10 times as far away from a transmitter as Station B, the signal will be 1,000 times higher at Station B.

To solve this problem of rapid attenuation, one could use a dish antenna, which effectively concentrates incoming and outgoing signals to make them stronger. However, few people would wish to carry a dish antenna around with them, and even if they did, they would not know where to point it.

Instead, cellular radio systems tend to be used to combat and even exploit rapid radio attenuation. With cellular service, which is not limited to cellular telephony, a region is divided into areas called cells. Stations only have to be strong enough to converse with the nearest cellsite transmitter and receiver (transceiver). This does not require a great deal of power, allowing us to build inexpensive devices with long battery lives.

In addition, because radio attenuation is so rapid, we can reuse a frequency channel in nonadjacent cells. In adjacent cells, signals at the same frequency may be strong enough to cause interference, but signals at the same frequency in nonadjacent cells will be too weak to interfere with one another, allowing them to use the same channel. As a broad rule of thumb, if you divide the number of cells by seven, this will give you the average number of times you can reuse each channel. For example, if you have 20 cells, you can reuse each channel an average of about three (20/7) times.

Inter-Device Communication: Bluetooth

It is tempting to think of HADs as interacting mostly with remote servers. However, there is a growing tendency of people to have multiple intelligent devices that need to communicate with one another. For instance, a HAD might need to synchronize its files with those of a desktop PC or notebook. To give another example, if a user wishes to print from a HAD, he or she would like to communicate wirelessly with a printer instead of hooking up cables. Also, while a cellphone may be a good way to contact a remote server, a user might wish the output to go— wirelessly—to a device with a larger screen, such as a PDA or a notebook computer. Finally, we will need a way to communicate with nanoservers (discussed earlier) at our location and even with the nearby HADs of other users.

For such needs, some mobile devices are being equipped with Bluetooth wireless transceivers. Bluetooth is a low-cost technology that is limited to a few devices within a very small area. It can be viewed as a personal area network, connecting the several devices we may carry with us in the future, as a desk area network that connects devices in our personal office or as a conference room network that allows a user's HADs to work with those of other participants or with a projector or printer in the room.

However, Bluetooth goes beyond simple connection service. The Bluetooth Alliance is also developing higher-level standards for message exchange, for the synchronization of files between a HAD and a desktop PC, and for other purposes.

Named for Harald Bluetooth, the 10th century Norse king who first unified Denmark and Norway, the Bluetooth technology hopes to unify communication between nearby intelligent devices. It will allow devices to work together regardless of what wireless LAN or metropolitan area network technology they use for longer-distance wireless networking.

Bluetooth can support up to 10 "piconets" in an area. Each piconet can have up to eight devices. This allows several people in an office area to use Bluetooth to link their devices together independently of one another.

Bluetooth is fairly slow, transferring data at only 721 kbps with a back channel of 56 kbps. On the positive side, it can support three simultaneous voice channels.

Although Bluetooth will be relatively inexpensive, inter-device communication can also be handled through infrared transmission—the same technology you use on your television's remote control. Infrared speeds tend to be even slower than Bluetooth speeds, but the reduced speed may be worth the reduced cost. Another longer-term possibility is to use human skin to carry signals between on-body devices. However, human skin capacitance changes when we touch large metal objects, changing propagation characteristics (Osborne, personal communication, August 2000). Wiring can also be woven into clothes. However, while there are many potential options, cellphone vendors appear to be committed to Bluetooth. If this commitment continues, Bluetooth should become dominant.

Wireless LANs: 802.11

Owners of HADs may use their devices within their office environments. In such cases, they may wish to access the company's intranet and electronic commerce sites via a wireless LAN.

For radio LANs, the IEEE LAN MAN Standards Committee's 802.11 Working Group has defined a series of radio LAN standards. These 802.11 LANs use a cellular approach. The LAN is broken into small areas, each of which is served by a device called an access point. The access point acts like a cellsite's transceiver. It controls all communication within its area. In addition, access points connect the HAD to the site's wired LAN, allowing wireless users to interact with wired LAN servers.

Initially, 802.11 radio LANs only operated at one to two megabits per second and were quite expensive. However, the 802.11 standard's speed has already been increased to 11 Mbps and should become even faster in the future.

In addition, prices are falling to attractive ranges. Wireless PC Card adapters for notebooks cost about $200 today, while access points cost about $1,000. Some companies now feel that by saving costs on wiring labor, 802.11 radio LANs can pay for themselves.[1] One potential problem is that both 802.11 and Bluetooth use the same frequency band (2.5 GHz) and probably will interfere with one another. So combining 802.11 for LAN use with Bluetooth for personal area networking may cause problems.

Metropolitan Area Wireless Networks (MANs)

Although Bluetooth has slightly confused the wireless LAN picture, we can create both large LANs and small personal area networks with fairly well standardized technologies in the forms of 802.11 and Bluetooth respectively.

Once we leave the customer premises, however, the standards situation becomes chaotic. Quite simply, there is no dominant standardized way to communicate with mobile devices within a city. We need to overcome this chaos and develop good standards for wireless metropolitan area networks (MANs) that serve a city and its suburbs.

The need for speed.

One problem with traditional wireless metropolitan area networking has been low speeds. Although this will change in the next few years, as discussed below, a typical cellular data transfer speed today is about 10 kbps rather than the megabit speeds enjoyed in wireless LANs.

However, although such low speeds are completely unsuitable for Web browsing with rich Web pages containing graphics, audio and other dense information, most early applications will use all-text documents with relatively low speed requirements. For example, consider a cellphone display with six lines of 20 characters each. Each character usually requires one byte (eight bits) of memory. The 120 characters on this screen, then, will require about 1,000 bits to be transmitted. Even at 10 kbps, it will only take a tenth of a second to send this screen. For PDA-size screens, the time to send the screen increases but is still brief.

Proprietary mobile services.

Most countries have proprietary low-speed radio services that have been in use for several years. The US, for instance, has Ardis and Mobitex RAM. Typically, these older services offer low kilobit speeds and are quite expensive. They tend to be used to link the traveling employees of a company. Given the high costs of these services, they are unlikely to be used for general HADs.

Cellphone transmission today.

The lowest-common-denominator default wireless service is cellular telephony itself. We can use our cellphone to surf the Web directly, or we can connect a HAD with a keyboard and larger display to our cellphone via Bluetooth to use the cellphone for transmission and the HAD for information display and input.

However, cellphone transmission speeds are slow. Wired modems can send and receive at 33.6 kbps, but cellular data service is slower because it must cope with the comparative unreliability of radio transmission.

Around the world, most cellular telephones follow the General System for Mobile communication (GSM) standard. GSM can send and receive data but only at the very low speed of 9.6 kbps. In addition, an adapter to connect a GSM phone to a notebook computer or HAD is quite expensive, sometimes costing almost as much as the cellphone itself.

In the United States, today's PCS systems usually can deliver data at speeds of about 10 kbps, again with a PC adapter. In addition, there is an older Cellular Digital Packet Data (CDPD) standard which allows systems to download data at 19.2 kbps but can only send data in very small chunks of about 150 characters, which is barely enough for mobile telephone needs. In addition, CDPD often allows little or no data uploading and is only available in some regions of the United States.

Higher speeds coming soon.

Tomorrow will be very different. Higher speeds are coming soon for GSM customers. The General Packet Radio Service (GPRS) standard is about to be implemented in some GSM systems around the world. GPRS will raise speeds to download to as much as 130 kbps (although most systems will only work more slowly) and will be an always-on technology that will allow access immediately when the user needs it. For the longer term, the Enhanced Data rates for Global Evolution (EDGE) standard should raise the download speed to as much as 384 kbps. For Web browsing, both speeds will be sufficient for sending visually rich Web pages. GPRS should be available as early as this year (2000). Edge will take another two or three years to appear and may be overtaken by even faster technology.

3G Wireless

Far higher speeds will become available in Japan as early as 2001 and in Europe a year later. Third-generation (3G) wireless systems will raise speeds to between 384 kbps and 2 Mbps. At such speeds, the gap between wireless HAD access and desktop access via cable modems and DSL will no longer be a serious issue. In Europe, a fairly generous 155 MHz of spectrum has been set aside for terrestrial 3G communication. Another 75 MHz has been allocated for high-speed satellite service. However, 3G standards are in flux today.

Fixed Wireless and Satellites

Although we have been talking about wireless communication in the context of mobile HADs, not all wireless networks will be useful for mobile devices. Some systems will require a dish antenna, which will not be practical to carry around. In the United States, for instance, there is a dish-based fixed wireless service based on the Multichannel Multipoint Distribution Service (MMDS) standard. Fixed wireless will allow up to 1.5 Mbps transmission downstream and 256 kbps upstream. Aimed at desktop PCs, it will compete with cable modems and DSLs. However, its dish will make it unsuitable for mobile HADs.

The satellite picture is very uncertain. Certainly, some satellite systems will use fixed dishes, but some may support omnidirectional antennas to allow HAD access.

USER INTERFACE ISSUES

A major application design issue for HADs will be the limited user interfaces of these devices. Although small size, light weight and low cost make HADs attractive for traveling users compared to notebooks, HADs lack the "real estate" to allow large screens and rich input devices such as full keyboards and mice. They also lack powerful microprocessors and the ample memory that even the smallest notebook computers enjoy.

Several approaches hold promise for making limited devices easier to use. In all cases, however, it is important to realize that the HAD market is highly price-sensitive. While desktop and notebook computers typically cost $1,000 to $3,000, intelligent cellphones tend to cost $100 to $200, and $500 is a key price point for PDAs. Good ideas that cost too much are not likely to be adopted rapidly.

Processor, Memory and Battery Limitations

As just noted, HADs today use slow microprocessors and have limited RAM. They have no hard disk drive at all. This means that applications must be kept small. It also means that security and network functions must be limited. As noted later, the Wireless Application Protocol (WAP) specifies modified "lightweight" protocols for network transmission and security.

On the other hand, microprocessor power and RAM density are increasing rapidly. As noted earlier, HADs soon will have as much processing power as today's full-size machines, and even in two years, they will be much more powerful than they are now. When we look at the processing power of today's cellphones, pagers and PDAs, we should not imagine that tomorrow's HADs, even within these categories, will be similarly underpowered, even with requirements to sacrifice some speed and memory for longer battery life.

Output Limitations and WAP

Even PDAs have small screens. Intelligent cellphones have even smaller screens that can only show a few lines with a few characters per line. Somehow, HAD output technology must live with these restrictions.

The Wireless Application Protocol (WAP).

Most cellphone vendors are now in agreement about how to attack the problem of tiny screen size. They have developed a family of standards called the Wireless Application Protocol (WAP) through the Wireless Application Protocol Forum.

WAP gateways.

When you use the Internet today, your browser or e-mail program talks directly to a server host. WAP uses a different architecture. Your HAD actually communicates directly with a WAP "gateway host." The gateway then communicates with Web servers and other server hosts on your behalf.

For example, when you transmit a request to download a Web page, that request first goes to your WAP gateway server using WAP-based HAD-gateway transmission protocols that operate over the Internet but that are much simpler than TCP. The gateway then communicates with the Web server via normal Internet and World Wide Web protocols, sending the request and getting a response. The gateway then encodes the Web page it received from the Web server to reduce the number of bits to be transmitted and sends the page to the HAD via WAP protocols.

WAP protocols typically use IP or UDP to deliver WAP protocol messages. This allows WAP to function over the Internet. Instead of using TCP at the transport layer, however, WAP uses the Wireless Transaction Protocol, which has less overhead than TCP because it dispenses with functionality that is not needed in wireless environments. WAP also adds a session-layer protocol, the Wireless Session Protocol, to maintain sessions between the HAD and the gateway if there are interruptions. While TCP must reestablish connections from scratch, WSP can simply resume the connection at the point at which it was suspended. At the application layer, information is compressed to handle the low bandwidths of many wireless connections.

Gateways can reduce memory and processing requirements. For instance, a WAP gateway can store your World Wide Web bookmarks file, your e-mail address book, cached Web pages you have visited recently and even your electronic wallet.

Wireless Markup Language (WML).

Full Web pages with graphics and other visual elements cannot fit on a cellphone screen or even a PDA screen. The very richness that has made HTML so attractive on full-size computers makes it unsuitable for HADs.

The WAP Forum responded to this problem by creating the Wireless Markup Language (WML) to be used in place of HTML. WML, a document type within XML, can format text information to fit nicely on a small screen.

A card deck metaphor.

HTML uses a Web-page-with-links metaphor. This is useful in computers with mice, but many PDAs will not have mice. Without a mouse or another pointing device, clicking on a link is very difficult.

In addition, although Web pages resize themselves automatically to a screen's width, a page with frames will not do so or will have frames so small that they are useless. In addition, although pages can become narrower to fit on screens, having to cursor up and down through correspondingly longer pages can be very daunting.

Instead, WML uses a card deck metaphor. Each screen is a single card in a larger deck. Hitting a button will take the user to another card in the deck or will take the user to another deck. In most cases, the user will simply go to the next or previous card in the deck. The card deck metaphor works even with the few buttons on an intelligent cellphone or PDA.

Creating WML pages and WML portals.

How will WML pages be created? One approach is simply to rewrite Web sites in WML. For many Web sites, this certainly will be a problem. However, many sites will wish to cater to the HAD market. To gain strong presence in this market, recoding in WML or even coding in WML exclusively will make sense.

We are even seeing the rise of WML portal sites designed for HAD users using WML. These portals give the user access to numerous WML Web sites. They even offer customization so that the most common choices for a particular user come up first, in order to reduce scrolling and keystrokes.

Another possibility is for the WAP gateway to translate HTML programs automatically into WML. Obviously, something will always be lost in translation, especially for graphics-oriented sites. It remains to be seen whether translation will prove effective.

Yet another possibility is the use of eXtensible Style Sheets (XSSs) when creating Web pages and even entire Web sites. XSSs separate content from formatting. It might simply be possible to create two style sheets, one for HTML and one for WML. The content and the XSS style sheet would then be sent to HADs (or to the gateway server, which would handle the formatting.) Again, however, the issue will be the acceptability of content loss during the formatting.

WMLScript.

Web pages often use scripting languages to automate functions through scripting applets (small applications). WAP offers WMLScript, which can do such things as control access to the user's telephone functions based on simple user commands that execute complex scripts.

Proprietary services.

Although WAP-enabled HADs are likely to dominate the market for devices with very small screens in the future, most of the first Internet-enabled cellphones have used proprietary technologies that limit you to a few Web sites today and that will not be able to talk to WML Web sites in the future. These proprietary systems may create serious convergence problems and market dissatisfaction.

Larger displays.

Although WML may be a necessary solution for some very small HADs such as cellphones, even PDAs have more screen area, and we may see the rise of devices with slightly larger form factors such as electronic books.

We may even see radically new screen technology. For instance, the experimental Toshiba DynaSheet technology uses a display that looks like a full-size sheet of paper. It is only one centimeter thick, weighs only 200 grams and can be rolled up when not in use.

For some users, there will even be eyeglass screens that project images directly into your eyes. The images produced this way can appear to be very large, for example appearing to be roughly twice the diagonal size of a television at a distance of six feet. Eyeglass screens can cover both eyes, or images can be projected into a single eye to leave some external vision. Of course, such screens disrupt vision and look weird to many people. They can also cause motion sickness if you are in a moving vehicle while wearing one. Most importantly, they are very expensive. While a device with television resolution costs "only" about $500, a device with computer resolution costs about $2,500. These prices will fall, of course, but in the highly price-sensitive market for HADs, they are likely to remain prohibitively expensive for general use for some time to come.

With such technologies, the cramped screens that drive WML will disappear from at least some of the HAD market. Full HTML pages may become the norm in a few years. In other words, WML may be mostly a transition tool, although it is likely to remain important for the smallest HADs such as cellphones.

Voice output.

Another option is to use voice output, that is, to have the HAD read aloud what is on the screen. Although this may make sense for some applications, reading a menu visually is much faster than listening to each of the choices being read aloud.

Input Limitations

While the small screen sizes of HADs create difficulties for application designers, input is also a problem. Although some HADs may have at least optional keyboards, full keyboards cannot be assumed by designers.

The need for simplicity.

Most cellphones will have only a few keys, and many PDAs will have even fewer keys. This radical simplicity can be very attractive for users who are not highly computer literate and do not wish to learn new information entry skills. In addition, people often are in busy situations when they use these devices, so it is important to keep the load on working memory to a minimum.

At the same time, not all users will be satisfied with radical simplicity and will wish for better ways to input information. The idea that people will use their HADs only a few minutes a day for simple tasks may not fit the realities of use in the future.

Key acceleration.

For intelligent cellphones, hitting numeric keys can give slow alphanumeric input, with each key representing three characters. With intelligence, the user can simply hit the keys without hitting shift keys to indicate which of the three characters is meant by each keystroke. After a few keystrokes, the system usually can guess the correct word.

Stylus input.

Another approach is to use a stylus for input. With styluses, users can point to things on the screen, enter text with printing or handwriting, and so forth. It is even possible to have a keyboard image pop up on the display so that the user can tap on individual keys. Unfortunately, stylus text entry creates many errors. More fundamentally, while styluses are useful for PDAs, how many people will be willing to carry around a cellphone with a stylus?

Voice input.

Voice input is also a possibility, especially in an environment where a user's hands may be busy. The intelligence to recognize a command from a very small repertoire of commands is not too daunting. With voice input, it will be possible to address specific objects on a screen, using commands such as "Next link" and then "Select." Given the small number of possible commands, voice input should be possible even in noisy environments. However, voice input sacrifices privacy, and constant mumbling could cause bystanders, who are already tired of loud cellphone conversations, to think badly of the HAD user.

The next big thing.

Perhaps some radically new entry method will emerge. The appearance of interactive terminal–host systems in the 1960s have risen to a flood of new input devices, including the mouse.[2]

SECURITY ISSUES

Security in WAP

In electronic commerce, almost all credit card transactions and other sensitive transactions are protected by the secure sockets layer (SSL) standard, which gives confidentiality, authentication and message integrity. Created by Netscape, SSL is now under the control of the Internet Engineering Task Force, which has changed its name to Transaction Layer Security (TLS).

WAP has modified SSL/TLS to work under the constraints of wireless HADs. It has called this version of TLS the Wireless Transaction Layer Standard. WTLS is almost as strong as full TLS and should provide excellent security between HADs and WAP gateway servers.

Note, however, that the Wireless Transaction Layer Security protocol only provides protection *between* the HAD and the WAP gateway server. It does not by itself provide end-to-end security including the link between the WAP gateway server and the Web server.

HAD Theft and Loss

Another security threat is the theft or loss of HADs. In 1999, 319,000 notebook computers in the United States were stolen, according to Safeware (Jailumar, 2000). This does not even count the accidental loss of notebook computers. Hand-held Access Devices, being much smaller, will be far easier to steal or lose.

The loss of a HAD through theft or neglect can have serious implications. These devices may contain stored passwords that will allow thieves to make transactions in the device owner's name or access sensitive corporate data. They may even contain sensitive corporate data in their memories.

It is important to make HADs useless to thieves or finders. One way to do this is to protect them with good passwords, that is, passwords that are too short or that are common words. Another is to encrypt files to make them unreadable even if passwords are compromised. However, encryption guarded by a weak password will provide little protection.

Such protections must be mandated by corporate policy, and such policies must be enforced through auditing and sanctions against violators. Policies must also be supported by the devices themselves. One popular Sprint PCS cellphone does not even disguise password keystrokes by putting asterisks or other characters in place of the password characters because its makers feel that it is too easy to make a typing error if the user cannot see the characters of the password (Hamblin, 2000)

HAD-Enabled Data Theft

Another security concern associated with HADs is that they may be used as tools to commit data theft. The location of HADs may be impossible to determine, allowing attackers to launch exploits from positions of anonymity.

In addition, HADs can be carried into sensitive areas, allowing outside thieves or employees without authorization to download confidential data. Synchronization tools will be very common, so downloading data will not even seem unusual to onlookers. In fact, wireless downloading may not even be visible because the HAD can be kept in the thief's pocket or briefcase most of the time.

Increased Security in Some Cases

Although HADs represent formidable security threats, HADs actually may increase security under some conditions. In hospitals, for instance, keeping a PC in each patient's room might allow an intruder to get access to highly sensitive patient data. If HADs were used instead, they would not be left in patient's room when they are not needed there (Robinson, 1998)

Radiation

One concern of HAD users is the amount of radiation that cellphones and other small devices give off when they transmit. There is growing fear that small transceivers may cause cancer or other brain damage. Certainly, judging from driving performance, people who use cellphones while driving appear to suffer at least temporary brain damage. Cellphone users also appear to suffer hearing impairments, judging from the way they shout into their cellphones in coffee houses and other public places. However, these problems may be unrelated to radiation.

THE FUTURE

The enormous cellphone explosion taking place around the world, especially in Europe and Asia, makes the cellphone the logical entry point for ubiquitous computing in e-commerce and internal intranet resources. Nearly every cellphone soon will be equipped with WAP technology or, in some cases, a proprietary technology. Given this enormous potential market, there should soon be a critical mass of portal sites for users with tiny screens and small keyboards. PDAs represent a smaller market, and their vendors seem to be more interested in proprietary solutions, but if many WAP portals appear, that should change.

A bigger issue is what technologies will be used for wireless networking. Given the critical mass of cellphone users, the obvious first step will be regular cellular telephony. For tiny text screens, the slow data transmission speed of today's cellphone networks will not be a serious impediment.

However, today's tiny displays and low transmission speeds should not blind us to how rapidly the pace of HAD processing and input/output technology will grow, driving us to providing ever richer content requiring higher transmission speeds. GPRS, EDGE and 3G wireless technologies will be implemented aggressively in Europe and Asia, giving the speed needed for larger displays and graphics. Although the cellphone will continue to remain small, HADs that are more powerful will be able to have full Web browsers, e-mail clients and other PC-like capabilities. Whether WAP will become only a niche technology for cellphones will be an enormous question for content developers.

Within the issue of HAD design is whether we will have a single HAD with many capabilities or several HADs linked together with Bluetooth wireless technology so that they effectively serve as a single device.

Wireless technology and security issues will be more complex. Quite simply, there are too many wireless alternatives, and if we have to build separate products for each, prices will remain high, and the market may be frozen as it waits for the situation to settle down. In addition, corporations and consumers are becoming ever more aware of security threats, and if HAD vendors do not respond adequately, security may seriously retard the growth of wireless HADs.

Another problem for HADs may be support. Just as millions of PCs came into corporations through the back door in the 1980s, hundreds of millions of HADs are arriving, and their owners, despite their fierce independence, are demanding service from corporate help desks. For intranet access, companies will have to install a new support infrastructure to keep HAD access healthy.

We did not consider operating systems or programming languages in this chapter because the picture is so murky. Palm OS, Windows CE, LINUX and other operating systems will compete for market share, and Java will battle with other programming languages and scripting languages for application development. However, while these issues are important for manufacturers, e-mail, Web browsing and other Internet applications are standards-based, so a PDA's operating system and programming language(s) are only important to the extent they compromise the user's ability to run other software.

For nanoservers, we will need a large number of new standards, including a local public announcement protocol that will allow a nanoserver to indicate its availability and purpose. In general, we need many new standards for local HAD-to-device communication at all standards layers.

Today, we have a telephone number (probably several), an e-mail address, a home page URL and other things that identify us and allow others to reach us. HADs could add to this complexity. On the other hand, a HAD that handled both our telephony and our e-mail could lead to the creation of a single identification number for all our activities or at least to the routing of information from multiple identity numbers to a single in-box for integrated handling.

A final issue is whether HADs will finally break America's lead in e-commerce and intranet technology. Instead of standardizing on GSM, the United States adopted an open technology regulatory system for cellphones. This has led to the fragmentation of the market with three different technologies—GSM, CDMA and TDMA—with GSM having a small part of the market. As a consequence, the US is not well poised to jump to GPRS as is the rest of the world. Unless the US jumps quickly into 3G technology, it may be left far behind as HADs outgrow their cellphone–PDA heritage. While European and Asian countries are moving aggressively into higher-speed wireless technology, most US carriers are saying that there is no need for higher speeds.

References

Hamblin, M. (2000, April 24). How to keep your handheld from falling into the wrong hands. *Computerworld,* [On-line] http://cnn.com/2000/TECH/computing/04/24/pdadisaster.idg/index.html.

Reuters, (2000, April 7). Cell phones rule in Japan. [On-line] http://cnnfn.com/2000/04/07/asia/wires/japan_phones/wg/.

Robinson, T. (1998, August 24). Wireless LANs: Just what the doctor ordered. *Internet Week*, [On-line] http://www.internetwk.com/trends/trends/trends082498.html.

Vijayan, J. (2000, April 25). Stolen laptop prompts calls for internal review. *Computerworld*, [On-line] http://www.nwfusion.com/news/2000/0425stolentop.html.

End Notes

1. In Europe, there is some interest in a competing wireless LAN standard, HiperLAN2, which offers quality of service guarantees. However, as the Ethernet-versus-ATM competition has shown, QoS is attractive only if capacity is marginal. In addition, rising volume has already begun to reduce 802.11 prices, while HiperLAN2 products will be high in price.
2. Although the mouse often is viewed as a new innovation, Doug Engelbart envisioned the mouse in 1962 and two years later built the first mouse as part of NLS, which implemented hypertext, including links that caused the reader to jump to another paragraph in another document on another machine.

Additional Reading

A good source for information about Bluetooth is http://www.Bluetooth.com.

Rysavy, P. (1999, October). Broadband wireless: Now playing at select locations. *Data Communications*, 73-82. This source gives a comparison of several wireless standards.

Saunders, S., Heywood, P., Dornan, A., Bruno, L., and Allen, L. (2000, January). Wireless IP: Ready or not, here it comes. *Data Communications*, 48-68 . This is a good source of general information on wireless technology and standards.

Agarwal, A. (1999, August). Raw computation. *Scientific American*, 60-63. This paper describes reconfigurable computers.

CHAPTER NINE

ERP + E-Business = A New Vision of Enterprise System

Betty Wang and Fui Hoon (Fiona) Nah
University of Nebraska-Lincoln, USA

INTRODUCTION

Companies have invested billions of dollars collectively in enterprise resource planning (ERP) systems with the objective of attaining an important business promise — complete enterprise integration. For companies faced with incompatible information systems and inconsistent operating practices, ERP has been a dream come true. ERP presents companies with the opportunity to standardize and automate business processes throughout the organizations, thus increasing productivity and reducing cycle time.

Although ERP systems have delivered value, it is becoming clear that the ERP model, which wraps organizational processes into one end-to-end application, may no longer be sufficient for today's fast-moving, extended enterprises. With the rapid growth of the Internet, the business environment has changed dramatically. The world has become a global marketplace. According to Gartner Group, the worldwide business-to-business (B2B) market is forecasted to grow from 145 billion in 1999 to 7.29 trillion in 2004 (King, 2000).

E-business has changed the definition of enterprise systems. Beyond the core business functions that ERP has traditionally focused on, e-business pushes the ERP from the inside core of the companies to the network edge. Companies are realizing that the most challenging part of e-business initiatives is not in developing a Web storefront but in extending ERP to accomplish business-to-business (B2B) and business-to-consumer (B2C) solutions. A new extended enterprise system emerges by integrating ERP with e-business, which creates business that is more agile, more focused and more competitive than traditionally structured business and tight B2B connections. With the help of the componentization concept, a seamless, end-to-end flow of information and process across the value chain of companies becomes realistic.

ERP AND E-BUSINESS

ERP is a structured approach to optimizing a company's internal value chain. The software, if implemented fully across an entire enterprise, connects the various components of the enterprise through a logical transmission and sharing of data (Norris et al., 2000, pp.12-13). When customers and suppliers request information that have been fully integrated throughout the value chain or when executives require integrated strategies and tactics in areas such as manufacturing, inventory, procurement and accounting, ERP systems collate the data for analysis and transform the data into useful information that companies can use to support business decision-making. ERP systems, if implemented successfully, enhance and redesign business processes to eliminate non-value-added activities and allow companies to focus on core and truly value-added activities. The following are two examples where ERP systems have dramatically increased the efficiency and productivity of companies: IBM has used ERP to reduce the processing time for updating pricing data from 80 days to five minutes and Chevron has used ERP to decrease its annual purchasing cost by 15%.

E-business stands for "electronic business," which involves communications and doing business electronically through the Internet. E-business is defined as "the use of electronically enabled communication networks that allow business enterprises to transmit and receive information" (Fellenstein and Wood, 2000). It can significantly improve business performance by strengthening the linkages in the value chain between businesses (B2B) and consumers (B2C). Besides increasing efficiency in selling, marketing and purchasing, e-business achieves effectiveness through improved customer service, reduced costs and streamlined business processes. Furthermore, e-business creates a strategic, customer-focused business environment for shared business improvements, mutual benefits and joint rewards. Companies use the Internet to implement customer-relation-management (CRM) and supply-chain-management (SCM) capabilities, which enable them to link their operations seamlessly with customers and suppliers. For example:

Nantucket Nectars, a juice manufacturer with 40% growth and $70 million in annual sales revenue, sells its organic juices through 150 distributors nationwide as well as general stores and juice bars in Nantucket. By using Oracle's ERP system and e-business platform, the salespersons can track sales and promotions through the Internet, and are provided assistance and suggestions to enhance their performance. The salespersons and distributors have access to commission reports, and they can track and adjust sales orders. Through consolidating its financial, compensation, sales and depletion data into a single report, Nantucket prevents out-of-stock and partial shipments. The forecasted need for 50% more labor force to handle customer service issues in the past was eradicated by integrating ERP system with e-business (Oracle, 2000).

By definitions and by their respective functions, traditional ERP systems take care of internal value chain (i.e., within a company) whereas e-businesses establish the value chain across the market and the industries. More and more companies construct their systems' architectures by integrating ERP systems with e-business. They use Web-based interface (corporate portals) with outside entities plus add-on modules such as CRM, SCM, etc. in the integration.

E-BUSINESS PUSHES ERP
TO THE NETWORK EDGE

In a traditional business process, after a customer order is received, the order information flows from department to department through order entry, manufacturing, warehousing, distribution and finance until the product is delivered to the customer and the payment is received. The key elements of the value chain have been controlled by separate and disparate information systems that could not communicate with one another. Not only did the companies not take an integrated view of their own business processes, but they also had an equally vague understanding of how their systems relate to the systems of their suppliers, competitors, business partners, distributors and customers. Hence, these transactions are typically carried out with minimal or no shared business processes.

In recent years, there has been a revolution in systems planning and design. Management takes an integrated company-wide view of its IT investments and choices, and implements an ERP system that integrates the core business processes of an entire company into a single software and hardware system. Customers, suppliers and business partners are consciously included in the business process, systems operation and systems development.

An ERP system is analogous to the internal technological hub of a company. When fully implemented as an integrated suite, it can be thought of as a company's

Figure 1: ERP system with five major processes

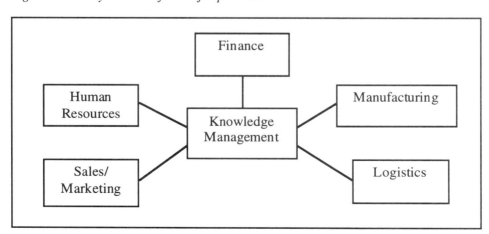

central repository. The five major processes in a typical ERP system are: finance, logistics, manufacturing, human resources and sales/marketing (refer to Figure 1). The focus of ERP systems is on the efficiency and effectiveness of the internal process. It offers a way to streamline and align business processes, increase operational efficiencies and bring order out of chaos.

E-business is focused on efficiency and effectiveness of external, cross-enterprise processes. While ERP technology supports business strategy, e-business opens the door to new strategic opportunities, which forces ERP to take one step further — to move from the single ERP system model to the extended ERP system model (refer to Figure 2). The Web technology provides the bridge between companies and their business partners to make e-business possible, while e-business makes the ERP system more transparent and outward. Instead of thinking about ERP within a company, we may view the ERP system along the value chain of companies in the same industry, or across industries. Companies are now turning their attention outward to engage in business with customers, suppliers and business partners through the use of the Internet and Web-based technologies. ERP functionality has to move onto the Web because that is where most of the core business processes are being carried out. The earlier example on the flow of a customer order and the steps in the process flow across the boundaries of the companies would now be handled by a number of different companies behaving as if they are one.

If a corporation decentralizes autonomous business units, they need to be able to access and share data between departments, managers and employees. With ERP systems, a transaction only needs to be entered once. The system can process the transaction across different software modules, resulting in highly comprehensive and integrated information that can be used for decision-making. While an ERP

Figure 2: Single versus extended ERP system

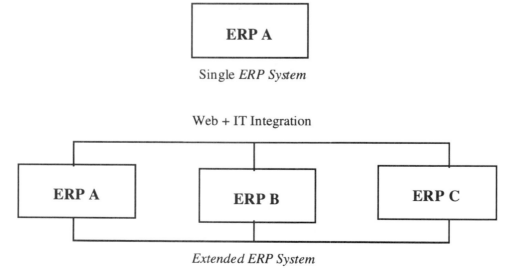

Single *ERP System*

Web + IT Integration

Extended ERP System

system can be viewed as a repository for data, information and knowledge, and it extends beyond functional boundaries by redefining enterprise wide processes, a Web-enabled ERP system forces companies to look at processes that span multiple enterprises (refer to Figure 3).

When e-business is integrated with ERP, the whole extended system provides a vision of business processes that span multiple businesses and enterprises. In the most ideal case, companies should be able to connect disparate platforms, applications and data formats across the value chain, including not only suppliers, but also customers as well. Furthermore, companies should retain the flexibility to change and add functions to applications as business needs evolve. Companies need to be able to adapt their ERP systems to the emerging world of e-business (refer to Figure 3).

ERP SOLIDIFIES THE FOUNDATION FOR E-BUSINESS

In a recent survey by *Information Week*, 66% of IT managers viewed ERP as their most important and strategic platform because it provides a solid foundation and information backbone for e-business. When ERP and e-business are properly implemented, they supercharge each other. E-business is the best vehicle to share business information with partners for creating major B2B synergies (Norris et al., 2000, p. 93). A fully integrated ERP system will capture and create accurate, consistent and timely relevant data, and assist in intelligent business decision-making. The impact of ERP/e-business integration is substantial, ranging from reduced inventory and personnel level to improved order and cash management. It also results in improved customer responsiveness, reduced IT costs and the availability of resources for value-added activities. The following case is an

Figure 3: ERP integration with e-business

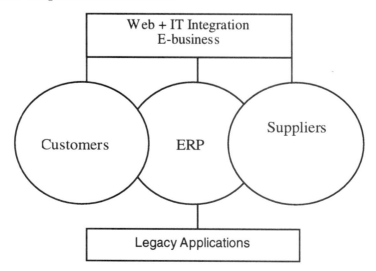

example where the full integration of ERP with e-business and SCM led to successful business (Sun, 1999; Whiting, 1999):

Colgate Palmolive Company, with $9 billion in consumer products business, has five regional divisions in North America, South America, Europe, Asia/Pacific and South Africa. The implementation of SAP R/3 in 1993 helped Colgate reduce its finished inventory by 50% and cut order receipt-to-delivery time for its top 50 customers from 12e to five days.

Because of its tremendous increase in international sales and the constantly changing manufacturing/distribution model, Colgate integrated its SCM-called supply network planning with its e-business platform from Sun Microsystems to leverage its existing ERP in early 1998. This supply network planning system together with the vendor-managed inventory (VMI) software helped Colgate-Palmolive manage its inventory at customer sites (such as Kmart distribution locations). By mid-1999, Colgate implemented the Web-enabled supply network planning modules in all of its North America manufacturing and distribution facilities. The VMI software was installed at about 70% of the customer facilities, which accounts for half of the company's sales volume. In the later part of 1999, Colgate implemented the production planning, detailed scheduling and demand planning of supply network modules, and integrated them with SAP sales and service applications and business information warehouse software.

Colgate is seeing a clear payoff on improved service to customers and suppliers. Since it achieved manufacturing efficiencies from ERP/e-business, the company has been having single-digit growth on sales revenues and double-digit growth on net income every year (Colgate, 2000). Now, the company is counting on its ERP/e-business to further the operating efficiencies.

The companies that have successfully implemented ERP systems will become the masters in helping other suppliers to integrate ERP and e-business to create a Web-based extended ERP environment. A well-run Web-enabled ERP system will make the entire value chain very powerful. Examples of successful cases include Sun, IBM, Compaq, Intel and Cisco in the high-tech industry; CitiGroup, Bank of America and Charles Schwab in the financial services; and Amazon.com in the retail industry.

A NEW VISION OF ENTERPRISE = ERP + E-BUSINESS

Although ERP integrates core business functions such as logistics, finance, human resources and sales-order administration, there are still many business processes that ERP cannot address. ERP falls short of meeting today's demands from customers for better services. With Web-based technology, information can move swiftly through the value chain, making companies anxious to add functionality to implement specialized applications that can meet their needs.

Componentization

The Butler Group, a British IT consultancy group, indicates it has seen a backslash against the inadequacies of monolithic application packages and argues that techniques to integrate applications can lead to better solutions without the stranglehold of inflexible functionality (Economist, 1999, p.32). The key question is how to continue adding new functionality rapidly at low cost while making it easier for organizations to implement and upgrade to a platform appropriate for e-business. The ERP vendors and customers are relatively quick to recognize the benefits of componentization.

Before e-business was taken into consideration, most of the ERP systems that have been implemented were delivered as monolithic code and did not employ the componentization concept. Barricaded behind complex, proprietary Application Program Interfaces (APIs) and based on complex, nearly indecipherable relational database schemas, ERP systems do not readily extend to e-business. With the popularity and widespread practice of the object-oriented approach, component-based techniques become essential quality requirements.

Componentization is the action of breaking up a large, monolithic ERP system into individual modules that would work together. Components are pieces of code that can be interchanged between applications. This idea is similar to the assembly of automobiles, airplanes and mobile phones. They are combined from parts that work together within an architecture. The parts are not a homogeneous set, but comprise many different types and standards. According to Sprott (2000, p.65), a component can be any form of implementation, provided it adheres to the concepts of separation, interfacing and standardization. Most ERP vendors are converting their ERP systems to a component-based architecture. When ERP is componentized, the internal functions performed by the system are represented using object-oriented blocks of code that can be used to create new applications (Callaway, 2000, p.116). The componentization of functionalities in ERP will make the internal and external systems more adaptable and reliable. Therefore, it will smooth the information flow along the value chain.

Based on the object-oriented concept, each functionality of ERP can be viewed as a separate encapsulated entity and treated as a component. By virtue of the independence of components, it is easier to manage, upgrade and modify a component-based ERP system. Granularity, scope boundaries and internal cohesion are important attributes of a component. A fine-grained component will be simple to upgrade because it involves fewer relationships but requires more management since there is likely to be many more parts needed to meet the requirement. In contrast, a larger component may be easier to manage but would require more effort to modify and implement because the scope of the functionality is much broader and the impact of changes is much greater. Since the components encapsulate individual business processes that other components can freely access, companies can more precisely control individual business processes. This divide-and-conquer approach allows the companies to do rapid concurrent development (Erlikh, 2000, p.17). Componentization breaks large-scale business processes into self-contained units of manageable size and makes it easier to deploy ERP systems in an e-business environment.

ERP and e-business applications can be assembled from Web-based components such as Online Analytical Processing (OLAP) components, batch components, application components and database components. A company implementing an ERP system would be able to select different modules or components from multiple vendors instead of picking a single vendor. Since an ERP system can be broken down into components by functionalities, the vendors would be able to quickly fix or add functionality to ERP systems. An individual component of ERP can be enhanced without affecting any other functional components. IBM research shows that only 20% of companies use a single ERP vendor. Almost 80% of companies use multiple vendors (IBM, 1999).

Using the Internet-enabled ERP as a foundation, componentization delivers one or more services. The service is the function that the component provides to the user (another server or client). As indicated by Sprott (2000, p.65),

> A service might therefore be something very simple such as a LOOK UP SYNONYMS service provided by a Thesaurus component, or as comprehensive as UPDATE NEW CUSTOMER INFORMATION service provided by a Customer Relationship Management (CRM) application. A series of services provided by multiple disparate components might be integrated into a common workflow that performs a unified business purpose.

It is very important that the interface and service provided are independent of the underlying implementation. For example, an implementation of ERP may be provided by a legacy database. With componentization, the legacy database can be replaced by an object-oriented database with no effect on the user of the service, provided the interface remains unchanged.

Flexible Customization

ERP vendors will come under considerably increasing pressure as they are forced to open up their products and to market components separately before the ERP market becomes saturated. It is becoming increasingly popular for components to be assembled by customers since companies need flexible ERP systems where new applications can be added fairly quickly and business intelligence can be extracted to fit into B2B and B2C solutions. The successful ERP vendors are beginning to provide customers with flexible and economical operational infrastructure that easily integrate with open market components. These vendors allow customers to exercise considerable choice in procurement to create customized solutions from readily and widely available building blocks.

A major advantage of component-based ERP is the incremental release and upgrade process. This is a benefit in the initial implementation as well as ongoing enhancement. Many ERP vendors and existing customers underwent considerable upgrade pain before they could achieve this result. The realities of upgrading are also not as simple as one might think. A complete integration test should be undertaken because of the high levels of interdependence between the components. The ultimate goal is to develop ERP components that are compatible with one another and that can be easily integrated with e-business and other applications.

COMMON ERP/E-BUSINESS PLATFORM (ORACLE & SAP)

Today, customers expect more than ever before. To meet these expectations, companies need to reach out and bring customers closer to their information systems and have them engage in product configuration, selection and Internet self-service (*Economist*, 1999, p.32). Also, it is essential for the vendors to set up a compatible e-business platform for system integration. Some major ERP vendors launched their Web-enabled ERP in the early part of the year 2000 to create the B2B and B2C solutions. Both Oracle and SAP set up Internet portal (hub) and use eXtensible Markup Language (XML) to manipulate data from internal ERP and push information flow across the value chain (refer to Figure 4).

The portal (hub) technology could provide the necessary access, while adding a variety of new features and capabilities for the users. XML is a meta-language for describing data so it can be interpreted in a more intelligent way. XML is designed

Figure 4: Extending ERP along the value chain

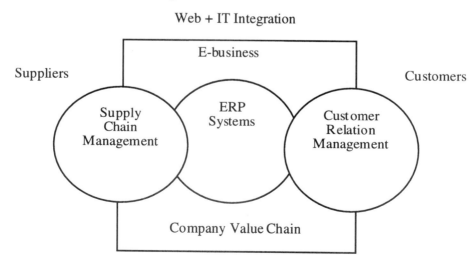

Web + IT Integration

to provide structured to semi-structured or unstructured data, the kinds of data that abound on Internet and e-business settings (PriceWaterhouseCoopers, 1999). XML uses a native Web approach that enables extensible data-exchange formats and provides the flexibility to create one's own data tags to develop a shared Internet file system (Fingar et al., 2000, p.253). XML revolutionizes the Web since it allows structured data—with standard names and consistent semantics—to be moved around the Web in a simple and straightforward way, as easily as HTML does today.

Oracle (Oracle, 2000)

Oracle, the number one player in ERP, and the dominant supplier of relational database to the Windows NT and Unix market, became a leading independent software company worldwide. Oracle's Internet Platform provides a comprehensive solution for ERP integration. Based on the popular hub-spoke-adapter architecture, Oracle uses XML to extract information from legacy and ERP applications. The information will be renderable through "Portlets" on the desired site (refer to Figure 5).

Its e-business (WebDB) platforms have the following functions:

- *Reduce complexity from interlinked applications and packages*
  The change in business requirements over the years has inextricably linked applications in a confusing tangle of connections across departments and business segments. However, no company can scrap its entire IT infrastructure and begin jam scratch again. Therefore, the portal platform has been used to provide better employee access to tools, applications and data.
- *Legacy heterogeneous environments*
  Legacy applications need to coexist with best-of-breed supply-chain, knowledge management and customer-relation applications on the Internet. It serves as a consistent mechanism for inter-application communication that facilitates cooperation among heterogeneous legacy applications.
- *Global operations*
  E-business breaks the boundaries of regions and countries. All operations are globalized. The portal platform is a better way for the companies to link applications and business processes to achieve their e-business goals.

Figure 5: Oracle's hub-spoke-adapter architecture for ERP/e-business

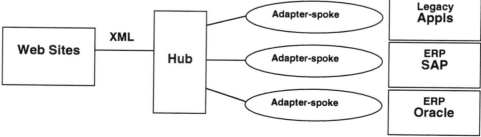

SAP (SAP, 2000)

Established in Germany in 1972, SAP possesses 33% market share worldwide. With more than 20,000 employees and an increase in revenue of 60% per year, SAP is another major ERP provider in the world. SAP uses the front-office market with a number of new Web-based applications covering B2B procurement, B2C selling and B2B selling — all designed to integrate with its market-leading R/3 suite. SAP believes this will be the key to extending its franchise into e-business.

R/3 is a client/server architecture product that uses the "best" enterprise business practices and supports immediate response to change throughout the organization on a global scale. R/3 currently contains modules for more than 1,000 business processes that may be selected from the SAP library and included within installed SAP applications, tailoring the application solution to the customer.

In early 2000, SAP uses an open Internet hub that provides both services and integration for companies to collaborate across business processes, conduct commerce, access personalized content and interact in professional communities (refer to Figure 6).

Its e-business platform consists of the following functions:

- *End-to-end Web business processes*
  The XML has been used to allow the exchange of structured business documents over the Internet to provide a common standard for different applications and IT systems to communicate and exchange business data. XML provides the bridge between different systems, companies and users. It provides an easy way to put flexible end-to-end business processes in place.
- *Open business document exchange over the Internet*
  The SAP Business Connector is based on open Internet communication standards. It uses the widely available hypertext transfer protocol (HTTP) to exchange XML-based business documents over the Internet. XML defines common business semantics to business documents such as orders, invoices,

Figure 6: SAP's platform for ERP/e-business

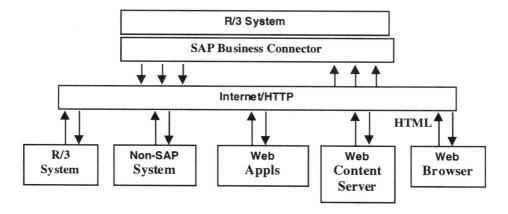

etc. With XML, the lingua franca of the Internet, business documents exchange across applications and systems are easily available.

- *XML-enabled SAP solution*
  The SAP Business Connector makes all SAP solutions accessible via XML-based business documents. It supports all major existing interfaces provided by SAP and empowers SAP customers to instantly benefit from SAP functionality over the Internet. This makes SAP solutions an integral part of their e-business solution. With the availability of Business Applications Programming Interfaces (BAPIs), customers can jump-start into the Internet age with their individual solutions by using R/3 with more than 1,000 BAPIs. The SAP's Application Link Enabling (ALE) capabilities are supported. Fully cooperative business solutions now require only a widely available and cost-effective Internet connection.
- *Flexible adoption of evolving business document standards*
  SAP Business Connector provides an easy-to-use graphical tool to convert and provide mapping between the SAP business documents and the XML-based business documents that are needed to collaborate with any business partners.
- *Web automation*
  The SAP Business Connector makes it easy to leverage the information and processes available at a company's Web site. For example, companies can use the SAP Business Connector to retrieve catalog information from a supplier's Web site and integrate the information with internal applications automatically and in real time.

CURRENT ISSUES

With the rise of e-business, integration becomes a challenging but mission-critical task in the corporate use of information technology. Some companies are reluctant to implement ERP/e-business due to the greater complexity involved in integration. The integration of ERP with other Web-enabled applications (CRM, SCM) is a complicated and timing-consuming process. The cost of software, implementation, training and maintenance will increase. The key e-business issue in application integration is to link e-businesses to other applications (that may be based on different technologies, business models and data models) without breaking the value chain (PriceWaterhouseCoopers, 1999, p.130). Enterprise Application Integration (EAI) software helps to integrate applications by packaging together the commonly used functionalities—combining popular enterprise packages and legacy applications in a predefined way. Therefore, EAI will make ERP/e-business integration and componentization simpler and more practical. In addition to the above issues, other issues remain in implementing ERP, integrating the systems and outsourcing ERP/e-business.

ERP implementations provide the backbone necessary for e-business. Without successful implementations of ERP, the capabilities provided by Web-based functions are limited. The growing number of horror stories about failure or out-of-control projects should certainly be brought to the companies' attention: FoxMeyer Drug argued that its ERP system drove it to bankruptcy before connecting its system to the Net. Mobile Europe spent hundreds of million of dollars on ERP only to abandon it when its merger partner objected. Dell Computer found that its system would not fit its new and decentralized management model (Buckhout et al., 1999, p.16).

Despite the promise and the high investment needed in implementing ERP systems and in linking ERP systems to the e-business infrastructure, statistics show that more than 70% of ERP implementations, whether self-created or designed by established ERP software vendors, fail to achieve corporate goals (Davenport, 1998, pp.122-123). The main reasons for ERP implementation failures are due to business and management problems. Companies fail to reconcile the technological imperatives of the ERP with the business requirements of the enterprise itself (Davenport, 1998, pp.122-123). If a company rushes to install an ERP without first having a clear understanding of the business implications within an Internet economy, the dream of integration can quickly turn into a nightmare. The logic of the ERP may conflict with the logic of the e-business.

Many companies implemented ERP due to its ability to bring order and efficiency through internal standardized business processes. However, every company has its unique business requirements and needs. Standardized processes that fit every organization are very difficult to develop. By implementing ERP, some companies have replaced proprietary processes that were better suited for their needs with standardized ERP processes. Since ERP business processes are often rigid and the components of the ERP from different vendors are usually not compatible, companies have found adapting ERP to new market demands to be difficult. In SAP R/3, most of the customers inevitably find that at least 20% of their needed functionality is missing from the package (Scott and Kaindl, 2000, pp.111-112). Componentization of ERP functions is in dire need.

According to Tse (*Economist*, 1999, p.32), a senior analyst at the Yankee Group, companies need to understand that e-business requires something close to building a second backbone system on top of ERP. They should also realize that it would be neither quick nor easy. IBM estimated that 70% of all codes written today consist of interfaces, protocols and other procedures to establish linkages among various systems (*Economist*, 1999, p.32). A software analyst at BancBoston, Robertson Stephens, said he spent 50% of his time on enterprise application integrations. The integration requires companies to provide more IT and end-user training. There is a longer learning period requirement for the daily operation. The sheer size, scope and complexity of these projects usually exceed expectations. The result is that companies often wait for years before they begin to see benefits. Lack of functionalities in ERP is forcing business processes to fit the software, and bolting on customized programs, while adding to the time and cost of implementation. Moreover, some alternatives, such as using work-around and customizing the software, increase the difficulty of upgrading to new releases of the ERP package

(Scott et al., 2000, pp.111-112). More often than not, projects wind up late or over budget. In the meantime, business time horizons have grown ever shorter. By the time companies have installed their ERP systems, their business has moved on and their original requirements have changed.

Outsourcing implies the use of external agents to perform an organizational activity. Companies consider outsourcing when: 1) cost saving is expected; 2) management wants to focus on its core business; and/or 3) the internal information systems function is perceived to be inefficient, ineffective or technically incompetent. Based on case studies, Lacity and Hirschheim (2000, p.324) suggest that outsourcing decisions may be a result of rational consideration and/or it may be a product of organizational politics, conflicts and compromises. Many companies are outsourcing their ERP/e-business implementation and integration to the best-of-breed vendors to simplify the daily operation and to better control the budget. This enables organizations to focus on their core businesses. Besides, many outsourcers price their services on a monthly basis with a fixed fee. This allows companies to better manage the cash flow and eliminate the large outlays typically associated with software rollouts and upgrades.

However, there are challenges in outsourcing ERP/e-business, most of which are strategic and technological issues:

- Renting remotely hosted ERP with e-business functionalities will have impact on the way independent software vendors conduct business. Therefore, it is essential that the vendors provide enough bandwidth and a high level of reliability to ensure that the applications perform at a necessary level for consistent and acceptable service and 24-7 availability.
- Success in ERP calls for extensive customization for power users. (In reality, ERP in midsize and small companies normally does not need much customization.)
- Companies should consider the possible leak of their business logic when outsourcing ERP. Manufacturers that outsource their ERP processes to a third party are launching themselves on a slippery slope to oblivion. For instance, when General Motors outsourced its ERP, it took them years to rebuild that infrastructure. A study of 40 US and European companies concluded that outsourcing led to problems and disappointments (King and Malhotra, 2000, pp.324).
- Outsourcing ERP/e-business may actually result in higher cost. According to *InformationWeek*, 19% of respondents said they didn't outsource ERP because they didn't believe it would be a cost-effective solution (Maeyaschuk, 2000).
- ERP/e-business outsourcing solution is only dominant in midsize and small companies. According to Mega Group, 60% of small and midsize companies are interested in outsourcing ERP (Grzanka, 2000). The large corporations are less likely to outsource their backbone systems.

FUTURE TRENDS

The rapid growth of the Internet will lead to a large increase in the number of ERP users. Companies are eliminating disintegrated legacy systems by replacing them with Web-enabled, integrated ERP systems. These integrated systems become part of the overall business strategy that connects an enterprise with its suppliers and customers, and transforms the entire value chain. Companies that intend to move into a net economy are beginning to emerge and focus on multi-enterprise systems integration and growth. They are forming strategic partnerships with major e-business infrastructure providers (Sun, IBM and Microsoft) to continuously integrate their ERP systems for reaching the internal and external performance target. Major ERP vendors (Oracle, SAP, BAAN, JD Edwards and i2) are constantly updating and releasing integrated ERP/e-business suites to support an open, collaborative and competitive business environment:

- The major ERP vendors will continue to build compatible and adaptable ERP components and develop extended ERP solutions designed to address the latest market demands. For example, Oracle's Release 11i is a business application suite that consists of Supply Chain Management, Order Management and new self-service software modules. It is tied to a Customer Relationship Management (CRM Release 11I and Oracle Exchange) application (Wilson, 1999, p.2). The whole software suite works seamlessly with one another to handle everything from customer service on one end to relationship with suppliers on the other. It is all re-jiggered to run on the Web. Based on the company's vision, anyone from giant corporations to tiny dot-coms can buy a single package from Oracle to run their e-business, rather than buying software from a host of competitors and trying to stitch it all together (Outsourcing-erp.com, 2000). If it works, it will move computing from desktop PCs to huge Internet servers that run anything from Web sites to complex corporate networks. Oracle's skills and technologies are taking the center stage. JD Edwards offers its OneWorld Software as a host service over networks. This application service is designed to be easier to deploy and adapt (Wilson, 2000, p.13). It will overcome the inflexibility of the ERP system on its implementation time.
- With the convergence of the Internet and wireless technology, users can access Web-enabled ERP systems anytime and anywhere through the use of newer and easier-to-use devices, such as personal digital assistants, smart phones, in-devices and biometric tools. For example, an accounting manager who is out of town will leverage his company's ERP with a personal digital assistant to review financial reports and give directions to his subordinates. He/she can log on to the system using his/her fingerprint or voice.
- The use of XML in B2B communications will enable a host of new relationships between companies, vendors, suppliers and customers. Exporting data from application suites and developer tools using XML will become a

standardized feature. For example, IBM translates generic XML information into device-specific formats that can be used on wireless devices.

- Outsourcers, ERP vendors and e-business infrastructure providers alliance together to provide more robust, scalable and compatible e-business platforms for the companies. PriceWaterhouseCoopers has built a strategic relationship with the Sun-Netscape Alliance (an alliance of Sun and AOL) to provide technology and services that enable companies to build business-critical e-business solutions that leverage investments in SAP R/3. Netscape Application Server for R/3 has provided a reliable infrastructure for Web solution (iPlanet) that allows customers to access PriceWaterhouseCoopers' SAP system in a secure manner (iPlanet, 2000).

- The future trend of ERP outsourcing is to explore into the applications service market. By the year 2003, offering ERP service over the Web will be a $2 billion business, as more than a dozen Application Service Providers (ASPs) are moving into the market (Gartner Group, 2000). ASPs take ERP and non-ERP applications from multiple vendors and put them together into a service. Rather than selling their creations in-house to corporate customers, they make their products available over the Web on a lease or rental basis. In addition, some mid-market companies are seeking to outsource their non-core business processes, such as payroll and employee benefit administration. According to a recent survey, 75 to 80% of a company's financial cost is tied up in labor or labor support. As stated by Marion (1999), any realistic attempt to reduce or manage costs in the finance and administration area has to focus not only on improved technology, but also on labor issues — the high costs of labor and the shortage of skilled labor.

CONCLUSION

If you're not doing business on the Web, you'll miss the boat. It's the wave of the future (Hamm, 2000, p.117). Given today's information age, e-business is the solution to dictate a successful information economy. However, companies can do little to move into this stage without the underlying (ERP) infrastructure in place as a foundation (Menezes, 2000, p.2). Today, extended ERP systems with front-end e-business connect an organization's "front office" (customer facing) and "back office" (business processes) operations to meet its global emerging market. Extending ERP means unleashing critical information and making it accessible to employees, customers and business partners, so that the various entities along the entire value chain can make better decisions.

Indeed, best practices consist of real-time, cross-enterprise, Internet-based flow of information, documents and processes, that is routed and driven in the most efficient and effective way. From a technical point of view, development and deployment of e-business models never stop. Companies should constantly reinvent to leverage changes in e-business technology and its ERP integration, or other business applications. New e-business models are emerging as companies in all industries are transforming themselves to compete in the Internet economy. Successful transformation requires new e-business strategies and processes, as well as robust and scalable application and technology platforms. With the right strategy and solid execution, an enterprise can transform itself to compete and grow in today's rapidly changing business environment.

REFERENCES

Buckhout, S., Frey, E. and Nemec, J., Jr. (1999). Making ERP succeed: Turning fear into promise. *IEEE Engineering Management Review*, Fall, 116-123.

Callaway, E. (2000). *Enterprise Resource Planning—Integrating Application and Business Processes Across the Enterprise*. Computer Technology Research Corporation.

Colgate Press Room. Retrieved August 23, 2000. (Masterfile) on World Wide Web: http://www.colgate.com/press/earn/.

Davenport, T. (1998). Putting the enterprise into the enterprise system. *Harvard Business Review*, August, 121-131.

Economist. (1999). ERP RIP? *The Economist*, June, 29-34.

Erlikh, L. (2000). Leveraging legacy system Dollars for e-business. *IT Professional*, May/June, 17-23.

Fellenstein, C., and Wood, R. (2000). *Exploring E-Commerce, Global E-Business, and E-Societies*. Prentice Hall.

Fingar, P., Kumar, H. and Tarun, S. (2000). *Enterprise E-Commerce: The Software Component Breakthrough for Business-to-Business Commerce*. Meghan-Kiffer Press.

GartnerGroup. (2000). *New and Upcoming Research*. Retrieved February, 2000. (Masterfile) on world wide Web: http://www.erphub.com.

Grzanka, L. (2000). ASPs and the renter's dilemma. *Knowledge Management*, May, 44-48.

Hamm, S. (2000). Oracle: Why it's cool again? *Business Week*, May 8, 114-126.

IBM. (1999). *Beyond ERP: Achieving Greater Return on ERP Investments*. Retrieved February 2000. (Masterfile) on World Wide Web: http://www.ibm.com/erp/nl1.

iPlanet. (2000). *Sun-Netscape Alliance's Vision for Net Economy Integration Amasses Global Support from Industry Leaders, Customers*. Retrieved August 22, 2000. (Masterfile) on World Wide Web: http://www.iplanet.com/alliance/press_room/press_releases/integration2.html.

King, J. (2000). How to do B2B? *Computerworld*. Retrieved February 23, 2000. (Masterfile) on World Wide Web: http://www.computerworld.com/.

King, W. R., and Malhotra, Y. (2000). Developing a framework for analyzing IS sourcing. *Information & Management*, (37), 324-333.

Lacity, M. C., and Hirschheim, R. (1993). *Information Systems Outsourcing: Myths, Metaphors and Realities*. John Wiley & Sons.

Marion, L. (1999). *Déjà Vu All Over Again: The Return of Time Sharing.* Retrieved February 2000. (Masterfile) on the World Wide Web: http://www.erphub.com/strategy_9907erp1.html.

Maeyaschuk, J. (2000). *ASPs Offer Benefits Through Economies of Scales.* Retrieved April 2000. (Masterfile) on World Wide Web: http://www.techweb.com.

Menezes, J. (2000). Shrinking Profits, Markets, Impact ERP, *Computing Canada,* January, 2-3.

Norris, G., Hurley, J. R., Hartley, K. M., Dunleavy, J. R., and Balls, J. D. (2000). *E-Business and ERP-Transforming the Enterprise.* PriceWatehouseCoopers.

Oracle. (2000). *E-Business Integration.* Retrieved January 2000. (Masterfile) on World Wide Web: http://www.oracle.com/ebusiness/integration.

Outsourcing-erp.com. (2000). *Big ERP Solutions for Mid-Market Companies.* Retrieved April 2, 2000. (Masterfile) on World Wide Web: http://www.outsourcing-erp.com/html/corpcare.html.

PriceWaterhouseCoopers. (1999) *E-Business Technology Forecast.* PriceWaterhouseCoopers.

SAP. (2000) *mySAP.com Marketplace.* Retrieved February 2000. (Masterfile) on World Wide Web: http://www.sap.com/marketplace.

Scott, J. E., and Kaindl, L. (2000). Enhancing functionality in an enterprise software package. *Information & Management,* (37), 111-122.

Sprott, D. (2000). Componentizing the enterprise application packages. *Communications of the ACM,* (4), 63-69.

Sun. (1999). *Colgate Palmolive Company—Sun Provides Global Network Computing Solution.* Retrieved August 22, 2000. (Masterfile) on World Wide Web: http://www.sun.com.

Whiting, R. (1999). Colgate goes live with SAP supply chain—company seeks to build on R/3 gains, *InformationWeek,* April 26. Retrieved August 2000. (Masterfile) on World Wide Web: http://www.techweb.com/se/directlilnk.cgi?IWK19990426S0029.

Wilson, T. (1999). Oracle suite integrates ERP, e-business apps, *InternetWeek,* October, 2-3.

Wilson, T. (2000). Handing off the burden, *InternetWeek,* January, 13. (Masterfile) on World Wide Web: http://www.e-business.pwcglobal.com/pdf/EbusinessandERP.pdf.

CHAPTER TEN

Security: The Snake in the E-Commerce Garden

Raymond R. Panko
University of Hawaii, USA

Security is one of the fastest-growing concerns in e-commerce and intranets. This chapter describes a number of attacks that hackers may attempt against companies and the methods used to combat each attack. The chapter also describes integrated security systems (ISSs), which automatically secure communication between two parties, protecting them from a variety of network attacks. Finally, the chapter describes potential risks from lawsuits if a company fails to adequately secure its systems and losses result.

INTRODUCTION

Hackers have defaced e-commerce Web sites, brought major e-commerce sites to their knees, stolen passwords (and threatened to post them unless extortion money was paid) and engaged in many other types of criminal attacks on e-commerce sites and on corporate intranets.

Yet as bad as things have been, they will be much worse in the future. Managers of e-commerce sites and intranets are engaged in an arms race with attackers. Both the stakes and the required level of security knowledge will rise dramatically in coming years.

The purpose of this chapter is to lay out basic security threats, principles, implementations and issues for e-commerce and intranets today. Specifically, we will look at the following.

- First, we will look at security threats, including interception and reading, impersonation, message modification, login attacks and denial-of-service attacks. For each of these threats we'll look at some basic security principles used to defend against it, including encryption for confidentiality, authentication, digital certificates, message integrity, firewalls, client PC security and server security.

- Second, we will look at integrated security systems (ISSs) for implementing security in practical situations.
- Third, we will look at a number of unresolved issues regarding security, including potential liability if your computers are taken over and used to attack the computers of other companies.

BACKGROUND: THREATS AND PROTECTIONS

It is important to begin a discussion of security by listing some major threats to security and the general steps that can be taken to thwart each of these threats. This section will examine interception, impersonation, message content attacks, login attacks and denial-of-service (DOS) attacks.

Interception and Encryption for Confidentiality

Interception.

The most obvious danger in network transmission is that someone will intercept our messages en route and read them. This would allow them to learn confidential information, such as consumer credit card numbers and business trade secrets.

Encryption for confidentiality.

Fortunately, it is relatively easy to provide *confidentiality* for transmitted messages, that is, the assurance that even if someone *intercepts* your messages, he or she will not be able to read them. We simply *encrypt* each message before we send it out.

The original message to be sent out is called *plaintext*. This name is somewhat misleading, because we are not limited to encrypting text messages. Our plaintext can be any type of file, including graphics files or video files.

We encrypt this plaintext to produce *ciphertext*, which we then transmit across the network. To anyone intercepting the ciphertext, it will look like a random string of ones and zeros. The interceptor will not be able to read it.

The receiver, however, can *decrypt* the ciphertext back to the original plaintext message. He or she can then read it, as we had intended.

Encrytion methods and keys.

Encryption requires an *encryption method*. This is the mathematical algorithm used to transform the plaintext into ciphertext. There are only a few encryption algorithms, so we cannot change our encryption method every time someone discovers our method. Therefore, we yield to reality and do not even try to keep our encryption method secret from attackers.

Encryption requires both an encryption method and a *key*. A key is nothing more than a string of bits (ones and zeros). When we encrypt plaintext, the resulting ciphertext will depend on both the encryption method and the encryption key. Different keys will give different ciphertexts from the same plaintext.

Because we cannot keep encryption methods secret, we must keep keys secret if we want to prevent interceptors from reading our messages. Keeping keys secret is critical to confidentiality through encryption.

Keeping keys secret is not enough. We must also make our keys fairly long. Otherwise, interceptors may be able to guess our keys by using *exhaustive search* in which he or she simply tries all possible keys. For instance, if our key is only two bits long, there are only four possible keys: 00, 01, 10 and 11. In general, if our key is n bits long, there will be 2^n possible keys. As the key length increases, the number of possible keys explodes, making exhaustive search vastly more difficult.

For consumer applications, a key length of 56 bits is common. Although 2^{56} is a large number, someone with a fast computer can complete an exhaustive search in a day or less. This would not make sense for stealing credit card numbers, but for an attacker seeking highly valuable corporate information, spending a day cracking a message may be well worth the time and cost.

Business-to-business applications need strong security. Today, key lengths of about 100 bits are considered strong, but we will need longer keys in the future to remain secure in the face of ever-increasing computer speeds for doing exhaustive searches.

Symmetric key encryption.

The simplest and most common encryption methods use a process called *symmetric key encryption*, in which a single key is used by both parties. As Figure 1 illustrates, when Party A transmits to Party B, Party A encrypts the outgoing message with the single symmetric key. Party B uses the same key to decrypt the ciphertext back to plaintext. For messages going the opposite direction, Party B will encrypt with the symmetric key while Party A will decrypt with the key. In other words, the single shared symmetric key is used for all encryption and decryption processes.

Symmetric key encrytion is very *fast*, placing a (relatively) small processing burden on computers and so allowing *long messages* to be sent using encryption.

Figure 1: Symmetric key encryption and public key encryption

Symmetric Key Encryption	Public Key Encryption

When A sends to B
  A encrypts with the single symmetric key
  B decrypts with the single symmetric key
	When A sends to B
	  A encrypts with B's public key
	  B decrypts with B's private key

When B sends to A
  B encrypts with the single symmetric key
  A decrypts with the single symmetric key
	When B sends to A
	  B encrypts with A's public key
	  A decrypts with A's public key

Symmetric key must be distributed securely	Public keys can be distributed unsecurely

Most encryption uses symmetric key transmission today, and symmetric key encryption's dominance will probably grow in the future.

The most popular symmetric key encryption algorithm is the *Data Encryption Standard (DES)*, which breaks the plaintext into blocks of 64 bits and encrypts each block with a 56-bit key.[1]

Although 56 bits was sufficient in the 1970s, when DES was created, it offers only weak security today. As a consequence, *triple DES (3DES)* was developed. In 3DES, each block of 64 bits is encrypted three times, each time with a different 56-bit key. This gives an effective key length of 168 bits, which is very strong security.[2]

At the time of this writing, the U.S. National Institute of Science and Technology is selecting a successor to DES. This new *Advanced Encryption Standard (AES)* will have much longer keys, making it safe to use for many years to come.

Public key encryption.

Figure 1 also illustrates another type of encryption, *public key encryption*. In this approach, every party has two keys. One is his or her *private key*. As the name suggests, this private key must be kept secret by the person. Everybody has his or her own private key, and everybody's private key is unique.

Second, everyone has a unique *public key* associated with their private key. As its name suggests, the public key does not have to be kept secret. You can give your public key to anyone, and you do not have to transmit the public key securely.

Suppose that you are Party A and wish Party B to send you a message confidentially through public key encryption. You would first send them your public key without security. As shown in Figure 1, Party B would then encrypt the plaintext message using your public key and send you this ciphertext over the network. You would then decrypt the message using your own private key.

Note that the sender always encrypts the plaintext message with the *receiver's public key*. Then, when a message arrives, the receiver always decrypts it with the *receiver's own private key*. In encryption for confidentiality, then, only the receiver's keys are important.

Figure 1 shows that when two parties communicate back and forth, there are *four* keys involved. Each party has his or her own private and public key. Each party encrypts messages with the public key of the other party. Each party decrypts incoming messages with its own private key.

Public key encryption is processing-intensive. As a consequence, public key encryption and decryption are *very slow*—about a hundred times slower than symmetric key encryption. This means that public key encryption has to be limited to encrypting *very short messages*. In fact, other limitations in public key encryption algorithms usually limit them to encrypting messages of at most a few thousand bits.

Why would anyone use public key encryption given these limitations? The answer is that there is no problem distributing public keys. In contrast, symmetric keys must be distributed to the two parties securely. Secure distribution is difficult. It is made even more difficult by the fact that *each pair* of business partners must have *a different symmetric key* to prevent others from reading their messages. If you deal with a hundred customers, you need to distribute a hundred symmetric keys securely!

Combining the symmetric key and public key encryption.

Although symmetric key encryption and public key encryption have very different characteristics, it would be wrong to think of them as competitors. In fact, they often are combined in security systems.

For example, symmetric key encryption has the problem of distributing symmetric keys securely. Fortunately, keys are fairly small, so public key encryption can be used to encrypt symmetric keys for secure distribution.

For example, suppose I wish to distribute a symmetric key to Party X. I first ask Party X for his or her public key. I then generate a random number for us to use as a symmetric *session key*, that is a symmetric key we will use only for our current communication session. I then encrypt this symmetric session key with Party X's public key so that I can distribute it securely to Party X.

At the other end, Party X decrypts the message with his or her private key, yielding the symmetric key. Now, we both have the symmetric session key. We can now begin communicating using fast symmetric key encryption.

Impersonation and Authentication

So far, we have been looking at encryption for the sake of confidentiality, so that an interceptor cannot read a message even if he or she intercepts it. However, reading intercepted messages is not the only security threat, and confidentiality is not the only security goal or the only security goal that requires encryption.

Impersonation.

Another major security threat is *impersonation*, in which an *impostor* poses as someone else (the *true party*). For instance, an imposter may wish to get access to a true party's sensitive files. To give another example, an impostor may place an e-commerce order pretending to be the true party. In general, successful impersonation is the key to bypassing safeguards against a large number of attacks.

Authentication.

To prevent impersonation, it is important to *authenticate* communication partners, that is, require them to prove their identities. Only after the other party has authenticated himself or herself will we accept them as the true party. In authentication, the party that must prove his or her identity is the *applicant*. The party requiring the applicant to prove his or her identity is the *verifier*.

Passwords.

The most common authentication approach is requiring the applicant to give a *password*. However, user-selected passwords usually are very short, making exhaustive search fairly easy.

In fact, *brute-force* exhaustive searches that try all possibilities may not be necessary. Most people choose passwords that are common words. There are only a few thousand words in any language, so *dictionary-based* attacks with password cracking programs may take only a minute or two to crack a password.

Biometric authentication.

As its name suggests, *biometric* authentication uses body measurements. Fingerprints, iris patterns and palm prints can all be used for authentication at varying costs and precision levels. Biometric authentication is very promising, because we always have our body with us. However, biometric technology is still immature and unstandardized.

One-time challenge–response authentication.

For traffic flowing across a network, the only way to authenticate communication partners is by looking at the messages they transmit. In general, there are two ways to do message authentication.

The first approach is *one-time authentication*, in which the applicant must send a single message authenticating himself or herself. If authentication succeeds, the applicant is treated as being authenticated in subsequent messages. Actually, the term "one-time" is a bit extreme. Often, the verifier will require "one-time authentication messages" at several times during a session, to ensure that no one has *hijacked* the connection (has taken over from the previously authenticated true party).

Figure 2 illustrates one type of one-time message authentication, *public key challenge–response authentication*, in which the verifier sends a *challenge message* and the applicant must send back a *response message* that only the true party could send.

Figure 2: One-time authentication with public key challenge-response authentication

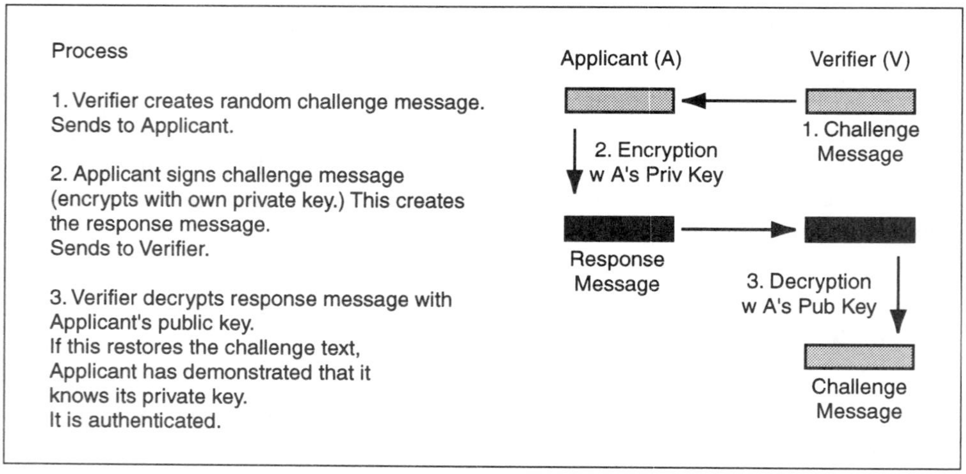

As its name suggests, public key challenge–response authentication uses public key encryption. In public key encryption, the verifier (and everybody else) knows the true party's public key. But only the applicant should know the true party's private key. If the applicant can demonstrate that he or she know the true party's private key, the applicant must be the true party.

The verifier sends the applicant a short randomly generated challenge message. This message does not even have to be sent confidentially. To create the response message, the applicant encrypts the challenge message with their private key.[3] The applicant then sends this response message back to the verifier.

If decryption with the true party's public key produces the original challenge message, then the applicant holds the true party's private key. Unless the true party has failed to keep this private key secret, the applicant must be the true party. The applicant is authenticated.

Public key challenge–response authentication is attractive because there is no need to distribute the public key secretly. On the downside, public key challenge–response authentication is very time-consuming because public key encryption and decryption are very slow.

Public key challenge–response authentication is not the only form of challenge–response authentication. Another is *shared secret challenge–response authentication*. This approach does not use public key encryption. Instead, both sides have a *shared secret*, which is a string of bits known by both parties. We call it a shared secret rather than a symmetric or private key because it is not used in encryption. Only bit strings used in encryption are called keys. The shared secret, in contrast, is used in a process called hashing.

Hashing is a process that always produces a small bit string no matter how long the hashed message is. For instance, the *MD5* hashing algorithm always produces a 128-bit hash, while *SHA1* always produces a 160-bit hash. Unlike encryption (and compression), *hashing is not reversible*. The brief hash does not contain the information needed to recreate the long original message.

As the figure shows, the applicant adds the shared secret to the challenge message sent by the verifier. The applicant then *hashes* the combined challenge message and shared secret. When the verifier receives the hash, it repeats the actions the applicant took. It knows the challenge message because it created the challenge message, and it knows the shared secret as well. It adds the shared secret to the challenge message and applies the same hashing algorithm that the applicant used. If this gives the same hash that the applicant transmitted, the applicant must know the shared secret. The applicant is authenticated.

Message-by-message authentication with digital signatures.

One-time authentication does not authenticate each and every message. This allows an impostor to insert messages within the stream of messages going between the authenticated applicant and the verifier. We would like to have *message-by-*

Figure 3: Message-by-message authentication with a digital signature

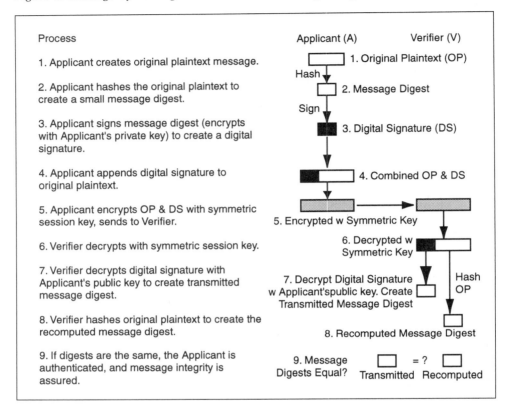

Process	
1. Applicant creates original plaintext message.	
2. Applicant hashes the original plaintext to create a small message digest.	
3. Applicant signs message digest (encrypts with Applicant's private key) to create a digital signature.	
4. Applicant appends digital signature to original plaintext.	
5. Applicant encrypts OP & DS with symmetric session key, sends to Verifier.	
6. Verifier decrypts with symmetric session key.	
7. Verifier decrypts digital signature with Applicant's public key to create transmitted message digest.	
8. Verifier hashes original plaintext to create the recomputed message digest.	
9. If digests are the same, the Applicant is authenticated, and message integrity is assured.	

message authentication in which the sender is authenticated with each message he or she sends.

Figure 3 shows message-by-message authentication using a digital signature, which is added to each outgoing message in the same way you sign every letter you send.

To create a digital signature, the applicant first creates the message to be sent. The applicant then uses MD5 or SHA1 to hash the message, producing a short *message digest*. These small message digests can be encrypted with public key encryption. In fact, the applicant encrypts the message digest with its own private key. The encrypted message digest is called the *digital signature*.[4] It is this digital signature, not the message digest, that is attached to the outgoing message.

The verifier reverses the process after receipt. The verifier hashes the message to produce the message digest again. The verifier also decrypts the digital signature with the true party's public key to compute the message digest. If the two message digests match, the sender must have the true party's private key. The applicant is authenticated as the true party.

Another message-by-message authentication approach is the *Hashed Message Authentication Code (HMAC)* method. HMAC authentication does not use encryption at all. Instead, it requires both the true party and the verifier to have a shared secret bit string. When the applicant sends a message, it adds this shared secret to the message and hashes the combination. This hash is called the HMAC. This HMAC is added to the original messages like a digital signature.

The verifier repeats the process. It takes the message is has received, hashes it again with the shared secret and therefore computes the HMAC. If this matches the HMAC arriving with the message, the applicant knows the shared secret that the verifier shares with the true party. The applicant must be the true party to know this shared secret. The applicant is authenticated as the true party.

HMAC processing is faster than digital signature processing. However, HMAC requires that shared secrets be distributed secretly, while digital signatures use public keys, which are distributed in the clear. However, as we will see below, the need for digital certificates adds security complexity to digital signature authentication.

The shared secret in HMAC creation often is a person's password. If this is the case, security will only be as strong as the password. Strong passwords must be supported.

Message integrity.

Even if the message is authenticated as having come from the true party, what proof is there that an attacker has not intercepted it en route and modified it before sending it on? Fortunately, both digital signatures and HMACs provide *message integrity*, which is the assurance that if the message has been changed, this change can be detected. Quite simply, if messages are changed, either deliberately or through a transmission error, the verification process will not produce the correct message digest or HMAC, because the bits on which the computations are made will be different for the verifier than they were for the applicant.

Authentication conspiracies.

The authentication procedures we have looked at all assume that the true party will prevent others from knowing its private key or shared secret. However, this is not necessarily a reasonable expectation. Consider a student taking an exam in an online course. The student could ask another person to take the exam for them. The student would give this person the student's password, private key or shared secret. The methods that we have discussed would therefore "authenticate" the impostor. Even biometric authentication would not be effective if the student stayed in the room while the impostor took the test. Such authentication conspiracies are serious potential threats to the integrity of distance education systems.

Digital signatures versus electronic signatures.

In 2000, the United States Congress passed an *electronic signatures* law, giving electronic signatures the same legal status as written signatures. This law defined electronic signatures very broadly. While it does include digital signatures, which, as we have just seen, use public key authentication, it also includes such things as clicking on a button to agree to licensing terms for software. Digital signatures generally have the advantage of *nonrepudiation*, meaning that if someone signs a contract with a digital signature, they cannot deny that they did so, because only the true party should possess the private key needed to create the digital signature. With many other forms of electronic signatures, such as clicking on a button, there is no way of distinguishing whether the act was done by the true party or by an impostor. This would make legal enforcement very difficult.

Digital certificates.

Public key authentication requires that we know the true party's public key. Certainly, an impostor could send us his or her public key claiming it is the public key of the true party. If we accepted their false public key, both one-time and message-by-message authentication would "authenticate" the impostor as the true party. *For authentication, we must get the true party's public key from a trusted third party, not from the applicant.*

In authentication, trusted third parties are called *certificate authorities (CAs)*. For each true party, the CA creates a *digital certificate*. This digital certificate, among other things, lists the name of the true party and the true party's public key. So if someone sends you a message which he or she claims is coming from the XYZ corporation, the verifier would use the public key in XYZ's digital certificate.

Of course, companies that misbehave can have their digital certificates revoked. So it is always important to check the Certificate Authority's *Certificate Revocation List (CRL)* to be sure that the digital certificate is still valid.

What prevents an impostor from getting their own digital certificate and then replacing their name with the name of the XYZ corporation? The answer is that digital certificates themselves contain *digital signatures encrypted by the certificate authority's own private key*. This digital signature will not check out using the CA's own well-known public key if the digital certificate has been modified.

Unfortunately, there are three problems with certificate authorities today. The first is that CAs are not regulated. There are no assurances of a certificate authority's legitimacy or of its internal quality control.

The second is that many CAs offer several classes of certificates. The lowest classes may only ensure that the certified party has an e-mail address. Naïve users may assume that digital certificates mean much more.

The third problem with digital certificates is that public key encryption requires a full *public key infrastructure (PKI)* that can manage digital certificates, create public key-private key pairs, distribute private keys securely, implement certificate revocation lists and do other tasks automatically. Until we get public and open standards for PKIs, companies will be tied to the PKIs of individual certificate authorities.

Digital certificates and public key authentication.

Note that *digital certificates, by themselves, do not provide authentication.* They merely tell you the true party's public key. This information is worthless unless it is then used in some public key authentication method, such as public key challenge response authentication or digital signatures. Digital certificates and public key authentication always must be used together.

Firewalls

When we connect to the Internet, we expose ourselves to everyone who uses the Internet, including thousands of potential attackers. This is not just a hypothetical danger. Nearly every company that connects to the Internet is scanned and then attacked in various ways. To thwart outside attack, companies often place boxes called *firewalls* between their internal networks and the Internet.

Packet filter firewalls.

There are two basic types of firewalls. The first is the *packet filter firewall.* As its name suggests, it examines the header of each packet—more specifically, both the IP header and the TCP header. This allows us to detect and discard bad packets. For instance, if the source IP address is that of a host known to be *within* our network, we should not be getting such packets from the outside, so the firewall should discard the message. Or, if the port number in the TCP header indicates that the application message is intended for an application whose messages we do not permit to cross our boundaries, the firewall would discard the packet.

Application firewalls.

Application firewalls, in turn, look at the application layer message itself. The firewall can pass or discard messages based on the behavior of that particular application. To give a simple example, if we receive a World Wide Web (HTTP) response message from a Web server to which we have not just sent a request message, we would discard the response message.

Application firewalls may also scan application messages for viruses, indications of pornography, spam (widely distributed junk e-mail),\ or other inappropriate content. Rapidly propagating viruses may make detection at the application firewall crucial because there will not be time to inoculate all individual computers against such threats when such threats appear.

In general, application firewalls are very strong because most applications have fairly predictable behavior. However, not all applications have highly predictable behavior, and we cannot build application rules for some applications at all.

Combining packet filter and application firewalls.

In addition, there are some simple attacks that packet filter firewalls can catch that application firewalls cannot. For these reasons, it is common to *place two firewalls in series*—first a packet filter firewall to act as a security "speed bump," then an application firewall for stronger checking.

The configuration of access control rules.

One problem with all firewalls is that they require the organization to develop sophisticated *if-then-else access control rules* for message filtering. There often are many such rules, and they often are *nested. If they are executed in the wrong order, attacks may get through them freely*. The correct configuration of firewall access control lists is one of the most difficult aspects of firewalls today.

Distributed firewalls.

Although it is important to protect the firm from outside hackers, internal employees who are already inside the firewall commit most computer crime. Many firms are now installing distributed firewalls within their networks, protecting different parts of the internal network from unauthorized access and manipulation from other parts of the internal network.

Login Attacks and Passwords

We have been focusing so far on how to send messages in a secure manner. But it is not enough to secure the network. We also need to secure the client machines and servers at the ends of our network connections. What good does it do to transmit credit card numbers securely if a hacker can steal them off the merchant's server afterward?

Client PC security.

If you have a browser, you already have public key authentication. Browsers come with private keys for use in public key authentication, the distribution for session keys and other matters.

Unfortunately, passwords typically are stored on the client PC. If an attacker can gain physical access to the user's client PC, they often can use stored passwords to bypass the most elaborate of safeguards in the rest of the network. Most people do not password-protect on their client PCs at all, or, if they do, they use absurdly simple passwords that are easily broken by dictionary attacks, which were discussed earlier.

Server security.

Servers have an administrative *master account* that can read any files, modify them, delete them and do anything else the sever administrator wishes to do. On

UNIX systems, this account is called the root. On Microsoft Windows servers, it is the administrator account. On Novell NetWare accounts, it is the supervisor account. The master account must have broad powers so that the server's administrator can manage the server. However, these broad powers make these accounts very dangerous. Multiplying this danger, other accounts can be given powers equal to the master account. Getting the master account's password is the goal of every hacker.

After obtaining master account status and tampering with the server, the hacker often creates a new account with equivalent master-level security powers. Using this *back door* account, the hacker will be able to get back in later even if the supervisor has changed the master password. Only if the administrator notices the backdoor account amid the myriad of legitimate accounts on the server will the back door account be closed down.

There are a number of "kiddie script" password cracking programs designed for hackers with little technical background. If the supervisor does not select a very good master password, a 14-year old child with little technical background may break into their system and cause serious damage.

Although most master passwords are difficult to crack, many users ordinarily create weak passwords that are fairly easy to crack. Although a hacker cannot do as much damage logged in as an ordinary user as they can if they are logged into the master account, they still can do a good deal of mischief.

Known security weaknesses and scanning attacks.

Another problem with server security is that security weaknesses are discovered occasionally in all operating systems. When this happens, vendors usually are fairly prompt about creating *patches* to fix these *known weaknesses*. Server administrators should then download and install the patches. Of course, not all do.

Hackers have created *scanning software* that can test a system for the presence of many known security weaknesses that have not been patched. The software then gives the hacker a list of known weaknesses and may also be able to supply the code needed to exploit the known weaknesses it finds.

Denial-of-Service (DOS) Attacks

It often is very difficult to break into a server by password cracking. However, there are a number of server attacks that do not require breaking into a server. The most damaging are *denial-of-service (DOS)* attacks that crash the server, clog communication lines to and from the server with spurious traffic or do other things that deny the server's services to users. Although DOS attacks can be spectacularly damaging, they are comparatively easy to do. Serious hackers deride DOS attacks as mere amateur vandalism. However, this is small comfort to the firm that has been brought to its knees by a DOS attack.

Single-message DOS attacks.

Standards specify the structure of TCP, IP, PPP and other types of messages that flow over the network. In some cases, either because the standard is deficient or because it is implemented in a particular way, a single *malformed message* may be able to bring down a server. When the server attempts to process the message, it may crash because it does not know what to do with the message.

Message stream DOS attacks.

Another DOS strategy is to send the target host a stream of messages that overwhelm its processing power. For instance, when one host wishes to open a connection to another host, it sends a TCP "SYN" message. When the receiver gets the SYN message, it prepares to open the connection. It sets aside RAM and other system resources and does considerable amounts of processing to prepare for the connection. A long stream of SYN messages, called a *SYN flood*, can overwhelm a server. The server will slow down or even crash if its system resources are exceeded in the attempt to open thousands of connections. Refusing further SYN messages may keep the system running, but this may also keep legitimate users from using the system.

SYN floods and many other message stream DOS attacks are fairly old, and patches have long been available. Yet despite the massive potential for destruction that message stream DOS attacks bring, quite a few networks are still vulnerable to them because firewall or router software has not been upgraded.

Distributed DOS attacks.

A single attacking computer may be limited in the amount of DOS damage it can inflict. In addition, it may also be possible to track DOS attack messages back to the attacker's computer. These considerations have led to a new type of DOS attack, the *distributed DOS* attack. Figure 4 illustrates such an attack.

Figure 4: Distributed denial-of-service (DOS) attack

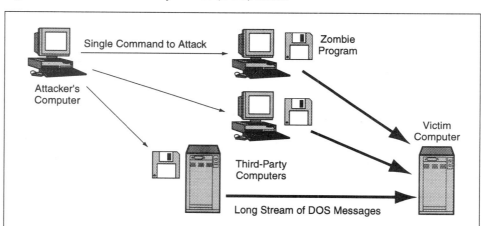

Figure 5: Integrated security system (ISS)

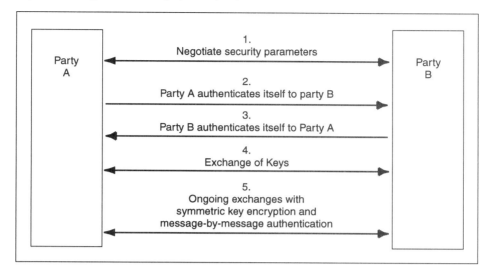

The attacker plants a "zombie" program in a number of programs by hacking into the computer or by tricking users into installing the zombie themselves. The latter is done by sending the user a *Trojan horse* program that masquerades as something else, such as a game, but that installs the zombie as well.

Later, when it is time for an attack, the attacker sends each zombie program an instruction to attack a particular target host. All of the zombies then begin sending a stream of DOS messages at the target host. Because the messages are coming from many different places, it is very difficult to design countermeasures without cutting off messages from legitimate users.

INTEGRATED SECURITY SYSTEMS

The security processes we have seen so far are confusing and complex, and we have only covered a few. Obviously, organizations cannot cope with such complexity without help, and individual users have to be shielded from almost all of this complexity. In this section, we will look at how integrated security systems do this.

What are Integrated Security Systems (ISSs)?

Fortunately, security in practice often is implemented in what we will call *integrated security systems (ISSs)* that provide a complete or nearly complete set of protections and do so almost completely automatically. Figure 5 illustrates the key elements found in almost all ISSs.

Initial negotiation phase.

The first step in ISS communication is to negotiate the security algorithms to be used during the communication session. For instance, if symmetric communication is used, the two parties must negotiate the specific symmetric encryption algorithm they will use. There usually are several alternatives from which they may select, for example, DES, 3DES, RC5 and Blowfish. Each of these may have alternatives, such as standard DES or DES-CBC. In the initial negotiation phase, the two parties must negotiate which specific algorithms they will use for all aspects of security in the remainder of the communication.

Authentication phase.

The next step is for each process to authenticate itself to its partner, using the one-time authentication algorithm they selected in the initial negotiation phase. This is likely to involve challenge–response authentication and, if public key authentication is selected, the retrieval and checking of digital certificates.

Key exchange phase.

Many security algorithms require the confidential exchange of encryption keys or other shared secrets. Using public key distribution, Diffie-Hellman Key Agreement or some other algorithm selected during the negotiation, the required keys and shared secrets will be exchanged.

Ongoing communication phase.

Now the two parties are ready to communicate securely. This normally involves the encryption of each message for confidentiality using symmetric key encryption and the use of digital signatures or HMACs for message-by-message authentication and message integrity.

Important Integrated Security Systems (ISSs)

In practice, there are several important ISSs used in electronic commerce and intranets. We will look briefly at the four most important.

SSL.

Netscape created an integrated security system for its browser-server communication. This was the *secure sockets layer (SSL)* protocol. Other browser and server vendors, including Microsoft, soon adopted SSL. Today, almost all electronic commerce transactions that involve credit card transfers and the transmission of other sensitive information are made using SSL.

Although SSL is sometimes disparaged by security experts, it is strong enough for consumer electronic commerce, and there have been no reported cases of credit cards being stolen en route. While it is true that SSL does not guard the safety of credit card numbers when they are stored after transmission on merchant Web servers, that is a job for server security, not network security, which is SSL's domain.

One problem with SSL is that while the merchant must authenticate itself to the customer, there is no requirement for the customer to authenticate himself or herself. Yet while merchant fraud is comparatively modest, consumer fraud is fairly common on the Internet. This weakness in SSL requires merchants to use other systems to check the validity of credit card numbers and other customer information. Fortunately, it is easy to get a separate system for validating credit card numbers.

Another problem with SSL is that it uses public key encryption for some of its work, and when it does, it slows the e-commerce or intranet server to a crawl. Reports of performance reduction when SSL is used range from 90% to 99%.

Netscape has turned SSL over to the *Internet Engineering Task Force (IETF)* for future development. The IETF is the agency that creates all Internet (TCP/IP) standards. The IETF is developing new versions of SSL under the name *Transport Layer Security (TLS)*.

IPsec.

The Internet Engineering Tasks Force has been giving most of its security attention to a family of standards called *IPsec (IP security)*. As the name suggests, IPsec works at the TCP/IP Internet layer (OSI Network layer), extending the Internet Protocol. IPsec works with both IP Version 4, which is the current version of the Internet Protocol, and IP Version 6, which is a new version designed to replace IPv4.

Figure 6 illustrates IPsec. It notes that there are two basic modes to IPsec. The *transport mode* provides end-to-end security between the two hosts, both on the Internet and within local networks. This may sound good, but it requires the two hosts to implement transport mode IP security, and relatively few hosts can do this today.

Also, because the IP packet must reach the destination host, transport mode security requires the IP packet to carry the IP addresses of both the source host and

Figure 6: IPsec integrated security system

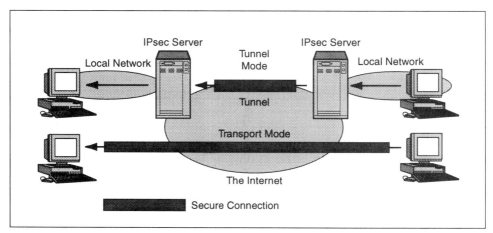

the destination host. This is dangerous because it allows an interceptor using a *sniffer program* to capture packets, analyze them and, among other things, create a list of host IP addresses within corporate networks. Creating a list of host IP addresses usually is the first step in identifying target hosts to attack.

IPsec's other mode is *tunnel mode*. As Figure 6 illustrates, tunnel mode transmission only protects packets as they are traveling through the Internet, not when packets are traveling within site networks.

The source host transmits its packet to the destination host. However, an *IPsec server* at the source host site intercepts the packet before the packet leaves the site network.

The source IPsec server *encapsulates* the original IP packet within a new IP packet whose IP header is addressed to the IPsec server at the other site. Sniffer programs on the Internet will only be able to see the IP addresses of the IPsec server sending the packet and the IPsec server receiving the packet.

The encapsulated packet normally is encrypted for confidentiality so that someone intercepting the packet on the Internet cannot read it. However, where confidentiality is barred by law or is unimportant, IPsec can send the IP packet as plaintext but add authentication.

The receiving IPsec security server decrypts and de-encapsulates the original IP packet. It then sends this packet to the original destination host.

One important aspect of IPsec is that it only uses symmetric key encryption and hashing, avoiding the slow speeds of public key encryption. Although public key encryption is sometimes portrayed as the wave of the future, in fact the trend is to avoid public key encryption in new integrated security systems in order to avoid its impact on computer performance.

Kerberos.

In Greek mythology, Kerberos is a three-headed dog that guards the gates of Hades. The *Kerberos* ISS receives this name because three computers are involved in security transactions. The first two are the computers that wish to communicate, the applicant and the verifier. These often are a client PC and a server, respectively.

The third party is the *Kerberos server*. When an applicant wishes to communicate with a verifier, it applies to the Kerberos server. The Kerberos server sends the applicant *credentials*, which consist of a *symmetric session key* to be used with the verifier and a *service ticket* to send to the verifier. This service ticket, plus accompanying authentication information, introduces the applicant to the verifier as legitimate and also sends the symmetric session key to the verifier. Now the applicant is authenticated, and subsequent communication between the applicant and the verifier can be done securely, using the symmetric session key.

PPTP and L2TP

Users could traditionally dial in from home using a telephone line and modem. They would dial into a remote access server (RAS). Today, they are likely to reach the RAS through the Internet instead of dialing in directly. Two protocols that are full ISSs give secure connections between the user's PC and the RAS over the Internet. The first is the *Point-to-Point Tunneling Protocol (PPTP)*. The second is the more sophisticated *Layer 2 Tunneling Protocol (L2TP)*. Both create a secure tunnel through which information can flow securely between the RAS and an authenticated user. Windows 2000 supports both, while earlier versions of the Windows server only supported PPTP.

Multi-Layer Security

SSL works at the transport layer, while IPsec works at the Internet layer, and PPTP and L2TP work at the data link layer. It is also possible to implement security at the application layer by having passwords for programs and at the physical layer by installing locks or limiting physical access. If security is implemented at more than one layer, this will slow processing and so raise costs. However, such **multi-layer security** is good because hackers often find weaknesses in the implementations of individual ISSs. With multilayer security, attackers still will be thwarted by security at other layers while the defective ISS is being fixed.

ISSUES

Although security is mature in some ways, there are troubling issues on the horizon.

The Arms Race

Security companies and attackers are engaged in a fierce arms race today. Numerous attackers around the world find new ways to exploit existing systems and then post their exploits on the World Wide Web, often with accompanying "kiddie script" software that almost anybody can use. Although exploits vary widely in the degree of sophistication required of attackers, there are many simple and effective exploits that teenagers with little background can use.

Although security companies and attackers seem to have a great deal of resources, companies that implement e-commerce and intranets are faced with the daunting task of implementing security on dozens and sometimes thousands of host computers. They must download and install patches to fix known security weaknesses constantly, because hackers can scan their computers to see which are open to specific exploits based on known security weaknesses.

Two things have to happen in the near future. First, the process of implementing security patches must be greatly simplified, in the way it has been done for antivirus programs. Antivirus programs have extremely simple ways of downloading information about new viruses and updating the antivirus program. Although patches for known security weaknesses are more widely ranging, we need to automate the patch downloading and installation process if we are to improve the very poor track record of corporations in implementing patches.

Second, companies must develop the attitude that security is worth implementing. Many companies have very small security budgets that are inadequate to purchase security products, install security patches and train personnel to configure security products effectively.

One problem in creating positive attitudes about security is that few companies realize how often they are attacked over the Internet. One way to improve security awareness is to install an **intrusion detection** product. These products log suspicious activities, often providing real-time warnings of security breaches. If companies realize how often they are attacked, they are likely to be more willing to implement security protection.

Who is Liable?

In early 2000, a number of e-commerce sites were attacked with distributed denial-of-service attacks. The impact, including loss of transactions and decreased stock value because of reduced investor confidence, was huge. We can expect many more such attacks in the future.

Who is legally **liable** for the damages caused by such attacks? Obviously, the person who conducted the attacks should be held liable. However, this often is a teenager who can barely be prosecuted and who has no money to pay for damages.

As noted earlier, distributed DOS attacks require the attacker to take over third-party systems and use these systems to attack the ultimate target. These third-party systems usually are viewed as victims. However, in most cases, they were used because the companies owning them had failed to implement security properly, including downloading and installing new security patches for known security weaknesses. In a court of law, it is distinctly possible that lax third-party companies that view themselves as victims could be held liable for damages. If this seems unfair, consider this analogy. How liable would you be if you left a loaded gun sitting on your lawn and it was stolen and used to kill someone in a robbery?

In addition, boards of directors have **fiduciary responsibility**, meaning that they are responsible for safeguarding the assets of their corporations. How liable are boards to their stockholders if the company is damaged by security breaches involving systems that could have been secured but were not?

Social Engineering

The most elaborate technical defenses can be overcome by simple **social engineering** exploits, in which the attacker dupes a user into divulging information he or she should not divulge. For instance, a common social engineering exploit is to call a user claiming to be the central services staff and asking them for their password so that the "technician" can fix a problem. More subtly, Java can be used to open a dialog box on the user's screen that tells the user that he or she has been disconnected and must retype their user name and password to continue. When he or she does, this information is sent back to the attacker. Another human engineering exploit is "shoulder surfing," that is, watching someone type their password.

As technical security becomes ever more sophisticated, the user will continue to become the weakest link in the security chain unless he or she is properly trained and unless policies are enforced. People must be aware of social engineering attacks and they must be trained to use passwords that are not easily guessed. As much as possible, good behavior must be enforced with technology. For instance, servers must be set to reject weak passwords. In the end, however, managing users must be done the old fashioned way.

Single Points of Take-Over

In security systems, we often have a few security hosts that safeguard or control large numbers of other hosts. These central systems can become **single points of take-over**. If they are taken over, the results can be disastrous. If the Kerberos server is taken over, for example, the attacker can allow himself or herself into almost any server while denying access to others. Even more centrally, some firms have policy servers that store all security policies. These policies are sent to other devices, such as firewalls, which implement the policies. If an attacker can take over a policy server, he or she can do whatever damage they wish, including locking out all legitimate users from all services throughout the organization. It is absolutely critical to recognize which servers are central and to provide extremely strong protection for these servers.

Additional Reading

CERT Coordination Center, Carnegie-Mellon University, http://www.cert.org/stats/cert_stats.html. CERT issues advisories for computer vulnerabilities, including viruses.

McClure, S., Scambray, J. & Kurtz, G. (1999). *Hacking Exposed*. Berkeley, California: Osborne/McGraw Hill. This is an excellent guide to how hackers break into systems and the actions they take after breaking in.

McLean, I. (2000). *Windows 2000 Security: The Little Black Book*. Scottsdale, Arizona: Coriolis. This is a readable but detailed guide to Windows 2000 security mechanisms. Good balance of theory about security mechanisms and how Windows 2000 implements these mechanisms.

Nichols, R. K. (1999). *ICSA Guide to Cryptosystems*. New York: McGraw-Hill. This is an excellent source for information about encryption algorithms and other technical mechanisms.

Schwartau, W. (2000). *Cybershock: Surviving Hackers, Phreakers, Identity Thieves, Internet Terrorists and Weapons of Mass Destruction*. New York: Thunder's Mouth Press. This is a broad and readable treatment of risks raised by attackers of various kinds.

Endnotes

1 The key actually has 64 bits, but only 56 bits are unique. The other 8 bits can be computed from the others as an error-checking safeguard.

2 Actually, the sender encrypts with the first key, *decrypts* with the second and then encrypts with the third. A variant of 3DES only uses two keys to encrypt three times, giving an effective keylength of 112 bits. In the third step, the sender encrypts again with the first key.

3 Yes, it is possible to encrypt with the private key. Decryption is then done with the public key.

4 Encrypting a message digest or other text string with one's private key also is called **signing** it with one's private key.

CHAPTER ELEVEN

Managing Web Site Performance and Reliability

Ross A. Lumley
George Washington University
Mitretek Systems, Inc., USA

An organization's e-commerce strategies either represent their entire existence for an Internet-only business or a significant investment by a traditional business. Competition on the Internet has resulted in many sites where a shopper can find the same goods and services. The differentiator for the market leader in a particular e-business is a positive shopping experience for the customer, which includes providing a reliable and high-performance Web site. This chapter describes a number of approaches to building reliable and high-performance Web sites.

INTRODUCTION

The business model of most organizations has seen a dramatic change in the last five years. Slightly more than five years ago the Internet did not allow any commercial business activity. The purpose of the Internet was for sharing information in a non-commercial environment. EPayNews.com (2000) shows the estimated revenues for US business-to-business (B2B) e-commerce goods for 1999 to be $43 billion according to Forrester Research, and it is expected to grow to $1.3 trillion by 2003. Revenues for US business-to-consumer (B2C) e-commerce goods for 1999 were estimated to be $8 billion and are expected to grow to $108 billion by 2003. The arrival of such a new paradigm for conducting business is resulting in new companies being formed to exploit this new economy model and established businesses scrambling to change their business model to compete in this new marketplace. E-commerce strategies for today's businesses either represent their entire existence for an Internet-only business or a significant investment by a traditional business.

Competition on the Internet has resulted in many sites where a shopper can find the same goods and services. Competition also has resulted in comparable pricing from the many sites. The differentiator for the market leader in a particular e-business is a positive shopping experience for the customer. Performance, availability and security are important characteristics in providing a positive shopping experience. The Graphics, Visualization & Usability (GVU) Center at Georgia Tech (1998) has found that the most frequently cited problem with the Internet is that it takes too long to view/download pages. The responsiveness of the Web site may determine whether a potential customer continues to do business or goes elsewhere.

Likewise, the strategy for putting together a Web site also has seen dramatic changes. From an approach as simple as taking a discarded server and running an open source version of a Web server application, today's large commercial Web sites have arrays of servers distributed around the world.

The traffic load of a popular e-commerce site increases by at least 50% on most weekends. In order to respond to this weekend increase, the Web master must increase the server capacity by adding additional servers to the Web site. Modern Internet traffic management techniques can add more servers automatically. It is very important in managing a commercial Web site that performance is managed proactively.

With the rapid adoption of the e-commerce business model, the stakeholder role has become strategic and includes key employees, business partners and customers. Without information regarding the stakeholders' perception of performance, the effectiveness of any enterprise application is in jeopardy.

This chapter will explore the strategies for building large scalable Web sites. The management responsibility for Web infrastructure planning should include performance and reliability. The growth in e-commerce and its strategic business role brings a challenge to IT management for providing an adequate network infrastructure.

A number of strategies have evolved during the last few years for building scalable Web sites. This chapter examines the traditional approaches to building an Internet Web site that can grow to handle large volumes of traffic. Next, the current array of product offerings is examined and finally, the future trend for high performance Web sites is discussed.

BACKGROUND

Managers of Internet-based businesses or e-commerce divisions of traditional businesses must take responsibility for the responsiveness of their Internet businesses. Menasce and Almeida (2000) raise a number of questions of concern for managers regarding Web site performance:

- Is the on-line trading site prepared to accommodate the surge in volume that may increase the number of trades per day by up to 75%?
- How can IT people justify to higher levels of management an enormous dollar amount for site expansion without showing any analytics?

- Is the number of servers enough to handle a peak of customers 10 times greater than the monthly average?
- How can we guarantee the quality of electronic customer service for different scenarios of traffic growth?
- In a business-to-business environment, sending and receiving sensitive data, conducting financial transactions and exchanging credit and production data depend on the secure and fast transmission of information. How can our company guarantee the quality of service required for implementing a supply-chain integration?
- E-business sites may become popular very quickly. How fast can the site architecture be scaled up? What components of the site should be upgraded? Database servers? Web servers? Application servers? Network link bandwidth?
- How can a small- or medium-sized company that cannot afford frequent hardware and software updates determine the adequate capacity of its e-business site?

Menasce and Almeida provide a comprehensive analysis of the quantification and projection of e-business performance including a range of strategies toward addressing these questions.

Basic Internet Operation

Before going into the details of how to make an Internet site scalable, let's first discuss the typical configuration of a large Web site. Figure 1 shows a Web site with a user connected to the Internet. We will start our tutorial on the Internet with the user entering a popular Web address into the browser. The technical name for the Web address is a Uniform Resource Locator or URL. The URL is a convenient way to advertise a Web site and easy for users to remember how to get there. However, the networks that make up the Internet communicate using a numeric address known as an Internet Protocol address or IP address. An IP address consists of four sets of numbers between 0 and 255 with each set separated by a dot. Thus the actual network address of a popular Web site such as www.popularsite.com might be 206.110.111.112. The URL is a much easier format for humans to work with and the IP address is a much easier format for computers and networks to work with.

Figure 1: Basic Internet operation

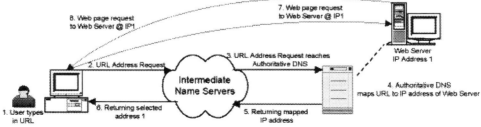

Once the user enters a URL, the browser must process the URL and convert or map it to an IP address. There are a number of ways that this is done, but the most basic way is for the browser to send a request on the Internet for the IP address corresponding to the provided URL address. The network service that performs this translation from URL to IP address is known as a Domain Name Server or DNS. Any intermediate Domain Name Server on the Internet may handle this request. The Internet Service Provider provides the first DNS for most user connections. Unless one of these intermediate DNSs knows the mapping of the desired URL address to its IP address, it will forward the browser's request on to a more knowledgeable DNS. The most knowledgeable DNS for a Web site is that site's authoritative DNS. This authoritative DNS knows the URL names of all the servers on its site and will complete the mapping of the URL address to the appropriate server's IP address.

The results of this mapping are returned to the requestor, which in this example is the user's browser. The browser will then use this IP address to request a connection to the Web server and request a particular page from the Web server. The Web server will retrieve the desired Web page and send the page to the user's browser. The browser then interprets the formatting information contained in the Web page and displays the page in the browser's window.

Scalability

Dictionary.com defines scalability as: "How well a solution to some problem will work when the size of the problem increases." This certainly applies to Internet Web sites. The management for an e-business must make sure that the capabilities of the site can rise to the need of the demand from visitors.

Estimating demand or traffic volume for an e-business can be especially challenging. Traffic can vary greatly by time of day, day of the week, day of the month and in response to advertising campaigns. If a site expects two million Web site visitors and instead receives four million visitors, then the administrators for the site must have a plan in mind to respond to the unexpected volume or else the site may experience substantial slowdowns and even outages. These performance problems can lead to turning away hundreds of thousands of visitors.

The basic strategy for scaling the capabilities of a Web site is to set up parallel server resources into what is known as a server farm. The server farm consists of multiple servers all of which are connected to the Internet in some fashion. However, most Web sites do not want to have a separate IP address and separate URL for each server in their server farm. This problem is dealt with in two ways, load balancing and load distribution.

This overall field is known as Internet traffic management. With the load balancing solution, the strategy is to setup the servers in the server farm behind a common IP address and use some method to direct each Web request to a specific server in the server farm.

In addition to meeting surges in traffic volume, a scalable Web site is also a more reliable Web site. Poor performance can just as easily result from a server failing as from increases in Web site traffic volume. As will be discussed below, products available for scaling Internet Web sites often provide the capability to add additional servers automatically if a server in the server farm fails.

Microsoft (1999) describes two dimensions to scalability, vertical and horizontal scalability. Vertical scalability increases capacity by increasing the specifications but keeping the same physical footprint and number of servers in the server farm. Vertical scaling has limits in that a physical server has a limit on maximum capacity. Site management is simpler but the hardware cost is typically higher than with horizontal scalability. Horizontal scalability increases capacity by adding servers. The focus of discussion in this chapter is on horizontal scalability.

Mourad and Liu (1997) describe empirical evidence that indicates a limit to the vertical scalability of the current generation of Web server applications. This is caused by multiprocessor platforms that do not provide the needed scalability to handle large traffic volumes. The reason is due primarily to the fact that current TCP/IP implementations are single-threaded which limits the potential of multiprocessor speedup for HTTP server applications.

Another popular approach to improving performance of Web sites is the use of caching popular Web pages. Arlitt and Williamson (1996) conducted a study of Web server workload characteristics and found that 10% of the files accessed account for 90% of the server requests and 90% of the bytes transferred. However, the trends in Web usage have shifted from static page requests to more dynamic page requests backed by database query results. Dynamic page requests are frequently not fulfilled by cached pages.

Internet Traffic Managers

Internet Traffic Management (ITM) products are becoming a standard component of any e-commerce Web site. Initially, ITM products will make the site highly available. Over the long run, as the Web site grows with increasing load, the ITM products will be essential for making the site scalable and in maintaining a high quality of service.

The Internet Traffic Management Center (2000) identifies eight real-world problems solved by Internet traffic management products.

1. Web servers and other computer systems fail.
2. No computer is big enough to service the load of a popular Web site.
3. Computers are not all equal.
4. The popularity of site content varies.
5. Not all site requests are equally important.
6. Bad things happen.
7. Networks are expensive—more expensive than most of us realize.
8. Parts of the Internet perform very poorly from time to time.

One of the primary tools used to build reliable and scalable Internet service is provided by a technique for redirecting incoming Web server requests to different servers in a server farm. As each new Web page request comes into the Internet site, the Internet traffic manager examines the request and, using one of the approaches discussed below, routes the request to the appropriate server.

Load Balancing vs. Load Distribution

The redistribution of Internet traffic can be done locally at a Web site as well as geographically to Web sites at different physical locations. Load balancing offers distribution of Web traffic within the same physical site, whereas load distribution spreads the Internet traffic across servers at different geographical locations. The techniques used by load balancers and load distributors are different and will be discussed in the following sections.

Figure 2 shows a single Web site with a load balancing solution to spread the load over the server farm. The other solution in Figure 2 shows a Web capability with three sites spread geographically across the Internet. Each of the servers at each of the sites has a fully replicated copy of the content so that each server can service any request. The load distributor determines the most efficient Web site to service each client's request and redirects the traffic to that location. The load distributor also provides a higher level of reliability by providing redundancy in the event that one of the sites is down or if an Internet routing problem prevents contact. A load distributor uses the Domain Name Services of the Internet to direct the client's request to the most appropriate Web site.

DNS-Based Load Balancing

The basic example described above for a request on the Internet is totally dependent on the mapping of the URL address to an IP address. This is accomplished by finding the authoritative DNS server for the requested Web site, and that

Figure 2 – Load balancing vs. load distribution

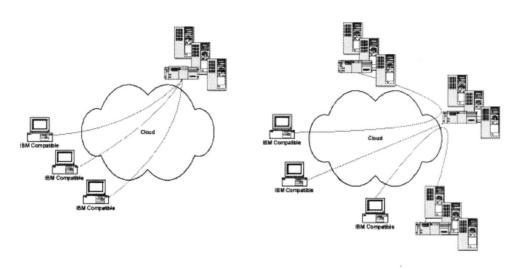

authoritative DNS server returns the address for the desired server. For a popular Internet site receiving many requests, it may not be possible for one Web server to handle all of the incoming requests. A large Internet site typically will solve this problem by establishing many Web servers all of which will have the same set of Web pages available.

The issue is how to spread the load to each of these servers. The original approach (see IETF DNS Working Group RFC 1794) to spreading the load across a group of servers is to equip the authoritative DNS server (i.e., the DNS server that knows the IP address of all the Web servers at the Web site) with more capability to decide which server should be given to each incoming Web request. There are several approaches to this allocation problem and we will discuss the possibilities shortly.

But first we will discuss the operation of the DNS approach. The basic concept of a DNS load balancer is to provide different IP addresses when mapping the URL address for the various replicated Web servers. Thus, one request from a browser may be given the IP address for Webserver 1, the next request will be given the address for Webserver 2 and so on. This type of load balancing is known as round-robin DNS load balancing. Round-robin DNS load balancing is one of the oldest approaches to Webserver load balancing and was first put in place at the National Center for Supercomputing Applications (NCSA) at the University of Illinois.

ISSUES, CONTROVERSIES AND PROBLEMS

The basic operation of the load balancing technique was described in the previous section. The strategy described was effective for early Web site scalability but has encountered numerous problems as the sophistication and complexity of the Internet has increased. Our attention will now shift toward understanding the nature of the problems, and then a number of solutions for dealing with the problems will be offered.

Problems with DNS Approach

A significant problem with the DNS-based load balancing strategy is the domain name caching that takes place across the Internet. Domain name resolution to an IP address takes place as a series of requests until a DNS server knows the full IP address of the target domain name. In order to reduce the traffic generated from domain name resolution requests, most DNS servers cache some number of domain names and their corresponding IP address. This way, popular domain names (e.g., www.yahoo.com) can be resolved quickly at an early DNS server in the chain.

Domain name caching defeats the advantage of the round-robin DNS approach to load balancing. One IP address resolved by the load balancing DNS server can be cached across the Internet and then all domain name resolution requests passed to the DNS server will be resolved with the cached IP address. Thus, the Web requests will bypass the round-robin DNS server and go directly to one server in the server farm.

Another problem with round-robin DNS load balancing is that it does not detect servers that are down and assumes all servers are equally powerful from a performance standpoint in handling Web requests. Thus, when the server farm consists of a mixture of server platforms with varying performance characteristics, slow servers will tend to be overloaded and fast servers will tend to be under utilized. This unbalanced loading occurs because the round robin algorithm receives no feedback as to how busy each server is in the server farm. More sophisticated approaches to load balancing monitor the health of the Web servers in the server farm.

Another increasingly important issue with load balancing is how to handle e-commerce sessions. If a user is connecting to a Web site to shop and possibly purchase goods or services, information about what goods are in a shopping basket and other status data must be maintained from one Web page browsed to another. When using many of the load balancing techniques, there is no guarantee that a client will connect to the server that has the knowledge regarding the shopping session.

SOLUTIONS AND RECOMMENDATIONS

The problems described above are typical of the simpler approaches to load balancing. As the e-commerce boom gained momentum, the need for sophisticated solution to these problems arose. The following sections discuss the commercialization of the ITM marketplace and the characteristics of the vendors and their products.

Types of Load Balancers

The commercialization of load-balancing technologies into off-the-shelf products has led to a product space of the following general categories:

1. Hardware appliance — a dedicated network device that tightly integrates and optimizes hardware and software to the task of load balancing.
2. Software — applications that run on standard system platforms and provide load-balancing services.
3. Switches – network devices enhanced with load-balancing functionality.

The advantages and disadvantages of each approach is discussed below.

Hardware Appliance

A hardware appliance is a closed system or closed box dedicated to the task of providing ITM functions. Hardware appliance load balancers provide a plug-and-play solution with minimal configuration required of network administrators. It often contains a computer system that resembles a personal computer. The hardware appliance runs a specialized operating system that is smaller than a PC operating system and is dedicated to providing the ITM functions. Because of the limited functions provided by the hardware appliance, reliability tends to be higher. The hardware appliance integrates the capabilities of ITM switches and ITM software.

It is built and tested as a closed unit at the factory and therefore quality control can focus on the performance and configuration resulting in a more reliable solution. Network managers often prefer a hardware appliance strategy as it closely matches the routers and other network devices with which they are familiar.

Software

Another approach to providing ITM products is to offer the functionality of a software application that runs on a standard computer. ITM software products are often more flexible in terms of how they can be modified and configured. However, the disadvantage versus the appliance approach is that the software must operate with an unknown configuration of hardware and software. For example, the performance of the network interface card (NIC) is very critical to the ITM software and yet the software may never have been tested on the specific NIC used in a given installation.

Network Switch

The network switch is an enhanced network device that still performs its network routing or switching functions but also includes the ITM functionality. The ITM network switch tends to be faster than the other approaches but does not typically look as deeply into the contents of each packet when making the decision as to which server to send each packet. The network switch approach uses a layer 2 or layer 3 network switch with integrated load balancing services. It does not require any separate servers to accomplish the load balancing.

Internet Traffic Manager Algorithms

The basic approach of using the DNS to redirect incoming Web traffic to alternate Web servers leaves open the question of how the Webserver should be chosen by the DNS. There are several answers to this question ranging from simplistic to complex. We will start with the simplest approach, which is to alternate between each Webserver in a round robin selection.

The basic question that the load balancing server needs an answer to is what kind of feedback can it obtain from the target servers in the server farm about their ability to receive more traffic. Some ITM products install an agent process on each of the target servers that it can communicate with and receive information about the target servers' condition. These agents were designed to provide details of the internal performance of each of the servers in the server farm.

Other ITM products depend on more passive indications of the load being applied to each Webserver in the server farm. Some of the passive techniques include keeping track of open connections to each server or using the standard network Ping protocol to gain insight into the responsiveness of each server. The ITM vendors have developed many other sophisticated approaches. Table 1 shows examples of some common load-balancing algorithms with a description of the unique characteristics of each.

Table 1: Load balancing algorithm

Algorithm	Description
Round Robin	Basic algorithm assumes all Web servers are equal and can handle any request to any information on the Web site. More advanced approach is to use a weighted algorithm where the weights can be used to account for different levels of performance from the Web servers in the server farm.
Weighted Ratio	Assigns weight to each server that can be statically assigned based on the relative performance of each server.
Fewest Connections	Monitors the active connections to each server and selects the server with the fewest number of connections
Fastest Response Time	Monitors the real-time response time of each server to a standard message and selects the server with the fastest measured response time.
Server State or Server Daemon Monitoring	A load balancer using a server daemon or state-based algorithm will constantly monitor the load and health of each server in the Web server farm. Server daemon monitoring uses an actual daemon process that the load-balancing machine polls to ascertain the load and health of each server.
Predictive	Selects server whose trend for observed performance is improving.
URL Parsing	The ITM device reads into the packet and HTTP header to determine the actual URL of the Web request. Based on the URL, a particular server will be chosen. URL parsing typically is used in combination with one of the other approaches.

A load balancer using some form of a server state algorithm monitors the availability and health of every server in the Webserver farm. Based on the status of each server, the load balancer selects the best server for each Web request. There are two methods that server-state-oriented load balancers typically use for monitoring server health—external and internal.

The load balancer may measure the state of each server by repeatedly sending ICMP Ping messages to each server and tracking how much time it takes to get a response. If no response is received after a number of attempts, the server is considered off-line and no Web requests will be routed to that server.

The ICMP Ping approach to monitoring server health does not provide any information on how the Webserver is actually responding. A more sophisticated method of testing server health is to send URLs to test the health of the Webserver itself.

Internal monitoring is accomplished by loading agent software on each Webserver in the Webserver farm. The agent sends internal status information to the load balancer such as the CPU, memory, disk and network utilization in addition to any other metrics maintained by the local Webserver operating system. Sophisticated load balancers may perform a combination of these algorithms and compute a weighted total for overall Webserver health.

How to Select the Right Load Balancer

The first selection decision is whether to use a hardware appliance or software approach. The ITM software products are attractive because of a lower cost since they allow use of off-the-shelf commodity-level server hardware. Generally, a hardware appliance or switch approach provides higher speeds and better reliability.

One complication with sites that require the maintenance of user information on an ongoing series of Web pages is how to send the user's Web requests to the same Webserver that has the "state" information for the user. An obvious example of this problem is seen in Figure 3 where the user is browsing for goods to purchase and is putting the selected goods into a shopping basket. The high-level communication protocol used for accessing a Webserver is called the Hypertext Transfer Protocol (HTTP). HTTP basically requires setting up a separate connection for each page requested. With each connection request, the ITM may transfer the request to a different server for every new request. If the information about the customer's shopping basket is maintained on the Webserver, then there needs to be a provision for sending each new request from the same user to the same Webserver. A simple approach to the persistence problem is shown in Figure 4 where the ITM load balancer keeps track of user IP addresses for some period of time and routes repeat visits by the same IP address to the same Webserver.

With every enhancement there are potential complications. One difficulty with implementing connection persistence is that many organizations use a proxy server to interface their entire internal network to the Internet. A proxy server essentially substitutes a special IP address for the user's internal network IP address. Thus every user accessing the Web site will appear to be the same user. The load balancer trying to maintain connection persistence may end up routing every Web request from every user behind this proxy server to the same server of the server farm. This may not be a great problem with smaller user communities behind a proxy server but it can be a serious problem with some proxy servers with large populations. One large population proxy server is America Online. All Web users from America Online appear to be one user and as a result could defeat using a load balancer.

One way to overcome this problem is to use both the user's IP address (which may be that of the proxy server) and TCP port number. The proxy server uses a unique TCP port number with each user request in order to be able to track the results of the Web request. This persistence problem also can be avoided if the Web site requires a secure connection. Under this scenario, the key to maintaining the connection persistence based on parameters used in a secure connection with SS is to use the SSL session ID.

Finally, the most recent approach to maintaining a persistent connection is with Web cookies which can include such information as user ID (if a login to the site is required) and last server used. Load balancers that can interpret Web cookie

Figure 3: Load balancing without persistence

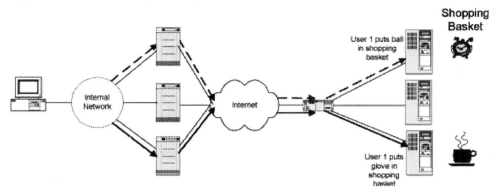

Figure 4: Load balancing with persistence

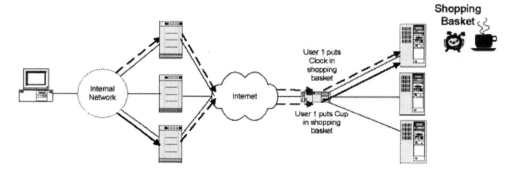

contents provide many possibilities for load balancing. The server servicing the Web request that results in the cookie actually defines the contents of the cookie. An example of more sophisticated use of the Web cookie is to store information in the cookie that indicates the quality of a customer in terms of how frequently they buy from the site. Then the load balancer can use the stored information on the quality of the customer and route requests from the best customers to the fastest Web servers. In this way a Web site is able to offer differentiated service based on the quality of the customer.

Clearly, all of the above complications illustrate the sophistication of today's load balancing products. Some of the features included in leading load balancing products include:

- Connection persistence
- SSL persistence
- Hardware reliability
- High performance
- Multiple port configurations
- Support for all IP protocols
- Deep HTTP header analysis (2000+ characters)

- Traffic prioritization for priority customers
- Full SNMP management
- Extensive SNMP and SYSLOG reporting
- Security
- Scalability and growth
- Complete redundancy

Therefore, the evaluation of available products should look for a balance of:
- Quality of service-based availability.
- Assured continuous operation with zero downtime.
- Simplified, consistent management across a breadth of protocols.
- Robust technical support and ease of installation.

ITM Vendors

The marketplace for ITM products has been soaring at rates comparable to the growth of the Internet. As discussed above, the vendors offer a range of products generally categorized as hardware appliance, network switches and software products. Table 3 lists a number of the ITM product vendors and the type of product each offers.

FUTURE TRENDS

Many of the features described above are moving in the direction of load balancers that look deep into the application layer of Internet packets so as to

Table 3: ITM product vendors

Vendor	Product Categories	Web Address
Alteon WebSystems	Switch	www.alteonwebsystems.com
ArrowPoint Inc.	Switch	www.arrowpoint.com
Cisco	Hardware	www.cisco.com
Coyote Point Systems Inc.	Hardware	www.coyotepoint.com
F5	Hardware	www.f5.com
Foundry Networks Inc.	Switch	www.foundry.com
HydraWeb Technologies	Hardware	www.hydraweb.com
Ipivot Inc. (Intel Corp.)	Switch	www.intel.com/network/ipivot/
Lightspeed Systems	Software	www.lightspeedsystems.com
Microsoft	Software	www.microsoft.com
RadWare	Hardware	www.radware.com
Resonate Inc.	Software	www.resonate.com

Table 4: Web traffic classification

Browse	80%
Search	9%
User Registration	2%
Add item to shopping cart	5%
Buying/checking out	4%

discriminate between different types of requests. Some of these products use this information to separate requests for static Web pages and search requests from shopping basket transactions or shopping basket checkout transactions so that these different types of requests can be sent to specific Web servers.

The future direction of the ITM industry is a movement toward more intelligent load balancers. Load balancing by sending Web requests to specialized servers can be used within an e-commerce Web site to provide the functionality that divides static pages, browsing, shopping and checkout. This type of load balancing is referred to as layer 7 management or HTTP header load balancing.

Enhanced network management tools can assist in forecasting trends for capacity management and real-time performance monitoring. A good network monitoring capability can help the manager know when and how to expand their Web server infrastructure to meet increasing user demand. Many products allow the manager to describe synthetic transactions that can routinely monitor the performance of actual use transaction types to assure that the critical transactions are performing well.

Microsoft has identified a strategy for scaling a Web site by improving the site's architecture. They recommend doing this by configuring specialized Web servers within the server farm. In this way the Web traffic might be segregated into categories based on the complexity of processing in response to the Web request. Thus, a request for a static Web page would be sent to one server while a request for a computationally intense Web page would be serviced by a different server.

To accomplish the Web server specialization described by Microsoft, it is necessary to use an ITM product that is capable of looking into the URL of the Web request and making a decision as to where to route the packet. Microsoft cites a study by Intel that showed all Web e-commerce traffic as falling into the categories shown in Table 4.

Intel found that browsing, registration and searching operations were done nine times more frequently than adding items to a shopping cart and checking out. Thus 90% of the e-commerce traffic can be handled by servers dedicated to static Web pages, while only 10% of the traffic needs to be routed to high-computation servers.

Microsoft shows that by following this strategy, the total number of servers needed to handle the static content portion of the e-commerce load could be reduced from 100 servers down to just 19 servers. Microsoft's Internet Information Server

(IIS) handles static Web pages rather efficiently, but processing requests for their Active Server Pages (ASPs) content creates a large CPU load. The conclusions of these findings were that matching the CPU-load factor profile in the distribution of Web requests across a server farm is much more efficient than randomly distributing the load.

One explanation of these results might be the impact of CPU caching of Web pages. With the large amount of RAM memory that can be installed on a Web server, a large percentage of static Web pages for a Web site may be kept in memory. However, by handling a mixed load of Web page requests, the Web server may not allow the cache to be maintained as consistently.

By 2002, much of today's ITM functionality will appear as standard features in routers, such as LAN switches and even LAN hubs. However, increased ITM functionality to analyze the CPU-load factor of each Web page request and then route the requests to the appropriate server will become more common.

CONCLUSION

This chapter has examined the importance of performance in e-business applications. It is clear that given the strategic importance of e-business strategies to most organizations, the management of such organizations must bear the responsibility of planning a robust and scalable solution to providing an infrastructure for building Internet-based business strategies.

While there are many strategies and issues involved with building a scalable Web site, one rather simple and popular approach involves the use of load balancing strategies. We have examined the underlying techniques used by load balancing products and reviewed some common uses of these products.

REFERENCES

Alteon WebSystems. (1999, June). *Firewall Load Balancing: Web Switching to Optimize Firewall Performance*. Retrieved May 18, 2000, from the World Wide Web: http:www.alteon.com.

Arlitt, M. F., and Williamson, C. L. (1996). Web server workload characterization: The search for invariants. *Proceedings of the ACM Sigmetrics Conference on Measurement & Modeling of Computer Systems*, 126-137.

Cardellini, V., Colajanni, M., and Yu, P. S. (1999). Dynamic load balancing on web-server systems. *IEEE Internet Computing*, 3(3), 28-39.

Dictionary.com. (2000). http://www.dictionary.com.

EPayNews.com. (2000). http://www.epaynews.com/statistics/purchases.html.

F5 Networks. (1999, April). *Building the Right Infrastructure for E-Commerce*. Retrieved May 22, 2000, from the World Wide Web: http://www.f5.com/solutions/whitepapers/ecommerce.pdf.

GVU. (1998, October). *GVU's Tenth WWW User Surveys 1998*. Retrieved May 18, 2000, from the World Wide Web: http://www.gvu.gatech.edu.

Hughes, L. (1998). *Internet E-Mail: Protocols, Standards and Implementation*. Norwood, MA: Artech House.

IETF DNS Working Group RFC 1794. (1995). *Internet Engineering Task Force*. Retrieved May 18, 2000, from the World Wide Web: http://andrew2.andrew.cmu.edu/rfc/rfc1794.html.

Internet Traffic Management Center. (2000). *Internet Traffic Management Products*. Retrieved May 18, 2000, from the World Wide Web: http://www.itmcenter.com.

Iyengar, A., Challenger, J., Dias, D., and Dantzig, P. (2000). High-performance Web site design techniques. *IEEE Internet Computing*, 4(2), 17-26.

Menasce, D. A., and Almeida, V. A. F. (2000). *Scaling for E-Business*. Upper Saddle River, NJ: Prentice Hall PTR.

Microsoft Corporation. (1999, September). *Building High-Scalability Server Farms*. Retrieved May 14, 2000, from the World Wide Web: http://www.microsoft.com/technet/commerce/bldhsfrm.asp?a=printable.

Mourad, A., and Liu, H. (1997). Scalable Web server architectures. *2nd IEEE Symposium on Computers and Communication*. Retrieved May 18, 2000, from the World Wide Web: http://dlib.computer.org/conferen/iscc/7852/pdf/78520012.pdf.

CHAPTER TWELVE

From Web Log
to Data Warehouse:
An Evolving Example

John M. Artz
George Washington University, USA

INTRODUCTION

Data warehousing is an emerging technology that greatly extends the capabilities of relational databases specifically in the analysis of very large sets of time-oriented data. The emergence of data warehousing has been somewhat eclipsed by the simultaneous emergence of Web technologies. However, Web technologies and data warehousing have some natural synergies that are just now being recognized. First, Web technologies make data warehouse data more easily available to a much wider variety of users both internally and externally. Since the value of data is directly related to its availability for exploitation, Internets and intranets help increase the value of the data in the warehouse. Second, data warehouse technologies can be used to analyze traffic to a Web site in a wide variety of ways in order to make the Web site more effective. This chapter will focus on the latter of these synergies and show, through an evolving example, how a simple data set from the Web log can be enhanced, in a step-wise fashion, into a full-fledged market research data warehouse.

BACKGROUND

For people who are not intimately familiar with data warehousing technologies, the first questions that arise are—what is a data warehouse and how does it differ from a traditional relational database? The standard definition for a data warehouse is "A data warehouse is a subject-oriented, integrated, nonvolatile and time variant collection of data in support of management decisions" (Inmon, 1996). This definition provides a good starting point, and closer inspection of the components of this definition does provide some insight into the nature of a data warehouse. First, a subject-oriented database is a database that is organized around subjects of interest to facilitate information exploitation rather than processing. This means that, by nature, the purpose of the data warehouse is to deliver information rather than to support processing. Integrated means that all data is accessible through the same interface and that underlying data sets can be linked using common keys. To say that the data warehouse is integrated is to say that users of the data warehouse do not need to be aware of the technologies used to manage the underlying data nor do they need to be aware of peculiarities in data set design when performing analysis across data sets.

Time varying is the most important characteristic that distinguishes a data warehouse from a traditional relational database. A traditional relational database represents the state of an organization at a point in time. Kimball (1986) calls this a "twinkling database" because records come and go but do not reveal a pattern over time. A data warehouse, on the other hand, represents that organization as it changes over time. To put this more precisely, a relational database is a snapshot of the organization at a point in time whereas the data warehouse is a collection of longitudinal data.

Since the data is time oriented it is also nonvolatile. The facts that were true last month remain true for last month. If they change this month then they are new facts for the current month. The only reason you would change historical data is if you were to discover that a fact from a previous point in time was recorded incorrectly. So the data warehouse accepts new data on some periodic basis, but existing data should not change. Finally, the data warehouse is used primarily for organizational decision making which means that it is not operational data, nor is it management information. It is data that is used primarily for forecasting and decision support. This means that the typical usage of the data will be at a much higher level of summary than transaction-level data.

Having given the broad view of the data warehouse, it is useful to take a few steps to further refine this perspective. The unit of decomposition in a relational database is the entity, which is generally defined as a thing of interest to the organization. Entities typically include customers, products, employees and the like. The purpose of a relational database is to maintain the current state of the entities—how many are there, and what facts are true about them at the current moment. Typical questions that one might ask of a relational database are—how many employees are there in the marketing department, which department has the most employees or which department has the highest average salary. These questions all address the state of the organization at a point in time.

The unit of decomposition for the data warehouse is a fact that represents a measure of a key business process. Units sold, dollars sold and gross margin are typical measures for some business processes although numbers of visitors, or time spent viewing a Web page are also useful measures for others. While the relational database tracks the status of entities as indicated by the values of attributes, the data warehouse tracks the success of business processes as indicated by the measurements of those processes.

The temporal nature of the data in the warehouse must also be emphasized as a key difference between relational databases and data warehouses. Kimball states "virtually every data warehouse is a time series" (1986). Whereas a relational database can be metaphorically thought of as a picture of the night sky, the data warehouse can similarly be thought of as a time lapse photograph of the movement of the stars. Information that can be derived from changes over time may not be available at all in a relational database.

For example, consider a relational database that contains inventory information. There will likely be a record in the database for each item in inventory. When a product is sold, the record in the inventory table is deleted. When a product is received at the loading dock, a record is added to the inventory table. At any point in time, it is possible to compute units on hand for any given product by summarizing the inventory table. However, if you were to need units on hand by day or by week, or the average number of units on hand for some time period, it would simply not be available because units on hand could only be determined for the current moment that the database represents.

One could argue that it would be possible to derive daily balances in the relational database and store them in another table. This observation is certainly correct; however, it also leads to other limitations in relational databases. First, an analyst may wish to summarize inventory balances in a variety of ways—by product, by warehouse location, by time interval, etc. These summaries may lead to questions that require high levels of summary such as product category, or greater levels of detail such as increasingly more specific time periods such as by month, then by week, then by day. These manipulations can be very complex and difficult in SQL. Data warehouse technologies make this kind of analysis much easier. Second, although standard SQL does provide a DateTime data type, it is very limited in its handling of dates and times. If an analyst wanted to compare inventory levels on weekends versus weekdays or holidays versus non-holidays, it would be difficult if not impossible using standard SQL. To determine if inventory shortages in two different products were coincident in time would not even be imaginable. Hence, current relational technology can nod toward processing of temporal data, but falls substantially short of actually delivering it.

Data warehousing technology overcomes these deficiencies in the relational model by representing data in a dimensional model. A dimensional model consists of a fact table (see Figure 1) and the associated dimensions. The fact table contains measures of the business process being tracked, and the dimensional tables contain information on factors that may influence those measures. More specifically, the fact table contains dependent variables while the dimension tables contain independent variables. Online Analytical Processing (OLAP) tools provide a means of summarizing the measures in the fact table according to the dimensions provided in the dimension tables toward the end of determining what factors influence the

Figure 1: A dimensional model

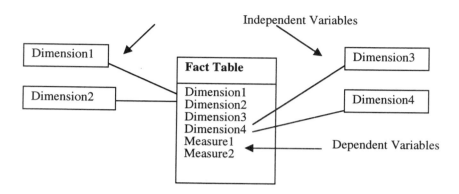

business process being modeled. Typically OLAP tools provide a means of easily producing higher levels of summary (roll-up) or greater levels of detail (drill-down).

Since information is usually collected at the transaction level, the data for the data warehouse must go through a 'staging' process where it is manipulated and summarized for the dimensional model. In addition, dimension tables may be constructed separately to enhance the possibilities for analysis of the measures.

The synergy between data warehousing and Web technologies can be seen most easily when the Web log (the file that records hits on Web pages) is represented in a dimensional model and then exploited using OLAP or data mining tools.

THE WEB LOG

A visitor to a Web site requests a page by typing in the address of the page, in a Web browser or by clicking on a link that automatically requests that page. A message is sent to the Web server at that address, and the Web server responds by returning the page. If the page contains graphics, the Web browser sends additional requests to the Web server to retrieve those files also. Each request that is processed

Figure 2: A typical Web log record

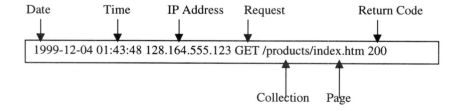

by the Web server is recorded in a file called the Web log, which contains a record of all activity on the Web site. The record typically contains the date and time, the IP address of the requestor, the page requested and the result. A typical record in standard format is shown in Figure 2. Formats vary and some Web logs contain additional information. But for the purpose of this evolving example, this minimal set is adequate.

From this simple log record, we can determine quite a bit about the traffic coming to the Web site. For example, from the date field we can ask: 1) When do we get the most traffic? 2) Is traffic to the Web site steady or cyclical? 3) Is there more Web traffic on weekends or weekdays? Answers to these questions might help the Web master in determining the best time to do maintenance or when to roll out new collections. From the time field we can ask: 1) Do visitors come during the workday or in the evening? 2) At what point during the day is the traffic the lightest? or 3) Is traffic spread out evenly throughout the day? Answers to these questions would be useful in determining when to do backups or when to take a server offline for maintenance.

Each request contains a path to the page from the root page of the Web site. If the directories are set up so that the beginning of the path name corresponds to an identifiable collection of pages, then we can determine the number of visitors by page and by collection. From this information we can answer questions such as: 1) Which collections are the most heavily visited? or 2) Which pages are the most heavily visited? Answers to these questions would be helpful in determining how to allocate development resources or which page designs are the most effective for attracting visitors.

Fields such as Date or Time can be combined with Collection to answer questions such as: 1) Are different collections visited more heavily at different times of the day? 2) Are different collections accessed more on weekends? or more generally 3) Do traffic patterns vary by collection?

The type of request is usually a "GET," however, other requests may indicate a form being submitted or a collection owner performing maintenance to the collection. Other operations might indicate a search engine probing the site or a hacker testing security. The Return Code indicates the final resolution of the request. A "200" means that the request was satisfied. A "401" indicates that the visitor did not have the appropriate authority to access the page. From these two pieces of information, we can answer further questions about the Web site such as: 1) How many requests are visitors versus collection owners? 2) Are there dead links? 3) Are permissions set incorrectly? or 4) Is there evidence of hacking?

A WEB LOG DIMENSIONAL MODEL

From just these six fields (Date, Time, Request, Collection, Page, Return Code) in a flat file format from the Web log, the Web master can determine quite a bit of information about the usage and traffic patterns on the Web site. However, by

Figure 3: A dimensional model based on the Web log

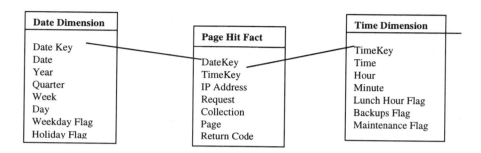

viewing the Web log as a data source for a data warehouse, it becomes an even richer source of data about the Web site. Figure 3 shows a first cut at a dimensional data model derived from the Web log.

By converting the Web log to a fact table and adding both Date and Time dimensions, it becomes possible to do additional analysis. For example, the Date dimension can identify specific days as holidays, weekdays, deadlines, sales or promotions or any other event that might be noteworthy for analysis. The Time dimension can identify time periods such as daytime, lunchtime or evening, although this gets a little tricky since visitors may be in any time zone when they access a page.

In the data staging process, the records in the Web log that did not reflect page requests would be filtered out. This would include the requests for graphics files that would substantially reduce the volume of the Web log. There may be other reasons why the graphics file requests would be left in, but for this example, the focus is on page hits.

With a little extra work on the dimensions, the model could be further expanded, as shown in Figure 4, to include dimensions for IP Address and Page.

Figure 4: An expanded dimensional model

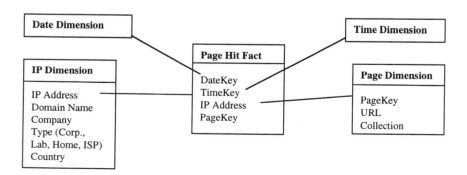

The IP Address dimension allows the Web log analyst to determine where the visitors are coming from or if certain collections attract visitors from different quarters. From this information it is possible to determine if the target audience is being reached. The IP Address dimension can be maintained at a variety of levels of granularity and completeness depending on the information needed. Keeping only three levels of IP address will usually identify a company or a service provider, but will not identify individual computers as four levels would. Three levels of IP address would require 16 million records, while four levels of IP address would require four billion records. Assuming a 100-byte record which provides ample room for the domain name, company name and country, this dimension table may get quite large. One option for reducing the size of this dimension table would be to snowflake (which is the dimensional model equivalent to normalizing) the table. This would reduce the duplicated character strings for domain name, company name and country to integer pointers into separate tables and reduce the storage requirements by up to 75%. Another option for reducing the size of this table would be to maintain records only for IP addresses that have actually visited the site. Even if a site has had 10 million unique visitors, this is still only 0.25% of the four billion possible IP addresses.

DWELL TIME

The model shown in Figure 4 contains a factless fact table. That is, a record in the fact table indicates that an event occurred, but does not provide any measure of that event. One of the things that Web designers like to know is how long did a person stay on a page. The time spent viewing a page is called dwell time and can be used as a measure of how useful the information on the page was to the visitor. Specifically, the longer the visitor spent on the page, the more valuable the information. Dwell time can be computed by sorting the Web log by IP address, date and time. This new sequence will show the log records by visitor. Consider the three log records shown in Figure 5.

Figure 5: Computing dwell time

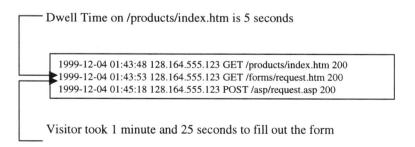

Dwell Time on /products/index.htm is 5 seconds

```
1999-12-04 01:43:48 128.164.555.123 GET /products/index.htm 200
1999-12-04 01:43:53 128.164.555.123 GET /forms/request.htm 200
1999-12-04 01:45:18 128.164.555.123 POST /asp/request.asp 200
```

Visitor took 1 minute and 25 seconds to fill out the form

Figure 6: A fact table including dwell time

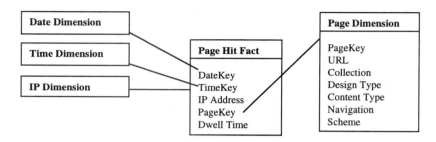

From just these three log records, we can determine that the visitor came directly to the products page, which means that they bookmarked the page or came to it from another site. They found what they were looking for in five seconds and went to a form to order the product. It took a minute and 25 seconds to fill out the form and the visitor did not look at any further pages. We can compute dwell time for each page by subtracting the time on one log record from the time on the same visitors next log record. This computation is not foolproof, of course. You cannot tell how long the visitor lingered on the last page they visited. Nor can you be sure that the user did not get interrupted with a telephone call while they were looking at the page. In a shared lab, one person may visit a few pages and then leave. The next person who sits down might very well have the same IP address and appear to be the same user. Hence, it is prudent to establish a cutoff threshold. For example, if there is more than a few minutes between hits, it may be a good idea to treat it as a new visitor unless the page is a form or has a lot of text, in which cases the threshold should be raised.

It takes a little more processing, in data staging, to compute dwell time, but now we have a dimensional model with a worthwhile measure rather than a factless fact table. The addition of this fact allows us to do analysis to determine what factors affect dwell time. If dwell time is a function of the visitor, date or time, then there is little that can be done by the Web developers to increase it. However, expansion of the page dimension allows the analyst to determine if dwell time is influenced by content or page design. Figure 6 shows a dimensional model with the dwell time and an expanded page dimension to capture information about the design, content and navigation scheme used on the page. This model is somewhat focused on determining what factors are likely to increase dwell time. It is not the only grain that can be derived from the Web log.

LENGTH OF VISIT

Another useful measure of Web site effectiveness is length of visit. Referring back again to Figure 5, it is easy to see how measures other than dwell time might be derived. For example, the total time between the first page request and the last

Figure 7: A dimensional model for length of visit

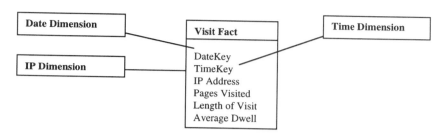

page request is a minute and 30 seconds. We don't actually know how long the visitor dwelled on the last page, but this measure will have to do. We also know that the visitor viewed three pages, averaging 30 seconds per page. Now we can create a fact table in which we have three measures of visitor behavior—length of visit, pages visited and average dwell time per page. This model is shown in Figure 7.

From this new dimensional model we can ask further questions regarding visitor behavior: 1) Does length of visit or pages visited vary by time of day? 2) Are visitors likely to surf longer in the evening or on weekends? or 3) Do home visitors visit more pages than corporate visitors? If the Web site has a well-defined target audience, answers to these questions might help the Web site designers develop more effective collections.

CONFORMED DIMENSIONS

Conformed dimensions in a data warehouse are dimensions that are shared across dimensional models, providing two benefits. First, construction of dimensions (such as the IP Address dimension) can be costly and time consuming. Using these dimensions across multiple dimensional models spreads out the cost. Second, having shared dimensions allows analysis across fact tables, which may provide even further insight into the processes being analyzed.

If the Date, Time and IP Address dimensions are conformed, the Page Hit Fact table and the Visit Fact table can share these dimensions. The resulting integrated model is shown in Figure 8.

Figure 8: An integrated dimensional model with conformed dimensions

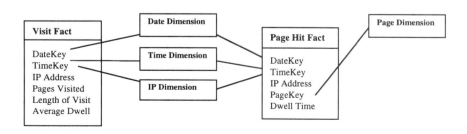

Now it is possible to answer questions that relate dwell time and pages to length of visit and number of pages visited. Note that the Visit Fact table contains the Average Dwell, but it does not contain the maximum, minimum or any character-istics of the distribution. For this information the Page Hit Fact table is needed. Further, the Page Dimension tells which collections were visited, making it possible to see if visit length is related to the collection or attributes of the collection.

SIZING THE WEB LOG DATA WAREHOUSE

The Date dimension would have one record for each day of operation for the Web site. At 22 bytes per record, the Date dimension would only require about 8K per year. The Time Dimension would require only 1,440 bytes, so little additional storage is required to add these dimensions. The IP dimension is a little trickier to size since it requires quite a few assumptions. However, assuming 10 million unique visitors, and a 100-byte record, the IP dimension would require one billion bytes or one gigabyte. If this dimension were snowflaked, the size could be reduced by as much as 90%. However, this storage savings would have to be weighed against the increase in processing time to join the snowflaked tables. The Page dimension would also have a 100-byte record, largely due to the URL contained in the record. A site with 1,000 pages would require 100,000 bytes for the Page dimension. A site with 10,000 pages would require 1,000,000 bytes or one megabyte for the page table.

To estimate the Visit Fact table and the Page Hit fact table, we will assume 100 hits per minute or 144,000 hits per day. Assuming the average visitor views 10 pages, this becomes 14,400 visitors per day.

The Visit Fact table would require 36 bytes per record. Assuming 14,400 visits per day, the Visit Fact table would grow at a rate of 518,400 bytes per day or roughly 15 megabytes per month.

Yet, the largest table would be the Page Hit fact table. The record size would be 32 bytes, and with 144,00 hits per day, it would grow at a rate of 4.6 megabytes per day or 138 megabytes per month.

At the end of one year, the Visit Fact table would require 180 megabytes and the Page Hit Fact table would require 1.6 gigabytes.

DATA MINING THE WEB LOG

OLAP techniques largely address summarizing the measures in the fact table in order to determine which attributes of which dimensions influence those mea-sures. Other techniques, called data mining, allow the analyst to look for hidden relationships in the data. A data mining technique called visualization presents voluminous quantitative data in a visual format, making it easier to visually identify trends. Consider a storyboard that is visually encoded with darker shades of gray to

Figure 9: A visualization of traffic to the Web site

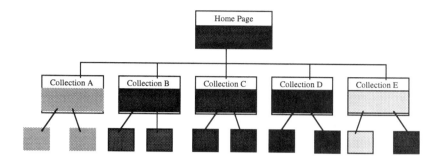

depict heavier traffic such as the one shown in Figure 9. From this visualization we can make several observations regarding the traffic to the Web site. First, we can easily see that Collection D is the most heavily visited collection. Second, Collection D is darker than the Home Page, which means that it has more visitors than the Home Page. If visitors were going through the Home Page to get to Collection D, then the Home Page would have at least as many visitors as Collection D. Hence, visitors must be arriving at Collection D via a bookmark or from another site. If we have news, sales or other time-critical information on the Home Page, it might make sense to move it to Collection D to make sure that visitors see it. Collections A and E are not very heavily visited, suggesting that the current set of top-level categories should be reexamined. Collection E has very light traffic, raising questions regarding its value on the Web site. Finally, Collection E has a subpage that is more heavily visited, again suggesting bookmarks or links from other pages. It may make sense to move this page directly off the home page. However, since we know that most visitors arrive via links, we may want to put a page at the current address that would automatically move visitors to the new address. The benefit of visualization techniques such as this one is that analysts can easily conceptualize traffic patterns without having to absorb large volumes of detailed data.

A MARKETING RESEARCH DATA WAREHOUSE

So far the dimensional models have focused on the behavior of Web site visitors in an attempt to determine which factors make them dwell longer on a page or extend their visit to the Web site. With some simple enhancements it is possible to extend the existing dimensional models into a full-fledged marketing research data warehouse.

Many sites require their customers to log into the site. Prior to activating the login ID, the visitor is asked to respond to a simple online survey form that provides some basic demographic information. This goes beyond the Web log, but allows

Figure 10: Integrated market research dimensional
model with conformed dimensions

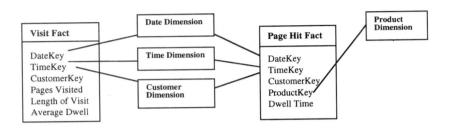

even more sophisticated analysis of visitor behavior. The program that processes the form can record the IP address, date and time along with the demographic information. With this information, the IP Address dimension from the previous model can be extended into a Customer dimension. If the site is designed in such a way that pages viewed can be translated into products viewed, then the Page dimension can be extended into a Product dimension allowing analysis of Customers viewing Products rather than Visitors viewing Pages. In fact, if sales are accepted online, sales events can be recorded in a sales fact table, even further extending the scope of the analysis into a full market research application. Not only would it be possible to analyze customer behavior with respect to products, but it would also be possible to tie that behavior to Web shopping behavior and ask questions like—Are visitors more likely to buy at certain times of the day such as lunchtime or certain days such as the first of the month or on weekends? Figure 10 shows the integrated dimensional models with two fact tables and conformed dimensions.

The example presented here started with a dimensional model of the Web log and evolved that model into a market research data warehouse. So as not to get too focused on the current models, it is important to remember that the purpose of a data warehouse is to provide quantitative time-varying information about the effectiveness of business processes. Consequently, a wide variety of other models could have just as well been evolved to analyze a wide variety of other activities, including advertising, information dissemination, security, software distribution and the like. If the Web site is an intranet, then customers become employees and the questions center around how well the Web site meets the needs of its users. The possible models are as varied as the possible purposes of a Web site. What is important to remember is that the Web server generates a large volume of time-varying data and that dimensional models within data warehousing technology are the most effective means of exploiting that data.

USING THE WEB TO GET TO THE DATA WAREHOUSE

Although the focus of this chapter was to show how data warehousing technology can be used to exploit the large volumes of data that are generated by a Web site, it is important to remember that these technologies are truly synergistic. That is, Web technologies can be used to advantage in data warehousing applications. A data warehouse that is not fully exploited does not return its full potential. Web technologies help make the data warehouse more accessible thus increasing its value.

The Web can be used in a variety of ways to make the data warehouse more accessible. At a minimum, instructions for accessing the warehouse can be put on a company's intranet, along with tutorials and documentation of the available data. Similarly summary data sets can be published, allowing users to download information into a spreadsheet or local database. In more advanced applications, server scripts can be written to extract customized summary sets from the data warehouse for further analysis on client machines. Finally, Web-friendly OLAP tools would allow anyone with proper permissions to access the data warehouse interactively, extracting custom data sets from the warehouse and analyzing them using browser plug-ins.

FUTURE TRENDS

According to Information Navigators, there are approximately 72 million hosts on the Web. Many of these hosts do not support Web sites, but many others (such as those owned by ISPs) have multiple Web sites. If only 10 million of these Web sites attract as few as 100 visitors a minute, then one billion records are generated every minute. This becomes 60 billion records per hour, or 1.4 trillion records per day. This is an enormous amount of information, providing great insight into the behavior of consumers and information seekers, among others. This huge volume of temporal data cannot be exploited effectively without data warehouse technology. Hence, the growth of the Web may well push the growth of data warehousing.

At the same time, data warehousing concepts continue to evolve. What started out as a dumping ground for used data is rapidly becoming a rigorously defined set of dimensional models to track key business processes. The technology is improving also. OLAP tools are making it easier to analyze dimensional data through visual interfaces, and data mining tools are making it easier to find useful patterns in large volumes of data. In today's tools there are gaps between SQL and OLAP, and again between OLAP and data mining. Data mining approaches are segmented between visualization, statistical and artificial intelligence. These disparate approaches will eventually become integrated in seamless tool sets that provide a variety of analytical techniques, along with some guidance on which approaches to use.

These OLAP and data mining tools will become more Web friendly as demand to access data warehouses from disparate locations increases. It is conceivable that at some point in the very near future, Web applications will become the primary source for data in most corporate data warehouses, while Web technologies will become the primary vehicle for accessing that data.

CONCLUSIONS

Data warehousing technologies and Web technologies are highly synergistic. Web technologies make data warehouse data more accessible to a much wider variety of users on both the Internet and intranets. Since, the value of data is determined by its usefulness in supporting decision making, Web technologies help increase the value of the data in the warehouse. Perhaps, more importantly, data warehouse technologies can be used to analyze the enormous volumes of data generated by a Web site. As Web sites generate large volumes of data for data warehouse and in turn provide easy access to that data, it is conceivable that these two highly synergistic technologies may become indistinguishable in the future.

REFERENCES

Adriaans, P. and Zantinge, D. (1997). *Data Mining*. Addison-Wesley.
Information Navigators Internet Growth Charts. http://navigators.com/statall.gif contained in http://navigators.com/.
Inmon, W. (1996). *Building the Data Warehouse* (2e). John Wiley and Sons, Inc.
Kimball, R. (1996). *The Data Warehouse Toolkit*. John Wiley & Sons, Inc.
Kimball, R. et. al. (1998). *The Data Warehouse Lifecycle Toolkit*. John Wiley and Sons.
Kimball, R. and Merz, R. (2000). *The Data Webhouse Toolkit*. John Wiley and Sons.
Westphal, C. and Blaxton, T. (1998). *Data Mining Solutions*. John Wiley and Sons.

About the Authors

EDITOR

Subhasish Dasgupta is assistant professor of information systems in the School of Business and Public Management, The George Washington University. He holds BS and MBA degrees from the University of Calcutta, India, and a PhD from Baruch College, The City University of New York, NY, USA. His research interests include electronic commerce, information technology adoption and diffusion, effects of information technology investment on firm performance, group decision making and global information systems. He has published in journals such as *Journal of Global Information Management, Logistics Information Management, Electronic Markets: The International Journal of Electronic Commerce and Business Media, Journal of Global Information Technology Management,* and *Simulation and Gaming Journal.* Dr. Dasgupta has also presented his research at numerous regional, national and international conferences.

CONTRIBUTORS

John M. Artz is an associate professor of management science at The George Washington University in Washington, DC. He teaches classes in information systems development, relational databases, data warehousing, and Web-based systems development. His research interests are in philosophical and theoretical problems in relational databases and data warehouses. Dr. Artz's previous publications include, "How Good is that Data in the Warehouse?" published in *Database* and "A Crash Course in Metaphysics for the Database Designer" published in *The Journal of Database Management.*

Kemal Cakici is a multimedia and research specialist in the Instructional Technology Lab and an adjunct instructor in both the School of Business and Public Management, and the School of Engineering and Applied Sciences at The George Washington University. He specializes in new technologies, educational applications of the different technologies, network systems and consults and provides solutions in identifying information technology strategies for companies. Kemal holds an MSc in mechanical engineering and is pursing a PhD in information and decision systems at The George Washington University.

Mary J. Granger is an associate professor of management science in the School of Business and Public Management at The George Washington University. Her research interests include information systems curriculum development, ethical and professional issues in the curriculum, computer-aided software engineering and database design. She has published previously in *Journal of Information Systems Education, The Journal of Education in MIS* and the *SIGCSE Bulletin*. She has also co-chaired working groups for the Introducing Technology into Computer Science Education (ITiCSE) conference.

Åke Grönlund is director of research education in the Department of Informatics at Umea University, manager of the North Sweden Informatics Research School and founding faculty of the Center for Studies of IT in the Public Sector (CSIPS). His research focuses on emerging uses of ICT such as electronic services in an organizational context, ICT strategies, business organization, use and usability. Current work includes electronic government, electronic democracy, and mobile work. He has served for many years as consultant in international European research and development projects in the field of electronic services development, management, and evaluation. Åke Grönlund can be contacted by e-mail at gron@informatik.umu.se. Web home: http://www.informatik.umu.se/~grpn.

Ashu Guru is a PhD student in industrial and management systems engineering at the University of Nebraska-Lincoln. He received his master of science degree in manufacturing systems engineering from the University of Nebraska-Lincoln. His research interests include computer simulation and database systems.

Beverley Hope is a teacher in information systems in the School of Communications and Information Management at Victoria University of Wellington, New Zealand. She completed a bachelor of science and MBA at the University of Kansas and a PhD at the University of Hawaii at Manoa. During her PhD studies she was supported by a scholarship from the East-West Centre. Beverley's research and teaching focus on quality, information management and IS research skills. In her work she takes a holistic or system view of organizations and the issues that face them. Her research has dealt with such issues as: information needs for service quality, performance measurement, extranet quality, developing data collection plans, computerized decision support and teaching research skills. She has presented and published at many regional and international conferences in information systems, decision sciences and evaluation, and acted as referee for several international conferences and journals.

Csilla Horváth is a PhD candidate in the Faculty of Economics at the University of Groningen, the Netherlands. She received her BBA degree in economics and her MS degree in mathematical economics from the Budapest University of Economic Sciences. Her current research areas are electronic commerce and modeling competitive marketing systems.

Ross A. Lumley is assistant professor of information systems in the School of Business and Public Management, The George Washington University. He holds a BS degree from the University of California, Berkeley, and an MS and PhD from the University of Texas, Dallas. Dr. Lumley's research interests include electronic commerce systems and business-to-business workflow systems, including performance and security factors.

John C. McIntosh is an assistant professor at Bentley College. He received his PhD degree from the University of Illinois, Champaign. His journal publications have appeared in *Journal of International Business and Entrepreneurship*, *Journal of Applied Business Research*, and others. His research focuses on the strategic use of information technologies and electronic commerce. He is also a frequent consultant for a number of businesses in the US and abroad.

Fui Hoon (Fiona) Nah is assistant professor of management information systems at University of Nebraska-Lincoln. Previously she was a member of the faculty at Purdue University. She received her PhD in management information systems from University of British Columbia. Her current research interests include organizational issues in enterprise resource planning implementations, evaluation of information systems for supporting individual, group and organizational decision making, using information technology to overcome human cognitive biases and theory building in information systems research.

Raymond R. Panko is a professor of information technology management at the University of Hawaii. His textbook, *Business Data Communications and Networking* (Prentice Hall, 2001), explores the broad realm of business networking, in which m-commerce and security promise to be key issues. Before joining the university, he was a project manager at Stanford Research Institute (now SRI International), where he conducted research for the Office of the President of the United States and many other research clients. He has also worked for the Boeing Corporation and Applied Magnetics Corporation. He received his doctorate from Stanford University. He can be reached at Ray@Panko.com. His homepage is http://panko.com.

Katia Passerini is a consultant in the Information Technology Group of Booz Allen & Hamilton and an adjunct instructor at The George Washington University. She specializes in multimedia applications and delivery over fixed and mobile networks, knowledge management and information technology strategy. Her prior experience in the field of communications and multimedia technology include for The World Bank, East Asia and Pacific Development Unit and the Instructional Technology Laboratory in Washington DC. Katia holds an MBA from The George Washington University, where she is completing a PhD in information and decision systems.

Jeremy Rose was born in Manchester, won an exhibition to read English at Cambridge and subsequently trained to be a musician at the Royal College of Music in London. After working for some years for the Rambert Dance Company and Music Projects London, his career was cut short by injury and he retrained at Lancaster, gaining his MSc in information management with distinction and later returned for his PhD. He took up his present post as senior lecturer in business information technology in the Faculty of Management and Business at the Manchester Metropolitan University in 1992. He collaborated with Peter Checkland on research projects, and has more recently worked with colleagues at the University of Aalborg (where he is visiting associate professor) and Georgia State University. He has published in management, systems and IS forums, and his doctoral studies focused on intranet development. Other research interests include IS development and evaluation, systems methodology, structuration theory and actor network theory, BPR, knowledge management and the health service.

Rens Scheepers is a senior lecturer at the School of Information Technology, Swinburne University of Technology, Victoria, Australia. Prior to his current position, he has been managing marketing and business systems in a large industrial research organization. His present research interest is the business use of Internet technologies in general, and specifically intranet and extranet implementation and management. He has presented his research at leading international conferences in Europe and the US and in a number of international journals. He holds an MBA from Pretoria University in South Africa and a PhD in computer science from Aalborg University in Denmark.

Keng Siau is a J. D. Edwards professor and an associate professor of management information systems (MIS) at the University of Nebraska, Lincoln (UNL). He received his PhD degree from the University of British Columbia (UBC) where he majored in management information systems and minored in cognitive psychology. Dr. Siau is currently the editor-in-chief of the *Journal of Database Management*. He has published more than 25 journal articles that have appeared in *MIS Quarterly, IEEE Computer, Information Systems, ACM's Data Base, Journal of Database Management, Journal of Information Technology, International Journal of Human-Computer Studies, Transactions on Information and Systems*, and others. In addition, he has published over 45 refereed conference papers in proceedings such as ICIS, ECIS, HICSS, CAiSE, WITS, IRMA and HCI. He has edited two books, two journal special issues and five proceedings—all of them related to systems analysis and design. He has served as the organizing and program chairs for the International Workshop on Evaluation of Modeling Methods in Systems Analysis and Design (EMMSAD) (1996-2000). Dr. Siau's primary research interests are in object oriented systems development using unified modeling language (UML), mobile commerce, enterprise e-business, enterprise resource planning (ERP) and Web-based systems development.

Betty Wang is a graduate student in management information systems at the University of Nebraska-Lincoln. She received her master's degree in accounting from the School of Accountancy of the University of Nebraska-Lincoln. She has more than 10 years of extensive industry experience in finance/accounting, strategic planning, financial management, project management, information technology management and general management with several large organizations worldwide. Her current research interests include business and technical issues in enterprise resource planning and e-business implementations.

I. Hakan Yetkiner is a PhD candidate in the Faculty of Economics at the University of Groningen, the Netherlands. He received his BS degree in management from the Middle East Technical University, Turkey, and MSc degree in economics from London School of Economics, United Kingdom. His interests are growth theory, dynamic trade theory and the Internet economy. Current research includes the economic implications of the general-purpose technology and market-place characters of the Internet.

Index